What Wisdom Whispers

Life Lessons in Love and Forgiveness

A Memoir

Andrea Broadfoot

Copyright © 2020 by Andrea Broadfoot. All rights reserved.

Published by Change Empire Books (Australia).

Printed on demand in Australia, United States and United Kingdom

Cover art copyright © 2019 by Bella Marie, used with permission.

Cover design and interior illustrations copyright © 2020 by Claire Blesing, Ville Creative.

Author photograph: Robert Lang Photography

EBOOK ISBN: 978-0-6488138-6-6

PRINT ISBN: 978-0-6488138-5-9

First paperback edition: July, 2020

www.andreabroadfoot.com.au

Special discounts are available on quantity purchases of What Wisdom Whispers for book clubs, organisations and others at www.andreabroadfoot.com.au

For orders by trade bookstores and wholesalers, contact the author at whispers@andreabroadfoot.com.au

Your support of the author's rights is appreciated.

Dedication

For my children who have taught me love, trust, strength, justice, and compassion, I am sorry I have learned the hard way, and ask your forgiveness for my failings. I love you both so very much. Thank you for your wisdom in my life.

For my mother, father and brothers who have stood by me with acceptance, love, unconditional support and a keen sense of humour and humanity throughout it all, the unbelievably bad times all the way through to the ultimate good. Thank you. I love you and am grateful for you all.

For our lineage that we might continue to be truth tellers that shine light in dark corners, so we can love, forgive, heal and be whole.

For my lover and soulmate Jack who stands beside me, honours my voice with kindness and diplomatic endeavour, while supporting me to be the best human I can be. Thank you. I love you. (Let's get together earlier next life.)

For the characters in my story, who have shown up throughout my life in the parts of family, friends, lovers, and colleagues, you teach me all I need to know through a divine alchemy of human interaction. Some of which has been excruciating, with the majority experience pure joy and soul growing, I accept it all with gratitude and the knowledge that I am fully responsible for my choices and the roles I have played that have journeyed us to here. Thank you especially to all my soul sisters (you know who you are) who have stood by me, and those who have moved on, the women who hold me tight, dry my tears, and laugh together until we cry. Because tragedy is comedy that just needs more time.

For my grandchildren and theirs, this is a memoir of a woman's life, which I dedicate to my heart's desire that you choose to love, honour and accept yourself now and forevermore, and experience this gift of life in your own special way, to be whole, complete and perfect. As you are. As we are. And so it is.

For Michael, and everyone else across the decades, who has asked me when I am publishing my book. This one is for you.

Acknowledgements

I honour the Traditional Custodians of the Country where I have the privilege to be born and grow, and where these events have taken place. I acknowledge their wisdom, connection to and care of this land which has never been ceded. I thank my Aboriginal friends, mentors and colleagues for sharing your stories and for your support and love, and I recognise Elders past, present and emerging.

I thank Mother Earth for holding me grounded, washing me in oceans of love, and inspiring me with the expansive skies of stars, moon and the sun we are gifted with each turn of the planet.

Thank you to Cathryn Mora of Change Empire Publishing, my dedicated book coach, editor, and friend who has mopped my brow, and maintained her encouragement across the time space continuum, to support the gestation and guide this birth of my first book. Cat, your commitment to cause is incredible, and I am grateful for your persistence to ensure my voice is heard in the world through What Wisdom Whispers.

Thank you to my beta-readers who invested time and presence to provide feedback to create a manuscript that is the best it can be. Special mentions to my friend Penny, who sent me a cheer squad in a letter after reading an early draft, encouraging me to complete the journey, and to Lisa an old school friend who generously gave her eagle eye for grammatical changes, and empathy for the shared anguish of traumatic and character building school experiences. Grateful to Michelle for daily ocean swims throughout the years, but regularly in the last eight months, which has cleansed and renewed me daily.

Lashings of love for Bella Marie for her channelled painting of Sacred She, who adorns the cover, the Divine Feminine who embodies forgiveness, the theme of our life work. Deep appreciation to Claire Blesing of Ville Creative for her beautiful cover design and website development, accompanied by regular gentle prompts and encouragement which has kept me on track, all the while growing the second baby of her own. I am blessed to be surrounded with the skills and wisdom of my fellow creatives and I thank you all for your support.

High fives to amazing artist and friend Rob Lang, from Robert Lang photography for the Salty Session ales after our photoshoot in his garden on the way to a wedding, where he captured the divine author photograph on the cover. Thanks to Hammad Khalid for formatting services and uploading to platforms that this book may be unleashed on the world.

Author's Note

My intention is that What Wisdom Whispers tells the story of my journey, and delivers a legacy of love, healing, and forgiveness.

A feature of the human experience is the nature of perception, filtered through our values, memories, language, attitudes, experience, beliefs, and focus. We are characters in stories of our own making, where whatever happens, at the very least, we get to choose how we respond. Because let's face it, shit happens.

This memoir is my story from my own perspective, and there is no intention to cause hurt or dishonour to any person depicted. I acknowledge that truth can hurt and understand that silence can be more comfortable, and this is just my rendition of truth, expressed at a moment in time. A story that is being voiced into the world, which I hope leads others to trust their own voice and speak of their individual experiences. For one person's story is another person's medicine.

Stories connect us as one.

Names are vital parts of who we are, and with permission some names have been retained.

Some names have been changed for ease of reading, and so characters are not confused.

Some names have been changed to protect the innocent.

Some names have been changed to release the guilty.

As you experience What Wisdom Whispers, as always, you get to choose how you respond.

With love,

Always and all ways,

Andrea

What Wisdom Whispers

Prologue

It was 1993. Mornings with our precious twin babies were sacred times. The golden first light serenaded by the birds in the trees around the garden, heralded each new day.

The twins were six months old when I woke that spring morning to hear them gurgling softly to each other. It was my cherished routine to bring our babies from their shared cot into our big brass bed so we could play. I gathered them into my arms, by now proficient at carrying two babies, feeding two babies, settling two babies, and took them back into our bed.

I cocooned the twins between my husband and I to ensure they were safe from falling off. Curling myself around their warm, still sleepy bodies they stretched and giggled, holding each other's hands, grabbing my hair and fingers.

We looked deep into each other's eyes. Pure joy lived there.

I looked over the twins to my husband lying beside us.

"Can you bring me a nappy please, hon'?" I asked quietly. I turned my attention back to our babies beside me.

There was a sudden unexpected movement in my peripheral vision. In a flash my beloved husband was now above me, and with a closed fist he smashed my head into the pillow.

I saw stars.

There was no time to register the shock.

Innately I went into immediate protection mode for the children, curling myself around them, holding them closely to protect them in case more violence rained down from above.

I flopped about on the bed, intermittently losing consciousness.

As I came to, I pleaded with him.

"Take the children out of the bed please, in case I squash them."

The father of my children gathered up our twins and took them out of the room.

I was alone as I vomited.

My body pulsed in and out of awareness as I lost sense of time.

Eventually I inched my way down from our high brass bed, out of our bedroom and crawled along the floor of the hall, pulling my body along like a caterpillar in need of a cocoon. I slithered across the lounge carpet and with difficulty pulled myself up into a lounge chair.

A languid observer, my husband watched my slow progress with mild interest.

Struggling up into the large genoa lounge chair, I sat back as my head flopped to the side involuntarily.

I strained to see my children.

I couldn't focus or hold my head up straight. Drool leaked from the corner of my mouth.

The babies were gurgling happily on bunny rugs in the middle of the lounge room floor.

"I think I should see the doctor," I slurred.

"He will know that I hit you," he replied.

"I think I am concussed," I said, drooling, my eyes closing of their own accord.

I was suddenly very tired.

"Have a rest," he said. "Go back to bed."

My mind made no sense of the situation. *How have I gotten here?*

From a blissful baby wake up call, to being bruised and battered before breakfast.

I peered at the children and at my husband, assessing the safety of my darling oblivious babies.

It was like nothing of note had happened.

I felt deathly tired and violently sick as I crawled my way back into our room and clawed myself up onto the bed.

Floating in a new world of my own making. I lapsed in and out of consciousness, vomiting intermittently, sleeping, and eventually waking with a raging headache.

After a few days, the swelling gave way to a black eye which emerged above my crooked eye socket. Half of my face was purple.

I went to the bathroom to check my face and I didn't recognise myself in the mirror.

I had changed.

Forever.

Chapter 1

My first memory is a dream I had when I was three. I was in my bed. An iron framed wire based single bed, four legs on the floor. In the dream I woke up in fear. A large plump snake was curling up the leg of the bed towards my pillow, on its way to strike me dead.

Sitting bolt upright, I screamed for Dad, whose room with Mum adjoined mine through the wall against my bed.

"Daddy! Daddy!" I screamed.

The snake's large head slithered relentlessly toward me, where I was shocked into stillness as the inevitable threat approached, eyes glistening pure evil.

The wall opened and I could see Dad with his back to me. He was sitting on his side of the bed, pulling his socks on ready for his early work start.

I screamed again in panic for him to come and save me from the snake, while it slithered ever closer to the top of the mattress where I sat, straining to the wall for the safety of a few more seconds.

"Daddy! Daddy!" I screamed again.

Daddy didn't hear me. His back stayed turned away. I was invisible to him. Panic rose in sobs of pure terror, while fate curled its way upwards to bite me. My screams woke me up. I sat alone in my bed. In the dark. Under threat, abandoned and afraid.

Dreams are powerful moments of creation. We choose what they mean and cloak our reality in their essence.

My dream coloured my life until I knew better, meanwhile I manifested the abandonment I thought I deserved in ever more creative ways in my relationships. Eventually I picked it to pieces through the spiritual journey that expanded throughout my life.

It is how we all grow, if we choose it, working through our self-worth issues to discover the truth within. There were many more years of lessons and their archaeological excavation to dig through before I reached that point.

In truth my childhood real life was much more wholesome than my perception of abandonment in a dream. A teacher that boarded with Mum and Dad while doing her training watched Sesame Street daily with me, and Mum credits Cath with teaching me to read by the age of three.

Voracious in my reading I tackled topics way beyond my years. I worked my way through the entire bookshelf, and got a library card, riding my bike down the street, and wobbling back with burgeoning book bag to avoid any parental censorship of my reading choices.

Mum and Dad were at work. I read every day and night, on the toilet and in the dark under my blankets at night with a torch. Whole worlds opened and I travelled time and space through my imagination on the magic carpet of words gifted through thousands of stories, tall tales and true.

True stories are the most powerful and they teach us so much.

Chapter 1

A true story of tragedy struck our family when I was four years old. My cousin Kirrily was three. We were close. Her mother is my Dad's beloved younger sister Janice, and for their own family, having lost another sister Marjory to meningitis when she was a toddler growing up, Janice was a precious baby girl for Grandma in a parade of older boys. Our families were strongly connected through our grandmother Olive Letitia Sarah Ann, the matriarch, and Dad's mother. We got together for supper and cards to celebrate every family member's birthday on my Dad's side throughout the years.

Aunty Jan and Uncle Alan lived around the corner with their three children. When Kirrily was three, Karin was two, and Steven had just been born, Kirrily slipped out of the house into the yard wearing her cowboy hat. Uncle Alan was still at work, due home any moment. The boat was parked in the yard with the cover on it. Kirrily climbed up into the boat and slipped down between the covers, maybe to hide from her Dad for when he arrived home. Kirrily loved to play hide and seek.

Minutes later, when Uncle Alan came home, he could see his beloved daughter through the glass windscreen of the boat. He waved, but Kirrily didn't move. Her feet weren't on the ground. The cowboy hat held her dangling just above the boat floor, and Kirrily had died. A freak accident in our family so protective of all the children, always. Such an unlikely tragedy that happened in mere moments.

Her loss devastated our whole family. I was seven when the death of my beloved cousin Kirrily hit home for me. Going to bed one night I was suddenly overwhelmed with grief. An aching space in my life that remained after my best friend and closest cousin left the physical plane ripped a new hole in my heart, and I sobbed, inconsolable. Mum came to check on me and was confused at first, but then she settled in to hold me, to listen as my distraught voice gushed forth with the stories of all that could have been, had Kirrily lived beyond three.

Forever after, Kirrily's accident affected the psyche of our family. Any hat strings were removed. At family gatherings the peace could be shattered at any moment when one of the aunties or uncles suddenly yelled frantically…. "Where's Bradley?!" … "Where's Sean?!"

We older children immediately stopped whatever we were doing, and sprang into action to locate the out-of-sight child and bring them safely into view.

A collective sigh of relief went up. Cards or conversations continued. The adults exchanged knowing glances. It put us on edge, but from then on, we all survived.

When I was four, I died too.

Dad noticed first.

I was standing at the window by the front door, with a little string handbag around my shoulder. My glazy stare to somewhere beyond had taken me from him.

"Andrea?" he called me loudly. "Andrea!" He screamed as he lifted me up into his arms. Limp, I flopped into unconsciousness.

He pulled the bag from my shoulder and raced me into the backyard. Out into the sunshine. Dad was calling to Mum with desperation. "Rosalie, call the ambulance NOW!"

Mum got on the phone as Dad laid me on the lawn.

"We need an ambulance now! Our daughter has stopped breathing," Mum's voice was urgent.

I was far away. Gone. My lips were blue, and Dad thought I had stopped breathing.

Dad began mouth to mouth resuscitation. Mum came out and stood above him, blocking the sun from my face. Wringing her hands and shaking.

I was fitting, shuddering, and flopping. My tongue slipped into my throat, making me choke.

Dad reached into my mouth for my tongue, to pull it forward. He rolled me over to clear my airway, willing me to take a breath.

"Andrea, breathe baby, breathe…." he whispered.

Chapter 1

I bit him to the bone on his finger.

I was alive and spluttering.

Dad was bleeding.

The ambulance arrived and whisked me into emergency, where they monitored my vital signs. There was no explanation for that momentary lapse of consciousness, the fit, the way I stopped breathing. The drama of life pulling me away for a moment that I might consider my options.

To live or not to live.

As it happened, I lived beyond four.

My parents were lucky. I was lucky. Throughout our lives we have stood beside our family who had it so much worse. Now there are grandchildren and great grandchildren.

When a child's name is called at our family events, we still stop and search, then return to normality with hearts beating just that little bit harder each time. It is a tradition that sticks like superglue.

We are fainters in my family.

Mum started it. With low blood pressure and a brilliant imagination, she fainted at her pain or that of another.

Our immunisations or childhood accidents were a family challenge where Dad had to hold it all together and get us to the hospital. On one such occasion I cried as I laid on the floor to receive the injection, while the doctor berated me for being weak and Mum for not parenting us fiercely enough, all while she wobbled against the wall struggling to stay conscious herself.

"Nothing a smack wouldn't fix," the doctor admonished as he jabbed me mercilessly.

Wit is another strong point. Mum had managed to stay upright and conscious. She held our hands as we crossed the road. "There was a prick at both ends of THAT needle!" Mum's acerbic comment made family history.

It was a wholesome upbringing, with the parents immersed in churchgoing, running the youth group, and Dad not yet discovered the delights of beer.

Fishing was our lifeblood. Mum's dad Sydney, our Grandy, and my Dad, had formed a close bond in his plank boat while fishing for whiting in Chinaman's Creek. My Mother's mum, Nana Ruby, babysat us during school holidays while the parents worked. I took up smoking aged eight, allured by her Craven A Special Mild cigarettes she bought by the carton.

It was like I was on a speed train to growing up. Books were my rite of passage and sanctuary. They taught me about the world through the voices of the writers which I imagined to be my own.

My earliest goals were to get my degree and travel to Europe. Travel the world. Instead, I stayed in bed. Under the covers straining my eyes with a torch to read the adventures of people and the planet.

*

Nana Ruby was a survivor herself. She made international news after spending all night in Spencer Gulf after fishing with Grandy, when their dinghy overturned. Nana was thrown into the sea and she was taken by the rushing tide. My mum was nine. They thought Nana was gone forever after search parties in boats and planes failed to find any sign of her.

Here is Nana Ruby Craddock's story in her own words transcribed by my Uncle David Craddock when he was still a teenager.

Dolphins and Darkness

> *It became apparent quite early in my married life that I was destined to be relegated to the ranks of fishing widowhood. My husband had been reared in a family where the sea was considered the natural environment and fishing the logical spare time occupation. I had been raised in a rural community, the major centre of which was a railway junction.*

Chapter 1

Shortly after our marriage, my husband, a railway locomotive driver was transferred from his position near the sea to my original hometown. It was in this uncongenial environment that the boatbuilding and family building began. The sea was only forty miles away and homebuilt car-top boats provided pleasant interludes between long, hot grease and soot-filled journeys as far North as Alice Springs on trains which were as unreliable as they were essential.

For me there were two choices; to enter the world of salt sea winds, tackle and bait or to spend my life in a continuous state of waiting. It was no choice really.

And so it chanced that in November 1953 my husband and I found ourselves moving away from the shore accompanied by the steady and reassuring whirr of the tiny outboard on the stern of our twelve foot white bondwood boat. It was clear and warm but with a brisk and dehydrating northerly sweeping down Spencer Gulf from the dry saltbush plain country around Port Augusta.

The area in which we fished was a tidal backwater interlaced with channels between mud islands which uncovered as the tide dropped. When the islands showed through, the water, confined to narrow escape routes, flowed swiftly out towards the main gulf channel used by the infrequent steamship traffic. We fished our way out with the tide and then it was our practice to wait for the turn of the tide and anchor at favoured spots on the way shoreward.

At about 4.00pm we were anchored in the swift flowing current between two islands, one of which showed the dark spade-like shells of razor fish, large anchored molluscs whose tender heart flesh is much prized by the fishermen for bait and by gourmets as a seafood delicacy. The other island we referred to only as the "Submerged Island" whose appearance above water level signalled a lower than usual tide.

The fishing had been slow but optimism is an essential part of the fisherman psychology. This was a ground that was best at slack water and promised large spotted whiting and perhaps a few schnapper. We decided to bait, cast and wait.

Several hours in a twelve foot boat can play havoc with the body's joints and so in this moment of respite, my husband stood up to stretch and survey the horizon with an earnestness which would make the casual observer sure that there was real purpose in the gaze. Having satisfied himself that what he sought was either there or absent, he stepped back towards the wooden thwart, placed his foot on a razor fish shell still wet and pearly after recent opening, and slipped backward.

In a desperate attempt to save himself he grasped the gunwale and we were over. I surfaced and grasped the boat. Syd spluttered up alongside me.

"Whatever you do, don't let go," he said. "This current would whip you away in seconds."

I hung on.

There followed a desperate series of attempts to right the boat. The motor was allowed to go to the bottom but the combination of the current and consequently a very taut anchor rope made all efforts futile. The tilting of the upturned boat, however, had allowed the empty vacuum flask to float out from under it. It hung in the turbulence close to the boat and I edged my way towards it. With the glass section knocked out it would make an admirable bailing utensil when the boat was righted.

As I neared it, it began to drift tantalisingly away. I let go, deciding that the five yards to it would give me a reserve of at least fifteen yards of swimming to return to the boat, reckoned on my far from legendary ability in water deeper than I was tall.

It was a ridiculous act. I called out as the boat receded into the distance but heard no reply.

Chapter 1

Because the boat was V bottomed, Syd had built into it removable floorboards, the main one being approximately three feet square and made from pinus flooring battened together. I saw this board only a few yards from me and struck out for it thinking of straws and drowning men.

I managed to get the board under the top half of my body and with my left hand clutched the farthest edge and used my right arm in a clumsy overarm stroke in an attempt to work my way back to the boat. I soon realized the uselessness of my efforts and decided that the end was in sight. I shouted, then cried a bit, then prayed.

How could I hope? The gulf was about eleven miles wide at this point. The current had swept me far from the mudbanks and shallows of the backwater and I was in the main stream. Shipping intervals were measured in terms of months and the fishing fleets did not operate here. It would not be until next day that we would be missed. A heavy resignation fell upon me, four children all at school orphaned by a slip of a foot on an innocuous shell.

I don't know how long the depression lasted. The sun, red-faced dropped towards the smooth bare hills in the west, the breeze abated and I was left in the centre of an awful silence. With impending darkness came a return of spirit.

"Damn it all woman, you're not dead!"

"You've been in the water nearly three hours now! You're still afloat aren't you?"

"That silly piece of board will support you for a long time yet. Hang on!"

In the dusk I could make out not too far distant a shipping marker buoy. I was elated. I could wait it out at least until searchers were mobilised. I made for it using my one-armed wallowing stroke. It looked so strong, stable and dry, a large Christmas pudding iced by the visitations of innumerable cormorants. On closer inspection my elation gave way rapidly to despair.

The top was at least three feet from water level and no handhold came to light in a careful circumnavigation. The sides were hung with shiny marine growth making a mockery of any hope I had held of a haven from the sea. During all this, I clung stubbornly to the board. It had saved me from death for this long, it might continue to do so. Reluctantly I parted from the inhospitable sea-sentinel.

My previous hopes made the ensuing despair even more dark. I was thirsty, exhausted and ready to let go. I began to think of sharks. The area is well known for them but no attacks on swimmers have been recorded. This was hollow consolation when I considered that very few people frolicked in the waters where I was at the time. It was totally dark at this time. I looked back to the East and could see the lights of cars, mere pinpoints as they sped along the road at the foot of the Flinders Ranges. It was not difficult to visualise the inside of the cars, people who were dry, safely on land and with company. It was then that I first heard the sound. A sneeze in the blackness.

"Choo!" followed by a gurgle then "Choo!" again. I had heard the sound too often to be fooled for long. Dolphins. The rounded backs and stark fins reappearing with an undulating motion accompanied by the whistling exhalations of air. We have always maintained, probably wrongly, that where there are dolphins there are no sharks.

Chapter 1

It was the lift I needed. I talked to myself, sang, prayed some more but the loneliness, the soul and will-destroying solitude had gone. I paddled and rested and paddled again in the continuous company of the playful and exuberant friends who had come to me unbidden and given me that fillip of spirit I needed. I do not know how long they stayed with me. Every muscle screamed for relief but life was with me and I thought about the old cliché about life and hope. It may have been hours, it may have been minutes later that my toes touched something. I was in two feet of water. I could not stand but I lay in the water and rested. I did not know whether this was a tidal flat or the western shore. I clung to the board just in case. Using it as a support, I forced myself onto my feet and looked back. Away in the distance I could see the sweep of spot lights far across the water.

"Syd must have made it", I said to myself and cried with double relief.

I soon discerned that I was in fact on the western shore of the gulf. On gaining dry land I carried my miniature raft up beyond the highwater mark and dropped it. I shall never forget the words I uttered – "Well done my good and faithful servant". I dropped to the sand and slept.

I awoke before daylight and began to walk. The lights of Port Augusta glowed to the North. There was no permanent habitation between me and them. My shoes were gone and in the weak moonlight ironstone and bindi eyes the vicious little prickles made progress difficult. I had not gone far when I was confronted by a flat and shining expanse before me.

"Water!" I said to myself. "If it's only one inch deep I won't go near it!"

I found out later that it was a smooth expanse of saltpan, easy and comfortable to walk on. I detoured through the ironstone and bindi eyes. At daylight the aircraft arrived. Far off the water was dotted with boats. The planes swept methodically over the area as I watched fascinated but frustrated by distance.

The sun rose higher and gained force. I knew I had to get water. The area was not totally strange to me. We had camped with our children down this way some years previously and an old man named Footner, a recluse who eked out a meagre living looking after station fences, had dwelt in a corrugated iron hut about a mile from the beach. The old man had baked bread in powdered milk tins and had kept us supplied during our camp on the shore.

I stuck close to the sea until landmarks became familiar. After a couple of hours the hallucinations started. The man towards whom I ran resolved himself into a straggly bush. The car in the distance did not materialise. My thirst was nearly intolerable by the time I sighted the hut and made for it. I reached it footsore, sunburned and exhausted. It was empty but the rainwater tank outside was not. Remembering story book warnings I drank sparingly and found an old bottle to carry a supply with me. The door of the hut was wired shut and I forced it with little difficulty. There was no food inside but the case of an ancient pillow provided me with tolerable footwear.

I struck off from the hut into the heat of the day, husbanding my meagre water supply. Some three hours later I saw figures moving far off in the heat haze. Clutching my bottle I ran and can faintly remember screaming "Don't disappear! Don't go away!"

They heard and ran towards me. One said "How would a cup of tea go, love?" It was hardly a statement likely to set Hollywood on its ear, but the words are still a part of a beautiful memory for me.

There's a newspaper photo of my mother aged nine holding a posy of flowers to greet her mother after she was lost at sea back in 1953. Years later, after my mother's oldest sister Margaret died, a box of letters was discovered. People from all over Australia and the world had written to Nana to congratulate her on her incredible feat of survival. They told their own stories too, of boils and afflictions, sons that had gone to jail, and husbands turned bad. Retelling their own daily tragedies to a stranger on the other side of the world. Sharing their tales of survival, weird, wonderful, desperate, and banal.

Chapter 1

Not that she ever said so, but it seems that Nana Ruby was a healer, too.

With a routine that kept my imagination well fed, my folks subscribed to the monthly *Readers Digest*. Piles of the magazines were well worn in the magazine rack beside the toilet. Pivotal pages permanently held open through the extra folding back, crispened by inadvertent splashes and the inevitable dry that followed.

My favourite section was the Drama in Real Life stories, where ordinary people turned into superheroes for a moment or longer, to save others, or survive some freak accident or incident.

Ordinary people who did incredible things fuelled my reading, in a mission to devour every book in the house.

That was who I wanted to be. An ordinary girl who stepped into the unbelievable world of real life by saving many lives. Mind blowing acts of courageous heroism.

Each night I dozed into sleep, dreaming of how I raced into the toppling building to save the neighbour's baby, or dangled from a high precipice by my fingertips, grasping the stained shirtfront of the old man lost in dementia, who had stumbled in the ten story car park.

I was always on the look-out for opportunities to leap into a burning building, avert a car crash by putting my body on the line, or catch a toddler falling from a high rise. This tall building rescue fantasy was even though we lived in small-town suburbia, where the trust homes met the privately owned abodes all on single level.

Daydreams included staying alive for months after the plane crash by eating my youngest brother piece by tasty piece. Sean was born when I was six, and was cute for a while, but three's a crowd, and by the time he was older, both my brothers ganged up in the eternal war of the sexes.

Dressed by Kmart, in chocolate coloured corduroy and various shades of orange, that flattened my even flatter chest, I roamed the neighbourhood looking for victims of circumstance I could rescue from imminent harm.

I had to act fast because I was sure I'd be dead by the time I was fifteen.

If not fifteen at least by the age of twenty-one.

Everyone died. I read it in the papers.

The girl my age, snatched from her bed in the suburbs, was front page news for months on end.

I often wondered how she slept right through the distinctive sounds of the screen on her window being sliced through with a knife that hot summer night, when she was taken from her bed.

Her pyjama top was found on a neighbour's lawn on their street some weeks later, folded neatly.

Sinister.

But the girl was nowhere to be found. Her name was Louise. I thought about her a lot.

I searched through the pages of the newspaper looking for updates on her fate. Every night the evening news was a sanctum of silence, as Dad nestled in his recliner chair, ready to snarl should any of us squeak.

Deathly silence was all I heard on Louise. Disappeared with no trace.

There was another one, too. A blonde girl taken from the side of the road, as she walked to the shop to get sugar in the city suburbs. I imagined her mum going out to the fence to peer down the road in the dusky hues of a dying day. Her eyes wide as she searched the fading light, pupils adjusting to the darkness which was her life from that evening forevermore.

A life where her daughter never ever slammed the door again.

Eventually the mother walked the suburban side streets to the shops to see if she had been seen, only to discover her daughter had never made it to their counter. Whisked away by men who moved in the darkness, sometimes in broad daylight, driving white vans, snatching girls who are yet to blossom into full colour life.

Girls like me.

Chapter 1

Squeezing the life out of them, or worse.

For some reason, getting to sleep was always a problem for me.

Contemplation of the full range of death throes imaginable does that to girls who read too much. Night after night I lay in my bed. Eyes wide, staring into the inky dark, broken only by the strip of light from the hallway, spilling under the door like so much blood.

One hot summer night I lay awake in a sweaty silk sheen, wondering what I would do to escape the clutches of the madman outside my window. The psycho determined to sneak me away from under my sheet into the covers of forever darkness. A noise pierced the gloom and I was on instant high alert with the unmistakable but almost silent clicking noise. Rhythmic and close by, coming from the window my bed sat right under.

Click, click, click, click…...

I imagined the shiny point of his sharp knife slowly slicing through the screen, tiny square by square to reach me.

Without waking my parents in the next room.

Just like Louise.

I slid my legs up and slipped the sheet off as quietly as I could.

Click, click, click, click…….

Monotonous and threatening, he had travelled from the city to find me, another dark haired ten-year-old, to snatch me from my bed. I was frozen in fear, awaiting my fate.

Click, click, click, click…

If he pushed the knife beyond the window and into my room, he could cut me now. I swung my innocent body away from the window. Bare feet hit the cool linoleum floor and I crept stealthy and scared to the door, hand outstretched desperate to feel the handle in the dark, to make my escape.

It all happened in an instant.

CRASH!!…..WHIRR!!…....flicker, flicker, flicker, flicker…..

I screamed and flew out of the room as the blind snapped itself to the top of the window, rolling ominously on the spindle, exposing the window bare.

Mum came running and met me in the hallway.

"He's coming to kill me! To snatch me from my sleep like Louise Bell," I sobbed, falling into Mum's arms. Dad pushed past us into my room, flicking on the light.

Mum held me tight, stroking my head.

Dad investigated the window closely then looked up to the blind still flicking against the curtain.

"Your blind flew up, Andrea," Dad said. As he pushed aside the curtain, the window was unmoved. There were no giant knife slashes, or even a gentle cut.

The screen was completely intact.

"It must have not been pulled down quite right." Dad pulled the blind down and tested it was firm on the spindle.

The curtain fell back into place and Mum led me into my bed. They both hugged me, and Dad padded back out into the hallway, to the safety of the light, and the dull monotonous roar of the television in the lounge room. Mum tucked me in under sheets so thin any sharp object was sure to pierce through.

"I was sure he was right here, Mum, ready to snatch me into the night, drag me out the window through the slashed screen." I cried into her arms as she held me close, leaning over me, wiping my hysterical tears.

"Who is here? You are safe darling," she said. "I can imagine that was scary, your blind flying up like that, but there is no-one here, except us. It is time to rest and get some sleep."

My sobs subsided to whimpers. Tired little squeaks and sighs. Mum squeezed my hand as she stood up to leave me alone with my monstrous imagination.

"If you struggle to sleep, come into our room, okay?" she patted my feet as she walked to the door. "And we'll leave the door open."

Chapter 1

"Okay," my heart rush was slowing to a more even beat. My breathing deepened but my eyes stayed wide to avoid more imaginings of disastrous deaths that night.

It was the time of the Truro murders. All those young women's bodies found in remote South Australia. Fifteen and sixteen years old some of them, killed in the prime of their lives.

The trial unfolded in the papers. I knew all the girls by name. Raped and strangled by a serial killer who was then killed in a car accident. He killed seven girls in just two months.

A killing spree cut short, with his accomplice left to face six life sentences for dumbly driving the girls so full of life to their last moments. He got good at helping to bury their bodies. Never questioning his friend or his motives, because the time he did, things became slightly unhinged.

He chose not to lift a finger to save those young women from the fate of death. Imagine if the killer had been wearing his seatbelt when the tyre blew on his car, sending it into a roll that stopped the carnage dead.

Just imagine. Imagine I did.

The voice in my head replayed all the details. It pondered how I could have saved those girls. Stopped them from hitchhiking. Stopped them from getting into that charismatic young man's car when their bus was late, or they were walking home from their part time job on a steamy summer afternoon.

If our paths had crossed. If I had seen them in time. If....if.... if....the meanderings and machinations of time twisting that their families and friends must have endured for the rest of their days. The voice in my head worked overtime with explanations and stories, insights, and alternate endings.

I remember the exact moment I understood that voice in my head was not actually me.

I was riding my bike when the revelation flooded into stark realisation. It was not me speaking in my mind. Instead it was a whispering of words that explained realities, calmed fears and bolstered moments with clarity and meaning.

The wind was whistling through my ears as I stood up on the pedals to pound out more power. A voice of calm wisdom washed through me. It was not like listening exactly, more a knowing of truth that sank through to the depths of me.

"You are cared for. You are loved. You can create a life of whatever you choose."

I pumped the pedals harder, attempting to outrun these whispers of wisdom.

"You are blessed. We care for you. You are perfect just the way you are."

Maybe it is God?

I looked around me and up to the sky for a sign.

The bike wobbled. I focused on the road in front of me to regain control.

"We are right here. Always."

I didn't think of angels at the time. Just a complete knowledge that the voice that was always already listening, was outside of me. It wasn't my own voice, but that of a guardian, a mentor, a wise one.

And they had my back.

This was a fortunate turn of events because there would be moments my life depended on it.

Chapter 2

Surviving childhood was extra challenging over time, with the arrival of two younger brothers. It meant I had to forge all the new frontiers first. As first born, it was my job.

Greg was sixteen months younger, and we were peas in a pod until Sean the love child was born five years later. It was then we commenced the interminable tussle over who was IN, and who was OUT, because THREE is definitely a crowd.

As the middle child, Greg lived up to the reputation and cried a fair bit.

He also refused point blank to eat.

Anything at all.

This exacerbated Dad's anxiety which was a potent mix of humour, love, laughter, and intermittent anger which freaked us out, coupled with bouts of deep depression that we didn't understand, all appearing at random junctures in our life.

We were never sure just what the mood might be.

Greg's concession to staying alive was a diet wholly consisting of vegemite sandwiches and glasses of milk. His birthday brought jars of vegemite in abundance from well-meaning neighbours and friends hiding behind smiling eyes, while they looked sideways at Mum with pure empathy.

Mealtimes became tense with foreboding as the control Greg wielded was whether he would eat, or not, and when.

Various parades of pleading, threats that were idle and carried out, silence, and yelling were the norm.

We would all sit down and stare at the plate in front of us.

I would begin to eat. Everything. Brussel sprouts even, although I struggled with peas and would consume them whole, in clumps, to avoid the taste. My frantic swallowing mechanism developed enough to avoid bringing them straight back up again.

Greg continued to stare dismayed at the plate of wholesome food before him.

"Mum," he said in a tiny plaintive voice, "I can't eat this. Sorry."

His big brown eyes would fill with tears, that wet first his eyelashes, then leaked down his face.

Dad at the head of the table would look across, eyes widening. His hands clenching the table.

"Greg, we are not going through this again. Your mother has made a beautiful meal for us all. Please just sit and eat it," Dad said. He sounded tired. He mostly started gently and worked up into a tirade of desperate frenzy.

"Dad. I am sorry. I just can't," Greg's eyes stayed down so as not to inflame the situation. Hoping that a vegemite sandwich might appear to save him.

Sean was still little and, in his highchair, while I gulped everything on my plate and averted my eyes from the train wreck that was teatime.

Mum sat there silently and ate her food, ready at any second to go and make the vegemite sandwich that would unhook us all from this drama. Always in full support of Dad, they were an amazing team in parenting, commanding our full respect and eternal love.

For about ten years the strain of mealtimes struck at the core of our dedicated parents in their endeavour to nurture us to adulthood the best they could. This came to a screaming halt when a microwave was introduced, the mushy food held its crisp, we started eating tacos, and Greg magically enjoyed a variety of foods for the first time.

Texture is everything.

It is fair to say our childhood was tinged with fear as Dad struggled with his share of stress related illness. There was the fear he would die, juxtaposed with the irrational fear he might kill us. Feelings experienced intermittently depending on whether he was depressed, hospitalized with some near fatal affliction, or chasing us around the house with his belt. This was usually after he arrived home from work, to find the siblings had just endured another post school world war three with each other. Survived only to be threatened with certain but improbable death by our father.

I got my own room and it had a lock on the door. It was my sanctuary during altercations with my brothers, long legs carrying me down the hallway to safety, if I could get the bolt across in place fast enough.

One afternoon after Greg missed the opportunity to grab and pummel me, I slammed the door in his face, and locked it, leaning my back against it with pure relief.

"Andrea, you bitch, open the door!" he screamed from the other side.

I sank to the floor as he kicked it with full force. His foot penetrated the plywood coating and created a hole in the base of the door. His demeanour changed to immediate regret and chagrin.

"Oh NO," he cried, "Look what I have done! What will Dad say?"

I could hear his fear and slid the bolt back to peer through a crack in the door.

The look on Greg's face was pure terror. Dad's arrival home from work was moments away.

I threw the door wide.

"We can fix it!" I suggested.

Mission handyperson was underway. We scoured the shed and found some wood putty and Greg used a kitchen knife to scrape it across the hole.

"It's the wrong colour!" he moaned. "This will never work!"

I scrabbled through my school bag and found a sticker big enough to cover the damage. Over the poorly placed putty we stuck a sticker, slightly awry but covering the fawn putty embedded in the white door.

We stood back and looked at our handiwork.

"He will notice straight away," Greg said.

"We could be lucky," I said as I wrapped my arms around his shoulders. "Anyway, we can both take the blame."

"Sorry Andrea, but you make me SO angry sometimes," Greg said, leaning into my shoulder.

"It's okay, mate, it's my job as big sister!" I said. We laughed weakly and awaited our fate.

Dad's car drove into the driveway, and we ran to sit in the lounge together, looking innocent. I buried my face in a book while Greg looked pained.

"Hey kids," Dad called as he shut the door behind him. "How was your day?"

"Great," I mumbled.

"Yeah, great," said Greg, not sounding great.

Dad tuned in on our faces as he entered the room.

"What's up?" he asked, sixth sense in probe mode.

"Nothing," Greg began, "Well sort of nothing."

I peeked up at Greg and watched the truth fall out of him sideways.

"Dad we were running in the house, and I know that you tell us not to, but we were, and my foot collided with Andrea's bedroom door, it was only a slight knock, and well….." Greg's true confession was on the table. I held my breath.

Chapter 2

Dad looked at us both.

"Running in the house hey?" he queried.

"Yeah Dad, running in the house, sorry," I said softly.

"Okay then, let's take a look," Dad led the way up the hall. The sticker precariously placed over the puttied hole had begun to pucker with the chemical reaction of being covered while wet. It had bubbled up and was starting to drip plastic.

We looked at the mess in horror.

"We tried to fix it, Dad," Greg stammered.

"I can see that mate," Dad replied. He was calm and collected as he leaned down.

"I might remove the sticker for now so it can dry properly, then we can sand and paint it. It'll be good as new!" Dad ripped off the sticker and it disintegrated into a pulpy mess in his hand.

"Nice try though, kids," he said, and he patted us both as he went to the bin.

And that was that.

From his outbursts of frustrated anger, to the next moment when Dad was loving, and full of advice designed to save our lives. He taught us to fish, drive, and how to fix the car. He loved us more than life. They were unpredictable times. Mum and Dad's early days of marriage were tight, and they lived fortnight to fortnight, with groceries on credit at Eudunda Farmers, paid for with their next pay.

Mum told us about how one day things were so desperate she prayed for money.

"Money was scarce. I was hanging out the washing. I decided to pray to God," she said with a small smile of memory shining pure faith on her face.

Please, Lord, give us some money... She had asked silently in her mind.

"I was hanging out your Dad's jeans. And PLOP, onto the ground in front of me dropped a twenty-cent piece! It was that instant! I burst into laughter and have never prayed for money ever again!" she laughed with delight.

Whatever their budget, we were shielded from their fiscal management strategies and got new bikes for birthdays, and once I came home from school to be surprised in my bedroom, which was full of new furniture and carpet.

My parents never missed taking us on annual holidays. We explored South Australian beaches and immersed in nature in the Flinders Ranges on camping trips, but settled on Tumby Bay for the annual January holiday when I was five. A tradition that continued forever.

The snake dream could have been a premonition. As soon as my youngest brother Sean could walk, he took to collecting reptiles in the scrub and brought creatures of all sorts back home, to either a glass aquarium in his room or to be released into our backyard.

Neighbours commented on the increase in snake sightings in Port Pirie around our home, which was part of the urban sprawl of suburbia meeting the low-lying saltbush scrub. My folks laughed them off, and proffered more fish from the unending supply in our freezer, presumably to distract them from their deepest reptile phobias.

We learned deep generosity and absolute acceptance of people from all walks and worlds from our parents.

After the Vietnam war concluded, refugees were relocated to regional South Australia. A family of four moved into the housing trust home across the road.

I got home from school and Dad was putting a big fresh snapper on a platter.

"It's for our new neighbours," Dad explained, and he walked over to welcome them to our neighbourhood brandishing the large succulent fish. Later that same evening, the family returned the favour with a massive platter of delicious spring rolls, the best I have ever eaten.

Mum was one of the leaders in the church. On Sundays we were always home for lunch late, often ferrying new people she found sitting in the back pew. People who had snuck into the service late for refuge or redemption.

Sometimes these people looked different to us, unkempt, sad, and often they were smelly. Mum didn't mind; whatever was ours was shared.

Christmases have ever been eclectic gatherings of the forgotten or lonely. Dad would pick up hitchhikers no matter how tattooed they were, and if they looked really dodgy, he would get Mum to sit in the back with us kids. That way, she could attack them from behind if required.

At school, my advanced reading age meant I sailed through the early years with teachers suggesting I skip Grade 3. I declined as my best friend would be left behind. As it happens a couple of years later, she relocated to the city, leaving me in desolation.

Fascinated by the holocaust in World War II, I devoured all reading material I could find on the topic. Both parents were working by the time Sean was at school, and censorship of my reading forays was impossible.

I proceeded unapprehended.

Diary of Anne Frank was written in my voice. I read accounts by women who authored the book using just their Prisoner of War number tattooed on their skin. Immersed in death and survival, rape, betrayal, and genocide, I lived many lifetimes in a few short years.

Our home was open to all and sundry with meals prepared to nourish the bodies and souls of our visitors. Saturday mornings was impromptu gathering time and I learned to cook at a young age, so would prepare cake or scones, while Mum made bottomless cups of tea.

The first meal I learned to cook was spaghetti Bolognese, and I would whip that up from age nine for the masses. In our home, we were seen and heard.

Mum would sit with me when I was sad at night-time, and tell me I could do anything I wanted to in the whole wide world. That I was loved, I was good enough, and I was cared for, whatever I chose. She would say that the greatest gift they could give us was independence.

Mum studied social work after Sean was born and taught budget management. She also taught family planning.

It was the seventies. In primary school I invited friends home to explore her suitcase of sex aids, condoms, and pamphlets, which educated our whole year level on the joy of sex in black and white.

On Thursdays Mum volunteered for Lifeline and they redirected the calls to our home phone. We had to remember not to answer the phone. Just in case a suicidal client was calling out for help on the precipice of some high place, plummeting through the lows of their lives.

Dad worked at the local lead smelter. He started as a fitter and evolved with the business, embracing computer technology, and worked his way into senior management by the end of his career. Mum worked there, too, when computers took up whole rooms. She did data entry but was forced to resign on marriage as married women were not allowed to have jobs in 1966.

Feminism was a key theme, not overtly, but innately. It was part of everything we saw and experienced in our upbringing. The respect Dad demonstrated to Mum. The fierce anger she expressed when his frustration spilled over into the occasional punching of doors. This habit ceased immediately when Mum threatened to put a hole in his boat for each new door he splintered.

Dad soon retreated from those outbursts and sought other more productive ways to express his feelings. We were encouraged to speak our mind, have our say, solve our own problems with their support and counselling, and take responsibility for our mistakes.

When Sean went to school, Mum went to work full time. Dad would finish at 3.30pm, so we had the best of both our parents. Sport was big and we played basketball, softball, hockey, and soccer.

When I was seven, my grade three teacher told us to call her by her first name only. I loved Shan so much. At a school camp while playing tyre forts with the boys who were hot and sweaty, they took their tops off.

I asked Shan if we could take our tops off too, and she allowed it. We played in pure freedom before the weight of sexual identity inhibited our humanity.

I asked Shan home for tea to meet my parents.

Mum and Dad loved her too. Shan changed my life with the true feminist values demonstrated and supported, equality for all, while being made to feel special, honoured and seen.

Whether it was the reading material, or the negative self-talk I berated myself with throughout childhood, I felt like I had lived a long time, over many lives.

My currency was storytelling, and I overshared. Telling all the secrets of my soul at school, I opened myself to ridicule, rejection, and judgement. It is a trend I expanded on with ever increasing regularity. Truth telling is important.

My smoking buddy was Delia, and together we also tried our hand at shoplifting down the main street. Temptation and acceptance were the shadow and light of my life, and was fully explored.

One day with school friends at the local shop, I stole some knickers from the box of sale items, shoving them down my corduroy trousers as I left. Huddled behind the fence of an empty block on the way home, I giggled with my friends as they marvelled at my skill.

They hadn't seen a thing.

Maria was a tall Aboriginal friend whose father was an award-winning boxer. She pulled on my arm.

"Can I have a pair to take home?" she asked, her eyes were shining with the adrenaline rush.

"No," I said, "I took the risk. You will need to steal your own." Maria shrugged and we all headed to our houses in time for dinner.

Next day at school, I arrived anticipating newfound popularity for my illegal behaviour.

The children were in small groups with their backs turned. Maria caught my eye and turned her shoulders away, shutting me out of the circle.

I walked past towards class.

"Knicker Pincher."

It was a vicious whisper. I couldn't tell who had said it.

The girls giggled. Looking furtively my way. Then the whispers got louder.

"Knicker Pincher, Knicker Pincher, Knicker Pincher," the chant was a taunt, I ran to class ashamed.

In class I was passed a note by one of the boys.

"Dirty Knicker Pincher," it read. I screwed it up and bowed my head.

Tears began to flow down my cheeks. The day was hot and eternally long. Shame filled my soul and as soon as the final bell rang, I ran for home.

It was unusual that Mum was home early that day. I ran through the house and slammed the door, falling face down on my bed sobbing.

Mum followed me in.

"What's up darling?" she asked. "Are you okay?"

"I've been stupid Mum," I spilled it out to my confidante and number one supporter, "I stole some knickers from the local shop and now the kids at school are teasing me, calling me 'Knicker Pincher'....they are cruel and I feel so bad about what I have done!"

Fresh sobs burst from me as Mum held me close.

"That's disappointing, Andrea," she said calmly.

Disappointing Mum was as bad as it got.

I howled louder and buried my face in my bed covers.

"When we do the wrong thing, we have the chance to fix it," Mum said. "Get your pocket money and the knickers, and I will go to the shopkeeper with you. You can take them back, apologise and pay for them."

"But I am wearing them!" I said distraught.

Mum hid a smile.

"Get the rest of the knickers and your money, wash your face and let's go," she said. "The anticipation and our imagination always make it worse than it really is. It is good to face up to when we do the wrong thing, say we are sorry and ask for forgiveness."

She squeezed my shoulder. I went to wash the guilty tears from my face.

Home could be like church sometimes.

Mum walked me around the shop, and stood beside me as I faced the shopkeeper, scared but resolved. I held out the contraband.

The shopkeeper stood peering at me over the counter with an angry scowl.

He wasn't very happy.

"Thanks for your honesty on this occasion," he said. "It is very sad to be stolen from. We work very hard for the products in our store and stealing undermines our efforts."

"I am truly sorry," I said. "It won't happen again."

"Good to hear," he said as he took the money proffered in my shaking hand.

He hesitated and peered at me closely.

"You know, I heard that a girl matching your description has been shoplifting down the main street. Have you got a friend with brown hair, about the same age?" he asked.

He looked down his nose at me, x-raying me with his eyes as he continued.

"You wouldn't know anything about that would you?"

My head became hot and my face flushed with shame.

"No sir, I don't," I lied. I turned and ran from the shop sobbing again.

I hid behind the same fence I had huddled with my friends the day before.

Mum came looking for me and when she walked around the fence, I was crying fresh tears of shame.

"Andrea, you have done the right thing owning up and you need to keep doing the right thing. You have choices, and choices take us places. Make good choices, darling. It's up to you," Mum held me as I cried then we walked home together.

The next day we were at Delia's place.

"Let's go down the street for a spot of 'Christmas shopping'," she said with a sly wink.

"No more shoplifting for me Delia. I can't live with myself," I stated the fact.

"But you are so good at it!" she exclaimed with a gentle punch to my shoulder.

"I know! What a skill right?" I was sarcastic. "We have choices Delia and I choose No."

I was resolute.

"Okay," she said, accepting my decision. "Let's go out for a smoke."

So we did.

It was at that moment our paths diverged. Choices defined my destiny. I started to focus more on my friends at church, and Delia did her own thing. I ended up baptised and Delia ended up in jail. It turns out that life truly is a 'choose our own ending adventure' of our own making. It is all about our choices and how we listen to our whispers of wisdom for guidance.

Intuition has saved me more than once. There was the time when I was twelve, visiting Shan's son, who had made a cassette recording of his KISS album for me.

We sat on his verandah, talking, and a group of his mates arrived on their pushbikes.

Chapter 2

"Wanna come for a ride to paradise, Andrea?" Flint asked, "We are heading out there now."

Paradise was along a dirt road through the flats in the scrub on the edge of town. It was a small paddock in the middle of a barren landscape, filled with unexplained hillocks of bright green if slightly itchy couch grass.

Like an outdoor living room, it was where the boys took the cask of wine they stole from the house next to the Seventh Day Adventist Church in grade seven, taking turns in swigging it until Stewart was vomiting so badly, he churned up his pink bubblegum at my feet.

We girls had accompanied them post-theft on the adventure, and watched as Tony loaded Stewart onto his bike to take him home, hoping his Dad didn't see him as they snuck him into the house. Stewart experienced a tough life, youngest of a range of brothers in a rough home.

I didn't think anything of it when Flint asked me on a bike ride to paradise. It was where we went. We pedalled hard and reached the grassy knolls, dropped our bikes and flopped in amongst the rolling grass lounge chairs.

The boys looked around. I settled on the opposite side of the circle. Innocent as a lamb.

"What shall we do?" said Tim, as he leaned back and looked at the sky.

"I know," said Philip, "Let's play truth or dare!"

We laughed.

Then there was a moment.

All the boys surveyed the circle, still laughing, and one by one their eyes settled on me.

I had a flash of recognition. I was not one of the boys here. I was the only girl, and some of these kids were older than Flint and me. Some of these boys I didn't know THAT well.

My legs took over the thinking, and in a flash, I was up and running. Jason reached over to grab me as I ran past, but that pumped adrenaline even faster through my veins while my legs took off at breakneck speed.

I didn't stop for my bike as that would slow me down. I just ran as fast as I could up the dirt road between the saltbush and swampy salt lakes towards town and safety.

Looking back as I ran, I saw that one of the bigger boys was in hot pursuit. Now I was really scared and began to sob as I ran. Sobbing took oxygen, and he soon caught me and turned back as he flung me over his shoulder. He started to carry me towards the boys who stood waiting on the road, watching with interest as the chase came to its inevitable end.

I was terrified.

I started to thump him on the back as I dangled down behind him.

"Put me down! NOW! Put me down!" I screamed and sobbed with terror.

Maybe it surprised him just how scared I was. Maybe I hurt him with my incessant beating. But my fearful reaction was enough for him to gently put me down on the ground.

He looked at me quizzically. It was like I was from another planet and he wasn't quite sure what he had caught. His hands hung by his sides as he watched me sobbing.

"Get my bike!" I ordered. "And DO NOT tell them I am crying!" The cries caught in my throat and I turned away to continue my walk towards town.

He walked away from me. Blood was thumping in my ears as I heard him yell back to the group.

"She wants her bike, AND she's crying!"

I kept walking.

When I reached our primary school on the edge of town, I went to the incinerator which was enclosed by brick walls on three sides. It was where the grade sevens hung out at break times. I wiped tears and sweat from my face, as my breathing slowed.

Flint arrived with my bike.

"Are you okay?" he said, concerned.

"I am okay, feeling a bit stupid, but I am okay," I said.

"I don't know what happened there, Andrea," he said. "You just ran off!"

"I don't know either, I just suddenly didn't feel right to be there as the only girl," I said.

"Fair enough, mate," he said as he punched me in the upper arm. "I'll go home from here. Enjoy the KISS."

"I will, Flint, thanks," I said and took my bike to ride home. Still shaken when I got there, Mum noticed I had been crying and followed me into my bedroom.

"What happened, love?" she quizzed me as I flopped on the bed.

"I don't know, Mum, I just didn't feel safe," I said.

"That's okay, love, always listen to yourself. You can trust what you feel, it can keep you out of trouble, and from getting hurt," she said as she stood to leave the room.

What I learned is that being female is not the safest thing to be. Things happen to girls, that we don't deserve or expect. My senses were sharpened, and I became alert and awake to threats. Threats imposed mostly by men. Men who cannot be trusted.

Chapter 3

From a young age I had big ambitions. I was seven when I decided I would be a lawyer. A whole life of exploration in the books I consumed, indicated that lawyers always win, while looking after people's rights in the process.

My sort of job.

Our dinner table discussions covered the social issues of the times and using debating techniques of a former life, I tackled my parents and their friends to create credible arguments.

Our laminated wooden look table, surrounded by deep brown glossy vinyl brown chairs, bordered with gold brass fittings sat on deep blue carpet in the heart of our home. As children we were part of the fabric of the family. We were all equal and close by Mum and Dad's elbows as politics, social justice or community issues were discussed.

My only goals were to get a degree and go to Europe, where I felt inexplicably drawn.

I was ten when Mum told me that the questions I asked her in constant curiosity, she hadn't considered until she was in her thirties. Perhaps legacy of the dinner table discussions, and my constant presence in listening to adult conversations. I wrestled with big ideas and concerns.

"How are babies made?" I knew the answer by the time I was four.

"Why do bad things happen to good people?" I read every newspaper I could lay my hands on.

"Where do we go when we die?" Mum was patient and explained the meaning of life and all its mysteries, honest with not knowing if she had no solution to share.

The folks bought the whole set of World Book Encyclopedia on a payment plan, and from then the answer was "look it up". I devoured those books.

At night I never slept before midnight, as thoughts of catastrophe and how I would save the world single handed, crowded out sleep. Often I cried, overwhelmed by the choices and horror in the world.

"You can be whatever you want to be," Mum crooned as she stroked my hair and held my hand willing me back to sleep.

To compound my sensitivities, I was accidentally traumatised when I snuck into the lounge behind my parents while they watched Alfred Hitchcock's The Birds. Horrific images burned my retinas and fear of birds seared my soul.

My parents sat transfixed to the screen, oblivious to me behind them, each in their own recliner. The blood curdling screams of actors drowned out my terrorised silent sobs.

Horror movies always seemed real to me.

"Why are the lights never on?"

"Why do people hurt each other?"

"How come fear is the driver of everything we see on television, apart from Sesame Street and the Goodies?"

Aside from my parents, I had guidance in my life through close connections with some of their friends. In particular, our accountant friend Nick, who said I was his protégé and challenged my perspectives with long dinner conversations. Another close family friend was Anna-Maria, who took me under her wing, taught me to cook tacos, and shared her cast-off wardrobe with me.

In the town I grew up there is an abandoned uranium plant, with tailings dams right next to the salt creek system behind the smelters. My Grandy had worked there when they moved from Quorn to Port Pirie. When they moved to Port Augusta, they left my mum to stay behind for her final years of school. Grandy ended up dying of cancer, but we will never know if it was the uranium plant or the power station residues that killed him.

Anna-Maria had swum in the tailings dams as a kid, and by her thirties, was fighting all manner of rare cancers that kept popping up in her body. She was a light in my life, who treated me as an adult and as a friend.

When I was fourteen, I rode a pretend motorbike into silent reading after lunch in our home class which held a range of different aged kids, where we met to sign in and out of school each day.

Everyone was already settled in as I rode into class on my invisible machine.

I did a wheelie on my motorbike and mouthed the noises.

"Vrooommmm, Vrooommmm, Vrooommm." I parked it carefully next to my desk as the other kids looked up, giggling. Anything for a distraction from silent reading.

As I dismounted and plopped into my chair, I looked up to see Mister Horsfall looking over his glasses at me. He was not happy.

"Andrea, after the session please wait behind so I can speak with you," It was more of a growl than a request.

The quarter hour of silent reading was eternal. Everyone looked sideways at me as they filed out to put books in their bags and head to their next class.

I waited in my seat, and then approached my certain doom.

"Yes, Mister Horsfall?" innocence seeped through my inflection.

"Andrea, I know that silent reading can be boring for some, and I know that reading is something you love, so distracting others from the task for your own enjoyment means they don't get the

Chapter 3

practice they need." He was serious. I was suitably sombre as the occasion demanded complete submission to avoid the inevitable result.

I nodded.

Sombrely.

"I understand, I am sorry, it won't happen again," I finished with a retreating flourish and flung my bag onto my back, readying to leave for my next class.

He wasn't finished.

"As punishment, you can write me 500 lines tonight," he continued and picked up his chalk.

He turned his back on me and wrote on the blackboard.

I will not ride pretend motorbikes into silent reading.

"Five hundred lines Mister Horsfall? Really?" I thought we were beyond all that slave rote labour by now, but obviously not.

"Five hundred lines. On my desk tomorrow." He was firm and the case was closed.

"Okay, sir, your wish is my command," I was sarcastic as I took my leave.

"I could increase it if you prefer," he said.

"It's alright sir, I get the message. It won't happen again," I left the room before he changed my mind.

That night the discussion, complete with true confessions of my transgression, took up dinnertime, as I told my parents of my plight.

Mum agreed with me.

"Five hundred lines? Surely there are more productive uses of your time. Couldn't he get you to pick up papers on the yard?" Mum queried, head tipped towards shoulder, brow furrowed as we pondered the alternative options.

"I know, right?" I said. "I was thinking of writing a poem instead."

"Good idea, love," said Dad, as he left the table to watch the news. As always, I had their support.

I went to my room and penned a poem, which I wrote out neatly and put in an envelope addressed to Mister Horsfall the next morning.

"This is my imposition Sir," I said. "I approached it a little more creatively. Hope you don't mind."

I gave him a shrug and a grin and took my seat, silently like obedient students do.

I watched him open the envelope and read the contents.

Why I Should be Quiet in English when Mr Horsfall is Teaching

I have to be quiet, what a bind!

Several reasons I must find

For behaving myself in Mr Horsfall's class,

Not playing the fool or being an ass!

Oh what can I do? What can I write?

I don't want to do another impo tonight!

I must be quiet for noise prevents,

Other class members from making sense

Of what Mr Horsfall's trying to teach

Bringing understanding within reach.

Chapter 3

But what about me? What reasons for me?

The teacher's pet perhaps I could be!

Maybe I should take an apple tomorrow

And watch Mr Horsfall suffer in sorrow!

"Why Andrea's not so bad," he'll think,

"Why am I mean to her? She doesn't stink!"

Another benefit quietness offers

Is not ending up in the Principal's office!

Having to explain my behaviour;

Please 'Man of Steele', be my saviour.

The teacher may even hold in reserve

The excellent marks I truly deserve,

If I fail to toe the line

And cause distress with my little rhyme!

Though this impo is tongue in cheek

It took much longer than prose, so meek,

So if I keep the promises I make

Let's keep it a game of give and take,

My discontinuing classroom larks

And this poem adds to my English marks!

THE END

He was trying to hide his smile, but it broke through at the edges.

"Okay, Andrea, this will suffice for your imposition for now. Please refrain from riding your motorbike into silent reading in the future. It can be parked out the front," he said, folding the paper and putting it back in its envelope.

That was the last it was talked about until the end of the year, when the school magazine came out. There was my poem. An imposition, my punishment, published.

An avid reader, my world expanded through books and my imagination. Horror in movies gave me nightmares for months, but in books it was not a problem as somehow my imagination set its own limits. Stephen King outlined the end of so many lives with descriptive deaths, all of which I devoured with delight.

Ghosts, mystery, and unexplained phenomena were staple fare. The holocaust in World War II which enacted the genocide of over six million Jewish people was a fascination from a young age. A strange way of making sense of the world which feeds itself on fear.

At school I was always teased for my vocabulary with the kids cruelly observing my penchant for big words and the ability to spell them. It was never an honour, I was always punished, and made to feel smaller than I already felt myself to be in my little lonely life.

"Knicker pincher, smart bitch, dictionary eater," the calls in the school yard cut deep, depending on the year of attack, and how my resilience meter was going.

Chapter 3

Once in early high school our teacher spelled vacuum wrong on the blackboard.

"Miss, Vacuum has one C and two U's", I called out helpfully. The teacher was immediately affronted and fought back.

"No, it doesn't!" she claimed loudly as she looked at the board tilting her head.

"It does, Miss," I persisted.

She wanted to escape the heat of thirty sets of thirteen-year-old eyes.

"I am sure I have it spelt correctly, but if you *are* right, I will buy you a Coke," she said.

It was the days of healthy canteen food options.

"If I am right, buy the whole class a Coke!" I challenged, stomach tightening as I backed myself in, and put myself in the firing line of the whole class.

The battle lines were drawn.

A dictionary was delved into.

Silently she changed the word to be spelled correctly on the board. Vacuum. One C and two Us.

At recess time the class gathered eagerly at the canteen window to claim their Cokes. Once the lids on the medium sized bottles were popped, they all raced off together.

I sat alone on the bench by the classroom in the sun to read, sipping my victory Coke. It was a short-lived moment of triumph for the collective.

Books opened my world and my heart. Imagination transported me across the seven seas and far up into the stars. Every main character was me; their voice was mine, their traumas and joys I shared, eager for lessons that expanded my soul.

I was fourteen when Mum put the local newspaper in front of me.

"See it?" she asked.

There in the display classifieds was an advertisement for a play reading. The local adult theatre group Studio 2 were looking for actors. The season play was Diary of Anne Frank.

A dream come true!

My voice was shaking as I called to register my interest. A few days later the letterbox revealed the script to review for the reading. My stomach is my feeling barometer. On the evening, it flip-flopped between terror and excitement as Mum dropped me off at the theatre.

"All you can do is your best, Andrea," Mum kissed me, "We are proud of you".

There was a room of people I didn't know.

Everyone sat in a circle, mostly adults and me.

There was another girl with dark hair, reading for the part of Anne who was in her early twenties.

The reading went around, everyone embraced their character and expressed their lines with full feeling.

I let out a blood curdling scream. Everyone jumped. I proceeded to read the final lines of the play, when Anne and her family are discovered by the Gestapo in their secret room above the factory. Tears rolled down my cheeks, as with hands outstretched, I was dragged away from my love interest Pieter.

In that moment I was Anne, channelling her fear, outrage, and terror at what happened next. Anne was me. I had read her diary many times, thought her thoughts, felt her blood running through my veins.

Fourteen and flung into the unknown in a world full of despots, depravity, and death. It was my life in my full colour mind.

I got the part.

By the time the production was ready for staging we had spent countless hours together as a group, perfecting the lines and action.

Nicole, the other dark-haired girl played my sister, my German teacher Mister Mickan from school was my father, and Pieter was a young teacher who I got to kiss in the final scene.

Chapter 3

We practiced many times.

"I think we need to do that again….", I said as I angled my head in the other direction and tried not to slurp so hungrily. "It doesn't feel *quite* right…"

Pieter kindly acquiesced to the consummate professional I professed to be.

Because of the number of lines I had in the show, the whole play was embedded in my heart. I became the onstage prompt for all the actors.

We did three shows over three nights. Beautiful flowers arrived at my dressing room before curtain call, and a family friend gave me a ceramic duck, for Missus Quack Quack, one of my lines in the play.

The highlight beyond the standing ovations was the news the doctor who had brought me into the world cried at the final scene. My kisses had reached perfection!

By the time I was fifteen I decided that law was too hard, homework gave me the right royals, and journalism was for me. I sought work experience in a whole range of workplaces to flex my writing skills. Angsty poetry filled my notebooks as I poured out my worries and teenage confusion.

My next great escape was applying for a student exchange with Rotary to New Zealand, with interviews and selection process happening as the play was wrapping up.

Mum and Dad supported all my adventures and funded my trip. In Auckland I connected with Rachel, who became my best friend and pen pal after I left the land of the long white cloud for home. In drama at school we read Romeo and Juliet. I was Romeo and Rachel was my Juliet. I was so enamoured with Rachel, I promised to name my daughter to honour her.

It was 1985 and the French bombed the flagship Greenpeace vessel, the Rainbow Warrior at Port of Auckland, which was on its way to protest French nuclear testing in the Pacific. We went down to see the ship listing in the water. History was being made all around me. New Zealand glowed golden green with gentle rolling hills, and stark white sheep dotted throughout the endless fields. My thigh muscles became strong and defined from walking up and down volcano craters to school. Dormant suburban basins resisting the pressures of deep time. A landscape covered with hopeful houses where eruptions could have been regular once. We didn't know the difference.

There were four forbidden D's to be an exchange student. The golden rules.

No dating, drinking, driving, or drugs. I only broke three of them.

In New Zealand you had to be 15 to get a driver's licence, and I was 15, so one of the guys from church took me for driving lessons. Another guy from church, whose girlfriend was overseas on an exchange to the US, asked me to the school formal. My host mother made me a beautiful lace and blue silk formal dress for my date.

There was a drug raid at Northcote college, orchestrated by the teachers one morning, when we first arrived at school. All the students smoking in the tennis court area were locked into that enclosure, then marched in single file groups to a classroom, where they were searched for contraband.

While sitting in the schoolyard, the rest of us observed with interest as little packets of stuff flew out of the windows at various stages, only to be gathered by other kids loitering in the quadrangle, stuffed in pants, pockets and bras, ready for re-circulation.

At the school formal there was a sweet burning smell I didn't recognise. Then I saw the kids sharing what must have been a joint on the dance floor. It wasn't passed to me.

The drink came at a family function, where I was offered a drink of Baileys Irish Cream and milk after dinner, and it would have been rude to say no. I broke the rules and survived to confess another day.

While in New Zealand I wrote regularly to family and to Anna-Maria, who was struggling with her chemotherapy treatment. Mum let me know she wasn't very well.

Chapter 3

I received a letter from Anna-Maria which was honest in her appraisal of her health. She was dying.

"I promise I will wait for you to return home," she wrote.

One night in bed in Auckland, two weeks before my flight back home I couldn't sleep.

I thought of Anna-Maria, I cried, I tossed and turned.

Restless I watched the bedside alarm clock numbers glow red, turning slowly towards dawn.

In the wee hours of the morning, I heard a whisper inviting me to sleep, I sighed, and slumber took me into peace, tears drying on my cheeks.

The next day the phone rang. It was Mum.

"I am so sorry, love, Anna-Maria couldn't wait any longer. She died during the night. She is at peace now with no more pain," Mum's voice broke. I began to cry.

"What time, Mum?" I asked.

When she told me, and allowing for the time difference, I realised that Anna-Maria and I had let go into sleep at the same moment. Right when I heard that whisper, willing me to let go.

Finally free to rest, we were together in spirit to the end as she promised.

Only I woke up.

Chapter 4

My life has been invested in a search for love. A forensic search for signs, as I scrutinise the universe, looking deeply in the eyes of passing strangers to see if love hides there.

Truthfully, I have always seen and sensed love everywhere.

Every morning the birds called their love from the trees in the trills of happy dawning. Entries in my journals recorded the weather and natural surroundings, before my heart poured out on the page.

Thoughts of deeper meaning were seeded in church from birth, and have expanded in a life journey of spiritual exploration, diving ever deeper. I can see love everywhere and definitely in nature. The nature of people reflects love too, but it is the love for ourselves and the other that is our greatest teacher this life.

It was at a Junior Christian Education Camp that I gave my heart to Jesus. The last service of the retreat was a celebration of the week. The hall was full of guilty teenagers when the young preacher spoke directly to my soul.

"Do you want to be free? Do you want forgiveness that means you live forever in rapture with God?" he intoned.

My heart responded.

Chapter 4

Who doesn't?

Tears began to fall softly down my face as I hesitated, then slowly raised my hand.

"Come to the front for redemption," he offered. "We have people here who will pray with you."

It was like I was taken over by an angel as I sobbed, rose to my feet and ran down the aisle to fall at the altar at his feet. His cool hand touched my forehead. Acceptance and love flooded throughout my body.

My whole face was leaking fluids, as two young leaders lifted me to my feet, and led me to the step outside to pray. They put their hands on mine.

"May Andrea accept the grace of Jesus. May He protect her and care for her, all the days and nights of her life," they held my sweaty hands, and wiped tears of shame from my face.

My heart broke open and light poured in. Behind us inside the hall, the dam wall of resistance overflowed, as young people followed my lead, making their own way to the front of the room to accept their dose of forgiveness.

When my tears ran dry, all I felt was calm peace. I claimed the forgiveness that was mine that moment, and was free. Free to live forever in the love that suffused my soul.

The experience confirmed my long-lived insight that I was not alone, and that voice in my head was not mine. Perhaps it was God's all along.

In the beginning there was the word. Bible study meant philosophical exploration of the word and the world. Stories of love, of hope, of loss, of betrayal, of forgiveness, and redemption. And the future, full of golden light.

My feelings have always been big, and thoughts deep. Like everyone I pondered the meaning of life, the origin of spirit, and whether that voice in my head was actually mine as a separate entity or part of something bigger.

Something whole, complete, and perfect, despite the chaos we create around ourselves in our physical being and doing.

Juxtaposed between Pink Floyd's *The Wall*, Christian theatre groups, and the sacred communion of relationship, my comprehension of life as servants of spirit, have oscillated from the sweetest prayers of light, to the darkest moments of isolation, despair and grief.

This is our human experience.

These are our patterns.

As humans we carry great weights and often, we carry the drama of others in vain attempts to protect them from the certain pain we inflict on ourselves through our stories and drama.

Meeting Clayton was predestined. Fate determined through my choices that carried me all the way to the end.

On the sharpened edges of all the different groups of kids at school, I was ever hungry for their acceptance. My creative story telling about my newfound fantasy love interest, ensured that all eyes were on me.

"Clayton came for youth group with his brothers and the WAY he looked at me across the supper table after the car rally, I can tell it's the real thing", I swooned, poetic and dreamy.

I was friends with Clayton's brothers at church, both straitlaced innocent young men and part of our youth group, of which I was the youngest.

Matthew was a star accountant, with countless cloth patches the evidence of chivalrous and practical awards, sewn in single file rows on the scout blanket which adorned his single bed.

Peter was doing a carpentry apprenticeship. I helped him with his studies, as constant childhood ear infections had caused slight deafness not picked up until grade two, which left him behind in his learning.

Both Matthew and Peter were too old for me, and while lovely, they were too... dare I say it? Boring.

But their younger brother Clayton? The possibilities lit me up.

Chapter 4

"Clayton drives a really cool HT Holden and wears wrap around black sunnies, golden hair growing over his collar," I reported at school on Monday after interrogating his brothers at church the day before.

My classmate's eyes were wide as I described our love unfolding in explicit virginal schoolgirl detail, coloured by scenes which secretly revealed deep lust and longing arranged on my mother's bookshelves.

Feelings that were explored through fiction and when breaking out of my heart were coddled by the church.

"He writes to me. AND we kiss."

"Long and deep."

Everyone shivered with delight.

Tingles in tight places, as our shared schoolgirl dreams of forever love sparkled as stars in our eyes. True love, so young with feelings so big they threatened to break the bounds of my skin.

After immersion in Mum's suitcase of family planning resources and reading the puberty guide, *Where did I come from?* I was on tenterhooks awaiting the first showing of blood that proved I was finally a woman.

It never came. Eventually I pretended to my girlfriends that the symbolic red stain had appeared in my knickers, and I, just like them was a young woman, fertile and menstruating. Except I wasn't.

I was different. Poised for womanhood that never arrived.

Clayton was four years older than me when he became my secret suitor.

So secret not even he knew of our entanglement.

The girls who usually teased or turned away, were lapping it up wanting more. My popularity grew, and those girls who scorned me at sports day and chose me last for basketball teams in physical education lessons, were putty in my hands.

In those moments I forgot the impact of the excruciating habit where teachers chose the two most popular kids, one male, one female, to then choose their teams, one at a time from a group of kids attempting to look like we didn't care. Those team captain types were suddenly my closest confidants, leaning on my legs, only just preventing real drool from escaping their parted lips.

My creative writing came in handy as embellishments ran riot. Recess and lunchtime became a tawdry expose of a fantasy world I cooked up for them to relish.

Finally Clayton did come to see his brothers for the weekend, and we met in person, at church youth group.

He drove a HT Holden just like his brother had said, and his golden sandy hair was even longer than had been described. He was wearing a paisley shirt and a cheeky grin.

Our relationship flourished. I created it to be so.

We did eventually kiss, and he wrote me a song in a card he made. He had adorned it with Dirty Harry film quotes written next to the souvenir ticket of our first cinema date, and the docket from our first lunch at the Central Hotel with salads like Nana made, was stuck to its border. Clayton was a romantic.

His accompanying note said to sing the poem he had penned while playing the blues with a harmonica in A Minor.

It was destiny.

Clayton was a preacher's son. He told me how when growing up, he was accompanied by his three older brothers and baby sister, as they sat patiently with their mum in the front row of church, twice each Sunday. Hair slicked back neat, their feet in long white socks and sandals, dangled at different heights from the pew. Their Dad preached love and forgiveness from the pulpit. The reward for faith in an unseen God.

Clayton told me how he often heard his mother crying in the night, softly, whimpering in the thin walled Queenslander they grew up in before they moved back to South Australia.

"Shut Up!", he heard his dad say, followed by a slap. "Open your legs now!"

Chapter 4

"As a child I would shield under the rugs, closing my ears," he said. It was a strategy he had learned to avoid the belt, or the kick from behind in the ribs, wielded by his frustrated father.

"My brother would have his back turned to the wall, feigning sleep. The sudden screaming cries of my baby sister, woken in the crib next to my parent's bed, pierced the night."

"I heard their bed groan a familiar creak as my mother escaped from under my father to tend the baby."

I was horrified.

Clayton took me to meet his mother and sister. His mum's place was adorned with photographs of her four boys, neatly dressed in white shirts, ties, shorts, long white socks and sandals. Their hair wet and flattened back and all sitting in an obedient row. Other frames showed his mother holding his baby sister, swaddled in crocheted layette, coloured innocent white.

I was sixteen when we shared a trip to the Grampians with his mother and sister. His mother told me how she played her role as the local minister's wife with five young children to feed, surviving only by buying loaves of stale bread on a predetermined budget. Meanwhile her husband feasted on cigars and the other men's wives he was marriage counselling, all in the course of his calling.

At the same time his unfortunate family were collecting cans from the bins around town, feeling prosperous to live in a state that paid refunds for empty drink containers. The boys rode their bikes, heavily laden with big bags of recyclables to be able to buy the essentials.

She told me about the various operations she endured to her hands and wrists from warding off her husband's blows. She spoke loudly of the hearing loss she suffered, after being taken on a flight against doctor's orders, after having her ears boxed. His mother was bitter and saddened.

Apparently, these were things ministers and other men did to their wives sometimes.

Those dark fearful nights concluded in the event of his parent's messy divorce, with his sister going to live with his mum, and his brothers all grown up and moved out. Prolonged family court proceedings ensued over his little sister, who refused to go and spend time with her dad.

"My Dad has a new wife now," Clayton explained. "A strong feminist who is doing her PhD in women's studies."

Clayton moved in with his dad when he came back into the city. Then he got a job in my hometown as a camera operator at the television station. It was true love.

Clayton introduced me to old cars, sixties music, and my first joint.

"How did I get to seventeen and not even *know* The WHO existed?" I asked him. My brain could not fathom how such big bands who had changed the world in the sixties were completely foreign to me, apart from the Beatles and Pink Floyd's *The Wall*, my Dad's go-to, which he listened at volume ten while sleeping in a beanbag between the speakers.

Comfortably numb.

After summer ended, I moved to the city to enrol in university and pursue my life dream. Clayton quit his job as television news camera operator to be by my side. We spent every moment together, twenty-four hours a day, seven days a week. We were best friends and when I shared the end of my virginity with him at age seventeen, we became lovers.

Not much study was getting done. My board arrangement in the leafy Eastern suburbs was threatened by my landlords because of Clayton's constant presence. We moved in together. The drives from one end of the city to the other cost time and money, and our love couldn't wait.

The summer I was seventeen turning eighteen, Mum and Dad attempted to coax me from the relationship. They convinced me that Clayton was not the one, that I would do better to focus on my university degree, and forget the boyfriend causing the distractions they saw.

"Andrea, we want the best for you darling, and you always wanted to get your degree and go to Europe," Mum was persistent.

Chapter 4

"How often *are* you at University Andrea?" Dad asked. "We are investing in your studies you know, and we want you to succeed."

Dad is ever practical.

I agreed with them.

Clayton drove up to see me for the weekend. I took him aside for a serious chat about our future.

"Clayton, it is over between us," I said. "I need to focus on my studies, get my degree so I can go to Europe."

I knew the story by rote. It was my childhood dream.

"But I love you, Andrea," he said, "You are the only one for me. Our love is forever."

I cried as I held him, but was resolute.

He left and returned to the city.

I had broken his heart.

My family travelled to the beach for our annual holiday. I was melancholy. Clayton drove over to see me. He cried and wrote me another poem. My heart melted.

We redoubled our efforts to sustain our forbidden love. We felt like Romeo and Juliet.

I went back to the city to start my second year of university, changing courses in an attempt to get into the competitive journalism degree through a side door.

I am not sure if Clayton ever actually asked me to marry him, so perhaps I created that too. It seemed the logical next step. I was eighteen when we went camping with friends in the Flinders Ranges, and visited Mum and Dad on the way, to announce our intention to marry in the summer.

Mum went to bed and cried.

She was still in bed when we arrived back after three days in the bush.

I was summoned to her darkened bedroom.

"You are so young," she sobbed. "Just take your time."

My dad stood outside their bedroom door and as I left the room, he opened his arms and held me close. Dad didn't say much at all. As a last stand, Mum and Dad told me they were going to boycott the wedding. Making me choose.

I dug my heels in, ever determined, just like Mum had taught me. Clayton and I drove back to our house in the city.

I retreated to our rental in the suburbs to plan the matrimonial event. A tight budget was understating it somewhat. I had a part time job and was studying on the opposite side of town.

Our home was ramshackle and abandoned by the elderly owner who died in the lounge, leaving a legacy trail of oily hand marks on the walls, as he moved about the house in his final years.

Our phone had been disconnected, because my meagre wage at the primary school didn't cover all the bills. Our front and back yards were full of long grass intermingled with weeds because we couldn't afford a lawnmower.

Clayton was a filmmaker full of potential, working on his art. He won the young filmmaker of the year award for a film about unemployed young people in the northern suburbs. Nineteen eighty-seven turned out to be the highlight of his career.

Following the film production, Clayton helped establish, and then volunteer at an organisation for unemployed people that taught filmmaking and music production skills.

Rock stars Jimmy Barnes and his brother John Swan were patrons who dropped in every now and again. In between dwindling university commitments and my range of part time jobs, it was where I joined Clayton to hang out during the week.

We spent Sundays at Clayton's dad's place for a barbecue lunch every week. We lay on the blue carpet in their front room and listened to the *White Album* by The Beatles, The Doors, the Kinks and *Pinball Wizard* by The Who, all on vinyl.

I couldn't imagine his father hitting anyone. He was quietly spoken and gentle, serene even. It was incongruous to think of the stories of abuse as we sat eating sausages and salad each Sunday.

Chapter 4

It was Mum's birthday in November. Suffering severe chest pains, Dad took her to the hospital. The doctor did a battery of tests. I was oblivious.

All the tests came back clear. The doctor met with Mum to discuss her case.

"I think you may be depressed," he said. "You know the meaning of 'crestfallen'?"

Mum wavered.

"It's a sinking feeling in the chest. Like a broken heart. It is definitely not a heart attack. We could try medication... for depression," he said.

Mum refused to take any drugs.

A month passed and one day there was a knock at the door of our ramshackle home in the suburbs.

Outside stood Mum and Dad. They had driven for three hours to the city, and waded through the weeds in the yard to knock on our dilapidated front door.

There were dirty dishes in the sink and not a surface to be seen in our home. I watched Mum take it all in, and I saw it through her eyes, silently resolving to focus more on housework in future.

"We have come to see you today, Andrea," Dad said, "Because we want to pay for your wedding."

It all felt a bit formal.

They were obviously chagrined at my proposal of a "bring your own plate" reception.

I swept off a surface, swiftly hiding the bong behind a chair, and put the kettle on. As I washed up some mugs for a cup of tea, I pulled the kitchen curtains across so the dope plants in the back yard weren't quite so obvious.

I didn't want to ruin what was a turning point in our relationship.

"Thanks so much, Mum and Dad, I love you and I have missed you," I said.

"That's alright, love," Dad said. "It's the right thing to do."

He looked pointedly at Mum, who smiled weakly, and reached out for my hand.

"We love you, Andrea, and you have our full support, whatever you choose, you know that," Mum said.

We smiled shyly at each other and sighed in unison.

So it happened.

We were married in a Uniting Church on a forty-three-degree Celsius Australian summer day. I wore the cream dress that Mum helped me buy for one hundred and fifty dollars. My wedding ring was a very thin gold band purchased for twenty-six dollars on the morning of the wedding.

Clayton's grandfather had gifted us a hundred dollars, thankfully, the week before the ceremony. Those funds also sponsored the groom's shoes, his white shirt and a three-dollar posy of flowers from the bucket outside the florist for my bouquet.

That scorching January day, I had just turned nineteen, and my knees were buckling before the vows. Dad hurried to get me a chair which saved my full faint to unconsciousness.

I nearly fainted three times during the service on our wedding day, in that big beautiful church adorned with stained glass windows of saints. It was where Clayton's father used to preach. It was a sign.

My parents paid for a beautiful reception at an Adelaide Hills pub beer garden. All our friends and family were there.

Afterwards we took our wedding money and headed for the city, where Clayton illegally parked the Holden out the front of a luxurious looking hotel, so we could book a night to consummate our betrothal as husband and wife. Clayton waited in the car.

I was still in my wedding dress. Confetti scattered as I ran into the front foyer of the hotel to ask the price of a room. The frangipanis in my hair held firm despite the heat.

A haughty concierge looked me up and down.

"It will be $250 for a *twin share* room," he said, disdain dripping from his posh accent like poisoned honey. I felt my cheeks get hot.

Chapter 4

Humiliated, I ran back out to the car.

There were a couple more experiences like that. I wished we had put wedding night accommodation on our list prior to the big day.

Eventually we settled on the Scotty's motel on the outskirts. The big Scotsman, in his tartaned landmark kilt on the corner, held ever silent bagpipes. He was our childhood signal that we had finally reached the city. It meant we were really truly, very nearly there.

We got in very late and had to wake the manager to sell us a room. We dragged our suitcase upstairs, discarding confetti like a breadcrumb trail back to safety. We shared our wedding night on a waterbed with its heat turned up to inferno.

We rolled around sweating, pulling aimlessly at sheets seeking relief from the heat, while the folds of the bed shed discarded condom wrappers and one used tampon, evidence of the work conducted at this inn before.

Our marriage started like that, uncomfortably warm, sexless, and cheap, all surely holy and promising signs of a bright new beginning in love.

Next day we ventured forth to Queensland, God's Country, in our fully laden HT Holden Station wagon, replete with dog Paisley and camping gear galore.

After driving across the centre of Australia, we arrived in Hope Street Warwick with one dollar and seventy-three cents in the bank, to stay with our best man's parents. We had enough money for one pie between us.

"We will have to get jobs," I said as I scanned the paper relentlessly. I called the newspaper to organise work experience, because they were advertising a cadetship as a journalist. My dream job.

I got the work experience but not the ongoing role.

Despite me being ever hopeful, there were warning signals.

My husband's persistent inability to hold down any sort of employment for more than the induction and first few days was astounding.

"Andrea," Clayton called. He walked in from work holding a long neck of beer in a brown paper bag, then swigged from the open top. He wiped his chin on the back of his hand.

"I got told today they won't be giving me any more shifts".

I sighed.

He had been kitchenhand at a local resort, and brought home some brilliant recipes, including blanched green beans in garlic and butter.

"I don't wash the dishes quite quickly enough," he said. "Apparently…"

He flopped into a chair and started to roll a smoke.

I did a hospitality course and vacuumed vast expanses of dark blue carpet in the local café, in unpaid work experience phases prior to unfulfilling waitressing jobs, while the boss with highly coiffed hair pointed out wayward crumbs on the floor.

Nervously facing each customer, I sweated, anxious to please and get it right, while being demonstrably clumsy with large hot stacks of plates.

Meanwhile Clayton continued his career in unemployment and grew his hair long.

We were crossing the street between the job agency and Centrelink when an old man yelled in our general direction.

"Get a job, you young yahoo!" he croaked loudly with venom as he passed us. We crossed without looking back.

"Old fucker," grumbled Clayton as he slumped into the welfare office.

I followed him in, and we waited our turn.

Chapter 5

It was in Queensland that I met Penny. Clayton got a new job at the bacon factory and was working a twelve-hour induction shift. I waited in town to take him home to our rented farmhouse, and dropped into the second-hand shop while I waited. I struck up a conversation with the jovial woman behind the counter. Penny invited me back to sit in the lounge at her place, once she shut up the shop.

"What are you doing here?" She asked like she could read my future.

"We need to get jobs," I said. "We got married in January and have been looking for full time work."

"You won't find much around here," Penny was matter of fact. "They don't like strangers in Warwick, particularly strangers from South Australia."

She talked like we had come from outer space.

Penny was the local pawnbroker and her Mum was the second-hand shop owner. Her Dad owned the real estate business with his office adjoining the shop. He had travelled Australia working as a soil tester when they arrived by ship from England, and found the best samples in the world on the Darling Downs.

They settled and bought land near Warwick.

"My parents got offered this stretch of land at the Gold Coast. A little shack community at Surfer's Paradise. Mum was adamant it was a good buy, but Dad shut her down. 'No, Mae,' he would say, 'What would you know about real estate?'" Penny reminisced.

"Turns out they could have bought the whole of Surfer's strip for 40,000 pounds."

My eyes widened and we laughed at the possibility. Surfer's strip was the mecca of the Gold Coast, by then home to high rise buildings and high rolling businesspeople.

"Of course, I could give you some cash jobs through the shop," she offered.

"Thanks, that would help out a lot while we get sorted," I said goodbye and went out into the dark to pick up Clayton.

I smiled to myself as I waited in the cold car park for Clayton to conclude his career at the bacon factory.

"I got a job!" I said as he slumped into the car next to me, stinking of raw meat, blood splattering his boots.

"Great, because I haven't," he said.

One day wonder, I thought.

I drove him home.

Penny always ensured I was the one going backwards, as we lifted lounge suites up the stairs of Queenslanders, homes perched high on stilts, every pension day. We became firm friends, along with her friend Mandy, who shared her house and kept her gun collection on her bedroom wall.

We had been there for nearly a year, with odd jobs just making ends meet, when my mother called.

They had discovered a family history of infertility and getting onto it earlier was better, especially if we ever wanted kids. Clayton and I packed up the HT Holden and the dog, and drove home all the way across Australia, to make an appointment with the specialist.

Chapter 5

So it was that at the age of twenty, after marrying and moving to Queensland, we returned to living on a farm twenty kilometres outside of my hometown. I was back in the place my whole life had been invested in escaping, in the midst of the recession Paul Keating said we had to have.

Jobs were scarce everywhere.

Using the skills learnt waitressing in Queensland, I won a part time job at a local restaurant, in the seaside village near where we lived. In between summoning up the courage to serve the customers, I washed dishes.

It was a friendly workplace most times with the usual temperamental managing chef running the kitchen. When I was focused on washing dishes and blinded by hot steam, the chef would come up quietly behind me, his hot breath on my neck.

"Hey honey, can I get between your legs?" his voice was a creepy whisper, and he didn't wait for a response as he reached down with sweaty hands. He opened the cupboard I leaned into, as I scrubbed filthy cooked on grease from his disgusting pots and pans. I clamped my knees together, as I shuffled out of his way and continued the job at hand.

I made a mental note to never be alone with him in the kitchen.

After a few months the local paper advertised for a copywriter. The job was writing advertisements for the local newspapers. To apply one had to design a range of advertisement slogans.

My campaign was 'Madwoman Eats Dictionaries'. I designed ten advertisements for fictional products, and included a madwoman devouring dictionaries, in a desperate commentary on life as a literate fringe dweller. I got the call for an interview.

When the day came, the advertising manager Stephanie, and one of the sales team waited on their general manager John to arrive. I sat sweating in the waiting area, with my whole life hanging on the plum role I had already imagined myself into.

The boss didn't show, and the start time for the interview was delayed.

Eventually, I was called into the office for the interview with only the advertising manager and sales representative. It went well, but once I got home my small wise voice nagged at me. I knew in my heart that the general manager was the decision maker, and without him at my interview, I didn't have a chance.

I picked up the phone, called the newspaper office and asked for him by name.

John's voice was smooth with laughter at the edges when he came to the phone.

"How can I help?"

"I had an interview for the copywriting role, and you weren't able to get there," I explained the situation. "As the key decision maker, I think my application is disadvantaged without the opportunity to meet you. I'd like to request a second interview," I finished in a rush.

I was scared witless but trusted my instinct.

He chuckled.

"That's a very good idea," he said.

We made a time, and I went to meet him. I got the job.

Forever after John told that story about me. How I rang to ask for another interview so I could meet him, as I knew that he decided the person for the role.

My call made John feel important, and it won me the start of the career I needed.

I had a husband to support.

The newspaper was a whole new world. There were deadlines and events, and we were the centre of the known universe in the local community. We knew everything first and were first on the scene.

I sat with the sales teams and put words to their campaigns for their clients, designed to sell products and ideas.

Everything was manual. My tools were a pair of scissors, glue, ruler, and I learned to use the bromide machine, taught by Jodie

Chapter 5

whose arms were shortened, one half missing and misshapen. Her mother was convinced to take thalidomide for her morning sickness when pregnant. Jodie was only a few years older than me.

Out the back on the computers were the typesetting and editorial teams. It was there that I met Kyralee, one of the typesetters and Richard, her partner and editor of the paper. Kyralee and I became fast firm friends, with the irony that she shared the name, but not the same spelling of my beloved lost cousin. It was a sign.

We had an amazing team and I loved going to work. Clayton came into town to see me on Friday lunchtimes when my pay went in. He waited for me at the club across the road drinking beer. The club was where we honed our skills at eight ball to wind down after the rush of the week's deadlines.

My Nana played eight ball competitively and I felt it as a birthright.

The BHAS club was the local working men's club that served the workers of the smelters where my Dad worked, the lifeblood of the town, serving cold beer and hot cheap meals.

One day there was a poster on the noticeboard, announcing world champion snooker player Eddie Charlton's regional tour, to promote nine ball for the upcoming Commonwealth Games. It was ten dollars to register, and we put our names down.

On the night, Eddie Charlton explained the rules at the outset.

"Nine ball differs from eight ball where you have 15 balls numbered 1 to 15 and you pot your small or big balls, leaving the eight ball until last, which when successfully potted at the end, wins the game. If you happen to pot the eight ball earlier than that, you lose," Eddie imparted the potted history of bastardised billiards with flourish.

"Nine ball has the balls numbered one to nine set up in a diamond rather than a triangle, and you have to pot the balls in order, one to nine to win." As he finished explaining the rules, he was chalking his world-winning cue.

The club was as packed with contenders and spectators, as the air was full of second-hand cigarette smoke. I was the only woman to register to play, and I slowly sipped beer as I watched each player try and fail. Eddie was resplendent in a vest and bow tie, with a quiet smirk as he dispensed of the locals one by one, to appreciative cheers from the crowd.

I stood up to play and chalked my cue. Eddie looked at me sideways and his smirk grew wider. A woman who dared cross the threshold of this holy war.

"You can break," Eddie was magnanimous, "It's mugs away."

I leant over the table, and focused intently on the diamond of balls set up at the other end. My shot sent the balls in a myriad of directions, breaking up the pack.

Eddie's eyebrows twitched as he stepped forward to take his shot.

We played ball for ball.

I miscued a couple of shots.

Then in an attempt to slice the three ball into a corner pocket, I cut it too fine and it hit the nine, sending it straight into a side pocket. Crestfallen at my failure, I went to shake Eddie's hand and sat down.

"You won," he said surprised, suddenly more crestfallen than me.

"What do you mean? I won?" I asked, confused. "I potted the nine out of turn."

"In nine ball, that is a win!" he said. "You made a valid attempt on the three ball in correct order and it sliced the nine into the pocket, which is a win!"

"Oh. My. God." I beat Eddie Charlton at nine ball. I stood up and shook his hand again, ever firmer just like my mother taught me.

"You have made my day!" I exclaimed.

By the look on his face I hadn't made his, and in the souvenir photo his smirk is more chagrin than pleased. I looked to the sky, knowing in my heart my Nana Ruby was immensely proud.

Chapter 5

Our newspapers were printed in a regional city a two-hour drive away. After collection they were dropped off to the various towns in between, with post-midnight delivery throughout our hometown.

I had connected with Michelle on the phone. She was the production manager. I offered to drive over to pick up the papers so I could see the production side in action. I wanted to do my job better.

Michelle was a consummate professional. So clear and kind, practical, organised, and supportive. She was totally focused on doing the job well each week, across the range of deadlines for the various regional newspapers produced.

When I got there Michelle showed me through the operation, and how plates were put together ready for print runs. It was when she turned away from me, to reach for something on a high shelf, that I saw the evidence.

Through her white shirt, I saw a tattoo on her shoulder blade.

This girl is not as straight as she makes out to be, I thought and then said as much.

Michelle laughed and we became great friends. Her Nanna lived in Port Pirie, so we caught up for drinks whenever she visited. My collection of Goddesses that guided my life was growing. When my own whispers of wisdom didn't cut through, it was my friends who clarified my worth and pointed out the best path to take.

Clayton was away one weekend, when I went out to play eight ball and share drinks with my newspaper work mates. Joining us was Allan, a visiting regional editor.

All my life I have demonstrated a level of naivete when it comes to attraction. Married young I was completely faithful and loyal, oblivious to any advances outside of my relationship. Besides, I saw myself as one of the boys, potentially a legacy of growing up with brothers and the fact that soccer was my first sporting love.

After a few drinks this night, Allan began to target me with his drunken affections. He had already told us his girlfriend was at home, awaiting his eventual return.

"C'mon gorgeous, kiss me, you know you want to," Allan slurred, leaning on me. I slipped away from him and moved around the pool table to take my shot.

"I am married *and* faithful," I said. We went on with the game.

Later, my colleague Stephanie invited us all back to her place for cocktails. Her husband was away too. She offered me a bed. A safer option than risking the drive twenty kilometres home after a few drinks.

Stephanie tucked me into bed in the spare room. Allan needed a place to stay too, so she set him up on the couch in her lounge-room.

As Stephanie closed my bedroom door, I fell asleep immediately.

Later I woke. I was frightened to feel someone in the bed behind me. As I became more aware, I realised this was not my own bed and those hands did not belong to my husband.

A man was groping me.

His erection was hard against my back.

"NO!" I yelled and struggled. I emerged from deep sleep into the stark terrified awareness that rape was only one thrust away.

I wriggled and resisted, getting louder, as I fought him off.

It was Allan.

Allan was demanding, then pleaded, and as he understood my fear was real, he suddenly switched to shame. He dived out of the bed and left the room.

I was left shaking, unbelieving, until eventually I slept again.

In the morning Stephanie came in and opened the curtains to blinding light. The memory of the night before sank in. Her eyes caught cloth on the floor, and she picked up a pair of solitary man's jocks, abandoned in his rush to depart the scene.

"Allan decided to leave very early?" she said, as she gingerly held the offending undies aloft.

I told her what had happened, sharing the horror of the experience, my fear and Allan's persistence.

Chapter 5

"All night I had said no," I said, "But Allan didn't take no for an answer. What does it take to make it clear?"

Stephanie gave me a hug. Her voice was firm.

"You must take his jocks with you," she said with fear in her voice "If my husband was to find them here when he gets back...." She trailed off.

I got up and dressed, and after a cup of tea, headed home.

Allan's jocks ended up in one of my casserole dishes, then left in Kyralee's car for a week or two.

I confided in Kyralee about my near miss, which would have devastated the special, exclusive connection with my husband, as my one and only intimate partner.

Not to mention being raped.

Some weeks later Kyralee brought the casserole dish with mislaid jocks to work, and we shared the story with our female colleagues.

Eyes grew wide, as Allan was a long-time, well-respected editor for the company, with a prominent family. Laughing hysterically by now, we cooked up revenge.

All our newspapers were connected by A3 faxes, so front-page proofs could be shared across the network, prior to being approved for printing.

I photocopied the jocks, and wrote a love note in thick black writing on the big sheet of paper, resplendent with the image of crumpled undies in the middle.

"Dear Allan, Thank you for a lovely evening the other week. You left these draped over the chandelier, Until next time, Love George."

All the women, the typesetters, journalists, and advertising team, cried with laughter.

We were shrieking with giggles, as I faxed it through to the front office of his newspaper, addressed to editor Allan.

We imagined the girls in their front office, taking that fax to their Editor in Chief. It was hilarious, and revenge was complete.

Until I got the phone call from my general manager commanding me to come into his office.

"Allan has made an official complaint about your facsimile," John said, very serious. "He denies any responsibility, and cites extreme concerns about the impressions the message has given, the subsequent response from his girlfriend, and your blatant attack on him personally and his professionalism."

There was silence. My eyes began to leak.

I tearfully explained to my general manager what had happened, and that my response was designed as a joke, after fighting the unwanted thrusting Allan from my bed.

John said he'd call Allan to work things out.

I went back to my desk, nervous and distracted. I was called back into his office that afternoon.

"Your claims have been rejected as false," John said. "You need to harden up, because these things happen, and there is no harm done."

"Harden up?" I spat. "That's what got me into this mess!"

A first warning was recorded on my file. My mother's social work office was just across the park. I phoned her sobbing and distraught. We met under the trees and I told her the whole story. She held me and assured me that everything was going to be alright.

Years later I saw Allan at the pub, and his eyes caught mine. He gave me a shy smile and a knowing wink. He nodded his head in respect, and forever after gave me a wide berth. Hopefully he had learned something. I know I did.

I survived, wiser and relatively unscathed, unlike so many other women I know, harassed, abused, raped and worse. We did fight back in our own unique way, and I was reprimanded for it, but those laughs that day in the office, as we wreaked our revenge on behalf of women everywhere, gifted us tears so sweet in that moment!

Within two years I was transferred into, and then retrenched from my media sales job, as the recession continued to play out. I had the personality for sales but just couldn't quite close the deal on white space, when the business owner was struggling to pay their receptionist. On the day I lost my job I called Dad, who drove straight to pick me up from where I was walking along the side of the road. I was sobbing, while holding my box of office memorabilia.

Dad patted my shoulder helplessly, as he drove me home to their place, while I cried, inconsolable.

"It will be alright, love," he said. "You deserve good things and it will all turn out okay."

One could only hope. And pray.

Chapter 6

I was twenty-one when I lost my job, and Clayton and I decided that the timing was right to have children. I needed to have in-vitro fertilisation, and by all accounts the treatment could take decades.

I went to a specialist, and endured blood tests taken every ten minutes, through a cannula embedded in my arm for a full day. After my levels were measured, I took a tablet treatment for a month, suffered another day of blood tests, hooked up to a machine that measured hormone levels. The test showed that the oral treatment would not be effective in lifting my hormone levels to a place where fertility was possible.

I visited my specialist and we worked through the options.

"So, can you make twins?" I asked hopefully.

When I was a kid, I pretended to have twins, a boy and a girl, while playing doctors and nurses with my best friend.

"We don't do twins," he said, matter of fact. "We aim for one healthy pregnancy, and a single healthy child."

Case closed, I thought.

That was that.

Chapter 6

The specialist prescribed injections that emulated the hormonal release of a normal cycle up to ovulation. I had regular blood tests to check my hormone levels. When they stayed low, the doctor increased the dose towards the end of the cycle.

Laying in the treatment reclining chair, the nurse inserted a probe, to check the number of formed follicles ready to be released from my ovaries on that first month. She took a sharp intake of breath.

"There are way too many there for any eggs to be released," she said.

I could end up the mother of ten in one pregnancy. It was too dangerous.

My world collapsed. I cried the entire three-hour trip home from the hospital.

Within days the hope bled out of me.

The second month our specialist kept the hormone dose down and when my level bounced up, I was in the 'normal range'. I was administered an injection of hormone, to release the eggs ready for fertilisation over twenty-four hours. Procreation was prescribed in the normal way between loving wife and husband. We were to make love as many times as possible throughout the next day and night.

Except my marriage was in no way normal.

Clayton and I visited the Central Market in the city on the way home. My eggs were flowing freely when Clayton started an argument over something trivial and disappeared down one of the crowded aisles. I searched among the banana stalls for my very own fruit loop husband, and after an hour without a sign of him, I eventually made my way to the carpark.

I waited in the car for futile hours. Hormones raging, sobbing and in disbelief at the sabotage he had inflicted after months of preparatory blood tests, drips, pricks, and probes.

I sat in the car abandoned in the carpark, fertile and alone. Three hours passed. As all the stages of grief and loss, anger and frustration waved through me and with no sign of Clayton, I drove back to my brother's place. It was eight kilometres from the city to the house. When I got there the house was empty.

I sat alone, infuriated, stricken, sad, and silent.

All that hope invested in my womb, into our future family, had come to this.

Some hours later there was a knock at the door.

There stood Clayton. He had walked all the way. Without looking into each other's eyes, we made forced frustrated love on the floor. Not the love story I had envisaged to welcome a beloved and much wanted child into our lives.

It was six weeks later, when the two test sticks I subjected to my first wee of the day, showed pink lines.

I went for a blood test.

When my doctor saw the blood test result, she advised I have a scan "to find out how many there are…"

I drank two litres of water in preparation. The jelly was slimy and cold, and the machine was pressed into my belly while the radiographer watched the screen intently. I was eight weeks pregnant. In my mind I whispered, only find two, please God, only two, not three… or more!

"We have TWO strong healthy heartbeats!" she said.

I laid back and cried with joy.

"Twins!"

My darling children. I nicknamed the babies Flotsam and Jetsam or Simon and Garfunkel. I eschewed all substances, ate healthy food, thought happy thoughts, and had daily naps so my babies could grow healthy and wise. I listened to my body and all She had to say.

I read Sheila Kitzinger, the guru on childbirth. I soaked up the research and information, presented in colourful illustrations and direct language.

Chapter 6

Sheila wrote about the prevalence of episiotomies in the UK, and the need for women to trust ourselves in the labour and birthing process.

I was invited to be part of a community engagement group to redesign the local railway station into a tourism and arts centre, and encouraged the coordinator to create a film as part of the project, promoting Clayton for the job as filmmaker.

Because regional hospitals are not equipped for twin births, I was sent to the city to await the birth of the twins for the last three weeks of the pregnancy. Clayton was still working on the film, so I was alone in the city, staying with family friends awaiting the arrival of our beloved twins.

As the due date approached, and at the very last minute I made one of the best decisions of my life.

I asked my mum to come into the labour ward with us.

Mum was quietly ecstatic.

Clayton loved Albert Camus and thought himself an existentialist. It was early in the morning on a Wednesday when they induced me, and Clayton watched on with mild interest while I laboured.

He got out his camera and filmed me from afar, taking in all the angles.

Mum fed me ice chips, rubbed my back, and held my hand. My dream of a normal labour was thwarted at the mid-point, with one sensor inserted into my vagina and plugged into the skin of the presenting baby's head, and another strapped around my tummy for monitoring the second baby's heartbeats.

Clayton waited until between contractions to ask if I'd like to step outside for a joint.

I ignored him and focused on blowing out the candle during contractions, which were getting stronger by the minute.

Mum wiped my forehead with a wet flannel.

They administered an epidural, standard procedure for twins in case they have to get the second baby out quickly. The first injection was administered by a gorgeous anaesthetist, who spoke to me gently, and waited until between contractions, to insert the needle into my spine. After minutes passed it was obvious the epidural hadn't worked, blocking pain to only half of my body, intensifying the tightening for the unsedated half of me.

Another anaesthetist arrived. He didn't wait until between contractions, instead inserting the needle into my spine as I lay hunched on my side, wracked with the powerful surges of labour.

The epidural made me unable to feel the lower half of my body, and unsure of how or when to push.

My daughter's head crowned. The first born would be our girl, who had been clearly female at all our scans. She was already named, and both were beloved.

My specialist's locum was from the UK. I caught a look of concern flood her face, while focused intently between my legs.

"We are going to need forceps to deliver, Andrea," she announced in a lilting English accent, as the midwife got in position.

The locum was still looking concerned as she picked up her scalpel.

"Andrea, you are going to tear, I am just going to make a small incision," she said, as she leaned forward, scalpel poised.

"NO!" I shouted. "You put that scalpel down NOW!"

I was unyielding.

She wavered.

"NOW!" I said firmly. "You will not cut me."

Sheila Kitzinger's advice was ringing in my soul.

Eyebrows raised in surprise, she put down the scalpel, and the midwife supported my daughter's head with the forceps. With a push she slipped into the world. They handed my perfect firstborn twin daughter to me. Wrapped up warm, her eyes were open, and she was silently staring up at me, squinting in the bright lights of the room. Calm and serene, she lay on my chest.

I held her close with one arm and kissed her moist downy head.

Chapter 6

The second born baby's gender remained a mystery until arrival. At scans every fortnight the baby had turned away, keeping all private parts secret until this moment.

It was ten minutes later when I birthed our second child. My joy on the silent Super 8 footage Clayton captured, can be lip read.

"It's a boy, it's a boy!"

Twins. A boy and a girl. Perfect. Rachel and Thomas. There had been lots of Thomases on both sides of the family, and Clayton even had an ancestor named Thomas Thomas. Thomas means twin. Rachel was named after my friend in New Zealand. Juliet to my Romeo. My much loved best friend.

The locum cleaned me up and administered one stitch. She left the room without a backward glance.

I was exhausted, exalted, and feeling surreal.

The midwife stood between my legs to gently clean me up.

"THAT was amazing!" she said admiringly.

"Two babies in one delivery?" I asked her.

"No, the way you put that locum in her place when she prepared to give you the episiotomy," she said. "I have never seen anything like it." She smiled.

"I was just scared to be cut," I said. But my quiet voice knew better. My wisdom had my best interests at heart and stepped in to be heard when it counted.

I relaxed back on the pillows awaiting the arrival of my babies so I could hold them close to my heart forever.

It was day three when Clayton arrived at the hospital to drive me and our twins home. I fought with the staff for permission to be released, as sleep was impossible in the busy ward.

"The old Valiant is leaking petrol," he announced. Clayton was nonchalant about the situation and we had no cash to fix the car anyway. Fortunately, it was raining, but as we drove along the highway with our precious newborns, images of burning infernos haunted my imagination.

We made it safely to our newly purchased stone cottage in Gladstone, bought with the help of my parent's funds for the deposit. Gladstone was a sleepy little town about forty kilometres from my hometown. Close enough, but far enough away. Our home was built in 1910, with a vintage rose garden along the fence and an apricot and oleander tree in the front yard.

Work on the film project meant that Clayton was working ten hours a day, seven days per week. Mum took several weeks off work to help me every day with the babies.

Three weeks after the twins were born Michelle and her boyfriend dropped in to visit and share dinner. Clayton did not come home at all. I made many phone calls in an attempt to track him down so we could eat together.

Finally, I called the leader of the project. The project coordinator spoke softly to me. He was calm but slightly guarded.

"I think he is with Anita, the producer," he said. "They are spending a lot of time together, getting the project completed."

"Right, fine, thanks," I said.

I hung up the phone and served dinner before it was ruined while Michelle and her boyfriend cuddled a baby each.

One of my gifts is seeing people's potential. Sometimes I marry it.

Going to work when the twins were just six months old broke my heart, but someone had to earn money for us to pay the mortgage and eat. I won a role connecting people with disabilities to volunteers, and then a job helping people with disabilities to get employment. I did freelance journalism for the regional newspaper and media monitoring part time. At the start in my main role, I worked three days per week, then four. My jobs kept us afloat.

We loved Rachel and Thomas so much. Gorgeous, gurgling, perfect human beings. Blissful eye contact, connected by breast feeding all day and in the middle of the night, our twins were settled siblings totally connected to us and each other. They held hands in the same cot and maintained a steady rhythm of being.

Chapter 6

The twins were still only six months old the morning I woke up and brought the babies from their shared cot into our big brass bed.

"Can you bring me a nappy please, hon'?" I asked Clayton, as I cocooned the babies between us.

In a flash he was above me, his closed fist smashed my head into the pillow.

I saw stars. Life changed forever in that instant. Trust was broken and it could never be put back into the box.

My face was still violent hues of purple some days later, when the phone rang. It was Mum sounding cheerful and bright.

"We were thinking we'd come out to visit," she said. "We haven't seen the babies for days!"

"Now is not a good time Mum. I don't think you should come out here," I trailed off.

Mum was silent. I heard my dad in the background, concerned.

"What has happened?" he was talking to Mum.

"Andrea? Are you okay?" Mum asked.

"You will see my face," I was ashamed.

"We are on our way," said Mum.

I hung up the phone and walked into the lounge to ask Clayton my burning question.

"What am I going to tell my Grandma when I see her this week?" I asked.

"Tell her I hit you," he said.

When my parents arrived, my brother Greg was with them. Mum rushed into the house, with Dad and Greg close behind. They saw my face and Dad took Clayton firmly by the arm. Greg was close by his elbow, standing tall with a frown.

"We were thinking we'd go down to the pub and have a little chat," said Dad. "Man to man."

Clayton looked wary but there was the promise of beer, so he joined them and they left.

Mum held me close.

"What has he done to you, Andrea?" she asked, tears in her eyes.

"I don't know Mum, it was totally unexpected, first thing in the morning, out of the blue," I said.

"This must be how his Mum felt, when his Dad hit her." I started to cry.

"I will put the kettle on and then I am taking your photo. I want you to be able to remember what he did to you Andrea. If he EVER touches you AGAIN!" As she turned away I could see her eyes glistening with tears.

I felt ashamed. It was all my fault.

The week after the punch to the face I was on the way home from Monday basketball and stopped in at the local supermarket. The woman working on the checkout stopped me for a chat. The name on her badge read Carol.

She leaned across her checkout to grab my goods, and punched in the prices with a series of high-pitched bleats.

"You're new in town, eh?" she stated the obvious. We had been in Gladstone six months, but the babies kept me very occupied in our home. I put the groceries in the base of the twin pram, under the babies. Our pram was as long as a B double truck fully laden.

I nodded; my eyes were hidden behind dark glasses.

"We're neighbours actually," she said, determined to strike up a conversation.

"Your dog shits on my lawn."

"Oh!" I said momentarily taken aback. "At least she's not shitting on mine."

We laughed. Her giggle was deep and luxurious, coming from the depths of her ample chest.

Carol looked down at my basketball uniform.

"Played in town today?" she queried.

Chapter 6

"Yeah, we got hammered," I replied and hesitated.

"What happened to your face?" she asked innocently.

"That's where I got the shiner, in last week's game." The words tumbled out. My lie to cover the deep shame I felt, and answer further questions that could come out of her mouth any moment.

"We've got a local association of basketball if you want a game here each week. We play A grade on a Monday night, and we'd love to have you," she said, as she hit the subtotal, and the till flew open at speed.

"Sure, I could do with a run, I'll discuss it with my husband when I get home," I said.

I paid her for the formula, nappies and baby wipes and pushed the pram filled with Rachel and Thomas, cooing loveliness into the bright hopeful sunshine of the day.

Chapter 7

For a few months, I had been regularly taking the twins to church. I pushed our pram across the horse track to the quaint steepled building. As they grew, I attempted to corral the babies, growing quickly to toddlers, into some semblance of sacred silence demanded by the grey-haired sages that religiously sat in the space.

"Do you think they could play more quietly during the sermon, dear?" The elderly lady behind me poked me in the back.

Her pointed nose threatening to drip, before her oozing eyes leaked into her spectacle frames, as she peered our way. Judgement burned me. I played with the children, one ear on the sermon, as I soaked up the forgiveness I sought.

The twins were joyous examples of pure love, and my insight that they were definitely a more sacrosanct study of eternal life and its promises, was dulled by the demands of the congregation as they steeped their Sunday in ceremonies that gave them the ticket to forever.

While hissing at me to hush my children.

Sometimes Clayton joined us. I never felt quite good enough, like I didn't fit in, or was welcomed.

Chapter 7

To help out, I collected books for a shipping container heading to Africa organised by the assistant pastor and his wife. His knock at the door was unexpected and I opened the door to streaming light and his shadow on the doorframe.

"Good afternoon, Andrea, I was just popping past, and thought you haven't been to church for a while," he was kind but pointed. "I wondered how you and the family are?"

I smiled. It is nice to be remembered and to be called on. It is all about the calling.

"Thanks, Roger, nice of you to think of us. It is a bit of a challenge with the twins at this stage, they make a lot of noise and we hate to be a distraction," I said. "Hey but I do have some books for Africa to donate."

I handed him a pile of books by the front door.

He looked me over, then peered closely.

It had been over a week since Clayton had punched me in the face. I was lucky to eat in a day, let alone look at my face in the mirror. There were times when I was getting dinner ready when my bladder called me to a stark awareness that I hadn't been to the toilet all day. My daily routine with the twins took everything I had. I had forgotten my bruised blackened eye, until I saw it mirrored in his face.

Hot shame flushed my face as I realised what a sight I must be.

Silent pity and concern flooded his.

"Are you okay, Andrea?" he asked. "What happened to your eye?"

"Ahhhh that," I said hesitating and then firming up my position as the safest story came to mind. "Elbow to the eye during basketball."

"Hmmmm, looks nasty," he said persisting. He knew the truth my eyes shared despite my shame, or maybe because of it.

"Yes, was lucky not to shatter the socket. I had forgotten about it. I only remember when people look at me and their face changes.

It is like I can tell what they are thinking," I finished lightly, skimming the surface of this slippery slope.

"Haven't seen Clayton at a service lately," he said, straight to the heart of the matter. "I knew his dad when he was preaching for the church in Adelaide."

Roger gave me yet another opportunity to spill the secrets that stayed in silence behind our doors. Maybe he knew what went on for Clayton's parents, the abuse and family violence, all mopped up under straightened ties, aligned with socks pulled right up. Jesus-like sandals on feet for all the sons, while their father concealed his transgressions under purple robes every Sunday.

Preaching the word of the Lord. Hope, forgiveness, love, and judgement day. His wife staring straight ahead in the front pew, her four sons beside her and her tiny daughter on her lap. Clayton's mother's bruises were covered by her clothing, because *her* husband was smart enough never to touch her face.

What would people say?

"Yeah, Clayton can't always get there with his filming commitments on weekends," I said. "But I will tell him you asked after him, and thanks for dropping in." I was already attempting to shut the door, despite his body blocking the entrance.

The pastor didn't make it into the hallway. The twins were having their afternoon nap and our conversation was shared in hushed tones on the doorstep.

Roger said his goodbyes and quietly closed the screen door. I stood watching him move down the path through our wrought iron gate between the roses and out into the world. A place where symphonies of love and acceptance promised eternal life from the heavens.

I closed the heavy front door and leaned with my back against it.

I have faith. That it will all turn out alright.

The old steeple held bells tolled for the ancient residents who limped to the service, where the droning of the lesson from the pulpit made me feel safe somehow. Despite my knowledge of the

Chapter 7

dark stories behind some of the men who stood to preach the word, I still believed in people's best, and the sacred intervention of the divine.

Church on Sundays became a chore too far. The stern looks of wizened old ladies, husbands long dead, with pearls adorning wrinkled necks did me in. They smiled stiffly with grimaces that overlooked the gurgles of joyous life at my feet, craning to hear the words from the pulpit that would surely save them.

I stopped going to church.

Our cottage had a long light filled hallway opening into a retro kitchen and dining room. I loved the generosity of the apricot tree in the front yard, and the fragrant rose bushes along the twisted arched wire fence, with its old gate which squeaked companionably when people arrived to visit.

Our hometown was the centre of a hard-working farming community with good rainfall and a healthy footy club. You can always tell the fortunes of the farmers in Australia by how well the local football team is going. There was an informal neighbourhood watch program, which consisted of the older couple next door regularly knocking to report sightings of cars going past, or unexplained parking on the other side of the road, and they noted the registration plates of visitors that called in when we weren't home.

It felt intrusive and safe as houses all at the same time.

Mum visited and held either Thomas or Rachel while I alternately breast fed, soaked, and washed nappies in huge buckets of bleach. I tackled stacks of dishes the size of small mountains. Between my various jobs, I nestled into home with the babies, looking deep into their eyes as I soothed them, feeding them with a breastmilk and formula blend to ensure they were getting enough and could thrive.

We hosted bible study at our house on Tuesday nights. One of my friends regularly spoke in tongues while we prayed in a tight knit circle.

Clayton stayed out in the shed, smoking rollies and brewing beer, while psychedelic sixties tunes played on the record player. He read his Phantom comic collection, a collectible series of early editions, surrounded by his favourite relics of yesteryear, old tins, wooden boxes, and pickaxe bottles.

In the lounge, Jan abruptly stood up and regaled us in the language of foreigner. She gripped my shoulder, with her eyes rolled back into her head and then spoke sudden English.

"Lord God Almighty, by your grace, will you send Andrea, Clayton, and the twins to the Flinders Ranges on the church camp, to rest with you Lord… to be cleansed?" The question hung in the air as Jan continued in a babble so beautiful, despite the language I did not understand.

We have no money, I thought as she chanted, holding my shoulders, asking the divine for our camping permit. I didn't really want to go to the church camp anyway. The voice in my head said as much.

"I have a vision of you, Andrea, a vision. You will touch many people. The people you touch will be like poppies in a field. Choose love," Jan's shut eyelids flickered, as her eyes rolled upward in the ecstasy of the insight.

I slumped into the chair as our eighteen-month-old twins slumbered in their beds, her handprints still warm on my body. I felt suddenly sleepy. Eventually they all went home, and I fell into bed and into deep peaceful slumber.

The next day Jan rang.

"It's a miracle Andrea, a miracle!" Jan was excited. "This morning I had a voice in my head as I did the dishes. It was telling me very clearly… *'All the money is not for you, all the money is not for you'*…"

"What money?" I was puzzled.

Jan was in a state of ecstasy, talking very fast.

"What money?? I thought the same as I drove into town to the post office box and collected the mail. *WHAT MONEY?*" she exclaimed. "There was a letter there addressed to me, with writing I didn't recognise," Jan continued. "I opened the envelope on the way home and a flutter of fifty-dollar bills filled the car. I nearly drove off the road!" she said with delight.

Chapter 7

"There is no explanation on or in the envelope. I don't know who it could be from! And I knew it was not all for me, after the voice in my head. It is a miracle! Some is for you so you can go on the church camp!" Jan shouted with joy, "You are blessed! Our prayers are answered!"

I was confused and attempted to slow my thoughts down as I took in this new development.

"But I didn't want to go on the..." the words seemed too ungrateful to be expressed out loud, so I changed tack. "You can't give us that Jan, it is for you, who is it from?"

"It's our miracle! This happens, mysterious gifts from God arriving without warning to show that He loves us. It's OUR miracle!" Jan giggled with joy as we concluded the call.

I hung up the phone and turned to Clayton. He looked quizzical as he stood by waiting to discover the reason for the very strange sounding call. Diligently I explained to my reluctant husband that we couldn't refuse Jan's miracle offer, never to be repeated. When the time came, we packed ourselves up with the twins and headed dutifully to the church camp, where we sang, prayed, laughed, and talked.

Clayton spent the time sloping away into the bush, having smuggled a couple of long necks of beer in the car for after dark.

We were cared for, so lucky and we loved each other.

That was then.

I was blindsided when my husband started abusing me at every opportunity. Anger curled from his throat with a cat-like stealth on attack. I consoled myself by writing down my silent protests with sarcasm in my journal, that I kept from his eyes. Not that he cared to read me. My poems and journal entries heaved with unhappiness. Rejection at every turn.

He knew exactly what cut the deepest. It happened in front of the children, his passive manner twisted into an evil snarl. He never really raised his voice. It was more of a threatening hiss with strong inflection on the invective, calling me cunt, bitch, whatever insulting insight came to mind that moment.

If I talked back, he left the room shaking his fist, sometimes punching a wall or door. He slammed the back door as he retreated out the back to his smoky shed.

His mother and her reconstructive surgeries were front of my mind, as I observed our life begin to mirror semblance of her experience. Perfect life of faith in God to all on the outside, with violence inflicted behind the closed doors of the marriage.

Son of a preacher man.

The man whose children I had borne became unpredictable and uncontrolled. He was in turn abusive, emotionally, physically, and psychologically. It didn't matter that he never hit me again. I began to have flashes of fear while my imagination worked overtime. As I washed two and three days' worth of dishes, I created large sculptures of clean saucepans, plates and utensils, reaching almost to the ceiling, carefully balanced with strategic entwining. I envisaged Clayton coming up from behind, to stab me all the way through my back, and deep into my heart.

My life was filled with the babies, workdays, and juggling the endless calls of the nappy bucket with an occasional sprint to the street for more formula. My muscles got bigger from shaking baby bottles. I returned to playing basketball three times a week after the birth, in two local teams with Carol and one in town with my Aunty Janice. I took out my frustrations on the court, and at the end of the season I won a tautology of trophies, one for best and fairest and the other a golden chicken for the most fouls.

At home I was the walking dead.

Chapter 8

Carol started to come over nearly every morning. She did the dishes, swept the floor, and put the kettle on. Her three girls were older than mine, and her two oldest daughters helped with the twins. It was a relief to have a friend in town.

We laughed a lot. Her husband worked away often, and Clayton spent his time in the shed, so we were left to our own stories and dreams, gilded by giggles.

There was a small group of twelve-year old children in the neighbourhood, that often walked past the house while I played with the twins in the front garden. The group started to visit and held the children while I did dishes or washed nappies.

When I returned to work to support the household, I missed my darling children terribly.

Clayton stayed home. When I arrived home after work, the twins would often still be in their pyjamas from the night before. Weet-Bix cemented to every surface. I changed and got stuck into cleaning, creating dish sculptures and cooking dinner, a daily pattern of creating order out of chaos.

Two years later, when the twins were nearly three, I found a request for tender that would assure Clayton some work. I showed Clayton the advertisement. It was a filming project that the local college was looking to produce.

"I haven't got the right equipment," he said. "I'd have to hire it from the city. Or we could buy a television camera?"

His suggestion hung in the air.

"How much are they?" I queried, while doing sums for the budget in my head.

"Ahhhh, about fifty thousand dollars," the numbers rolled off his tongue like silk.

I got up early to progress the tender proposal each morning before I went to work, while Clayton eventually rolled out of bed to make his coffee in the plunger.

I pondered how he could hold a job if he was never up early enough to make it to meetings on time. I continued writing the submission and collated the elements of the budget. I resolved to ask my parents to guarantee the fifty-thousand-dollar loan for the television camera that would launch Clayton into his career. It was time for him to fulfill his true potential as an award-winning filmmaker with his unique way of seeing the world.

"Dad?" I asked when he answered the phone.

"Yes, love," Dad said, "What's up?"

"We are going to start a film making business, so Clayton can work doing what he loves," I sold it like a pup. "I am writing a tender for a project that if we win, it is guaranteed work for Clayton for three years, but we need a TV camera to avoid the costs of the hire fees from the city. I have done a budget, and wondered if you could look it over, and if you agree, go guarantor for us to get a personal loan."

"How much, Andrea?" Dad asked.

"Fifty grand," I said it quickly, so it didn't sound so much.

"Just as guarantor? And you have the income to support the loan?" Dad asked.

Chapter 8

"Yes, Dad, I have done the numbers and I can cover it with my wages, considering our mortgage and living expenses," I was excited, "It would be a dream come true."

"Plenty of dreaming going on love," he said. I was too enthused to spot the sarcasm. "I'll talk with your mother and get back to you once we discuss it. And I will want to talk with Clayton to make sure he is taking responsibility and will follow through."

"Thanks, Dad," I said. "Love you."

"Love you too, Andrea," he said and hung up.

At our family conference later, we took a considered look through the tender proposal and bank loan paperwork. With their full support, I applied, and Mum and Dad signed to guarantee the loan that I would pay back. They bet their house on it.

The paperwork was at the bank ready for Clayton's signature and a couple of other forms he needed to complete. Then he could buy the television camera and get to work.

My style was to push it through, make it happen, and act. But this time something stopped me.

I distinctly heard the quietest of voices whispering in my ear.

Don't push this one. Let him step up and take responsibility. Allow him space, don't make it happen without him making a move.

This went against my grain. I was the breadwinner and had worked out the loan so that I could pay it back within 15 years. A large loan on a piece of specialised equipment I had no idea how to use.

Despite my excitement for my husband and his dream career, I held my enthusiasm in check and was silent. Every time I wanted to mention it, I stopped myself.

That still small voice held power and wisdom.

It was around this time that we met another family at the local swimming pool, and I invited Rochelle, Bill, and their two boys over for tea and playdates. Their second son was the same age as the twins.

Clayton and Rochelle became close while her husband Bill and I were at our respective jobs supporting our families. They took the kids out during the day, and made photographs of them, running between the haystacks of open lush fields in the surrounding farmland.

Six months later the loan papers were still at the bank awaiting Clayton's action when the reality of his illicit affair became so obvious that even I and my rose-coloured glasses could not ignore it any longer.

A mutual friend shared a cup of tea with Rochelle, who had revealed her latest artwork. The friend came to visit me straight after.

"Have you seen her latest painting?" my friend queried, while looking at me from underneath her eyelashes.

"No, I haven't. What's it of?" I asked as I stirred sugar into her tea.

"It's of a blonde woman holding a baby over her head in a gesture of triumph, and there's a brunette in the background," she said, watching my reaction carefully.

"Interesting. Who does the blonde look like?" I asked, knowing the answer already.

"It looks like Rochelle, and the brunette?" my friend continued, "Looks just like you."

Winter was looming when I challenged Clayton under the clothesline. Our underwear hung between us, a false sense of protection as I confronted him.

"So, are you fucking her?" I spat the words. "Tell me the truth."

He nodded.

I crumbled into the realisation that my life was over.

Any obligation I had to work myself to the bone, for TV camera technology that benefited only him, dissipated in that instant. In the aftermath, cuddled by sleepless nights in a cold bed, the awareness of what could have been was clear. I could have been in debt for fifty thousand dollars, paying for something I had no idea how to use, for another decade and a half.

Chapter 8

My wisdom whispers were worth listening to, no matter how it turned out.

The day after the revelation that broke our marriage I was crying before I was awake. My eyes leaked pain from deep within my soul while my heart physically hurt from the betrayal.

I decided that if I didn't tell anyone, it wasn't true, and things could stay as they were.

Unhappily married.

I dragged myself out into the kitchen to put on the kettle.

Rachel looked at me.

"Why are you crying, Mummy?" she asked with the innocence of a three-year-old. I couldn't answer as sobs closed my throat.

"Daddy has made Mummy sad," said Clayton as he scooped Rachel up into his arms.

I began to choke and ran to the bathroom to wash my face and pull myself together for the day at work.

That day I had a lunch meeting planned with a new colleague I had not met before. James was an older gentleman who radiated care and compassion. Grief overwhelmed me, and I blurted my situation onto the table between us, a bloody mess of heartbreak. James suggested we drive to the park by the beach, where he listened as I poured out my shattered dreams, the pain of betrayal, and the cutting truths of infidelity now known.

James listened and then gave me a big hug.

"I have only just met you, Andrea, but my sense of it is, that you are strong enough to get through this. I am sure you will come out the other side stronger than before," he said. And then he was gone.

That afternoon when I came home from work, Clayton's lover Rochelle was in the kitchen with a pair of scissors. Her head was down as she concentrated her efforts on the table surface. Clayton stood awkwardly in the far corner of the room, watching my face.

I looked more closely.

She had inscribed *"I want your life"* into the wood of our kitchen table.

Without stopping to consider if her words were remorse or a threat, I picked up the fire poker and raised it above my head.

"Get out of our house NOW!" I screamed at her to leave. I moved towards her around the table, giving her the door to escape. Rochelle dropped the scissors and ran sobbing for the driveway.

Clayton followed her into the yard, and I watched him hug her as he opened his car door for her, shuffling her inside, then shutting the door. They didn't look back as they drove away.

I sank into the chair, put my forehead on the table and sobbed.

Still I told no-one. An incredible feat for my open honest heart. Clayton's infidelity was an illusion.

I could pretend things were the same as they always had been. A dysfunctional marriage to the only man I had ever been with.

My silent grief was overwhelming. Every morning I woke up crying. My world changed in that instant of knowing. Information I could never unknow, but that I could keep secret and ensure it didn't interact with my reality.

Over the next three weeks my mother and Carol called to see how I was. I couldn't share the secret of my shattered marriage. Maybe they could feel what was going on. I was in complete denial.

One Monday Clayton went to the local pub to watch Rochelle play eight ball. I was home alone with the twins. They were asleep when Kyralee rang to chat, and the whole story bubbled up and blurted out of me.

"He's having an affair with Rochelle," I said. "You know the woman I introduced you at that barbecue last summer. They have been spending lots of time together while I am at work. He's admitted he is sleeping with her. He's with her now, at the pub."

"Oh, Andrea, the bastard! You know he has propositioned me as well?" Her truth made me cold. He loved Kyralee. They were born the same year, and our families shared a lot of time together over many years.

Chapter 8

"He what?" I exclaimed. "Oh My God! What is wrong with me?"

"Of course, I turned him down," she said. "I would never do it to you. Besides, he is NOT my type!"

Her bold statement cracked us both up.

"You can have him," I said, "It appears everyone else has!"

As we laughed, I began to cry. Sobs caught in my throat and tears rolled down my face.

"I tell you what," Kyralee said in her 'I have a plan' voice. "I'll drive out and watch the twins, and you go to the pub and confront him there. See if you can sort it out."

There is no talking Kyralee out of a plan. She is Wonder Woman in real life, our Kyras. In under half an hour she was at our house, ushering me out the door.

"What will I say?" I dug my heels into the linoleum of the kitchen floor, as she gently guided me out the back to the car.

"Say whatever is in your heart," she said. "I will be right here and will take care of the twins until you get back."

I drove to the pub and parked the car out the front. Taking deep convulsive breaths, I attempted to slow my heart down to a dull roar. As I pushed open the door, I knew my life had changed forever, but also believed that our marriage was worth fighting for.

I went to the bar and ordered a cider, taking in the scene, where Clayton and Rochelle cuddled close, at the other end of the venue near the pool table. Rochelle saw me first and pulled away as she caught Clayton's eye. She nodded her head my way.

Clayton's eyes got big and wide. He was defensive in his attack.

"Hey, where are the kids?" he yelled across the bar. "Have you left them home alone?"

My reply was quiet and determined.

"If you want to talk to me about our family, you come over here and discuss it." I turned back to my drink.

He staggered over and sat on the bar stool next to me.

"What are you doing here?" he questioned.

"What are YOU doing here?" I replied.

"Watching the eight ball," he said. "Did you want to step outside?"

"Good plan," I said as the eyes of every patron in the place watched us with interest.

We walked outside. My pleas came tumbling out.

"I just want our marriage back. I love you and want us to work it out," I said. "We have our children to think of."

I leaned on the bonnet of my car as I spoke, then realised I had parked right beside Rochelle's car.

He opened his arms wide and laid back on the bonnet of her car.

"If you love me, fuck me right here and now," he said with a laugh.

Beer had overtaken his senses. It all flashed through my head. The places he had slept with her in our home while I was at work. The secrets, the betrayal, the lies.

"When you are ready to talk sensibly, I will be at home with our children," I said, and got into our car, starting the engine. He remained on the bonnet of her car looking at the stars. I drove home.

When I got there Kyralee and I drank a glass of wine and talked through the options.

"So, he laid on the bonnet of her car and made you the best offer ever? I can see it now!" Kyralee shook her head. "In the end, Andrea, he is the loser. You have so much to offer, and if he chooses Rochelle, that is his loss entirely."

I was crying silently.

"I know, but it doesn't feel like that right now, it feels like the most incredible betrayal and complete rejection. And what about the kids? My plan was never to be single with children. Even though he spends most of his time in the shed and now with her, he loves them, and they love him," I said.

We sipped our drinks in contemplative silence, while Kyralee held my hand, until eventually she hugged me and left for home.

Chapter 8

About half an hour later the phone rang. I held my breath as I answered the call.

It was Kyralee sounding breathless.

"You will never guess what happened!" she said giggling. I relaxed as I sat down to listen.

"I have borrowed my mum's car and the lights are faulty, so I had them on high beam to ensure they would work, and then took the back-way home after the wine. I was near the railway line when I saw a car, and dipped the lights, which meant one of the headlights went out completely!" It was rapid fire retelling.

"Suddenly the other car's lights flashed red and blue. It was the cops! I pulled over, fully aware I needed to avoid any breath test, just in case. Anyway, they came to the window and asked me the registration number of the car I was driving, and of course as it is Mum's I had no idea. Next they asked me my mum's name."

I sat in silence listening to the drama unfold.

"You know how Mum just changed her name by deed poll?" Kyralee queried.

"Again?" I asked astounded. Kyralee's mother had a history of strange manoeuvres, regular name changes being just one.

"Again! And in my panic, do you think I could remember my own mother's name?" Kyralee started to guffaw. "So there is this cop, who has pulled over this woman with faulty lights, a couple of wines under her belt and no idea the make, model or registration number of the car she is driving, and better yet, she doesn't even know her own mother's name!"

I could see it now. Kyralee's fast talking manifestation to extricate herself out of another delicate drama would confuse even the most skilled constabulary. I laughed with her.

"So, what happened?" I asked, crying with laughter.

"They let me off with a warning and were so confounded, that they told me to drive straight home. They didn't think to breath test me!" Kyralee rounded off the story with the flourish of small victory.

"I made it and am here safe at home now," she said. "Has Clayton materialised yet?"

My smile slipped as I snapped back into my mournful reality.

"No, he hasn't," I said sadly. "I thought this could have been him calling, but no."

"He doesn't deserve you; you know. Sleep well sweetcheeks, I love you," Kyralee said, and we hung up.

I went to bed and lay awake, replaying the scene with Clayton at the pub in my mind. The humiliation, the drama, the rejection, ridicule dripping in his voice. I lay there for hours, waiting for the sound of the back door. None came. I fell asleep, distraught, and exhausted.

It was in the wee hours of the morning, before dawn when I woke, and realised Clayton was in the bed beside me. I sat up and hissed at him.

"What time did you get home?" I was furious. "I waited up so we could talk. Where have you been?"

"I slept at Rochelle's hall," he said, blurry from beer, awakening from a deep sleep.

"You make me sick!" I said. "You have made your choice, get out of this bed! NOW!" I yelled and started to flail and thrash, hitting out at him. He went into the twin's room and curled around Thomas who was blissfully sleeping.

"How DARE you!" I whispered, following him into the room. "This is not going to work out!"

He rolled over away from my anger. I thumped him on the back.

"You have made your choice," I hissed. "I am done."

He said nothing, and as I left the room, I heard him snore gently as he fell straight back to sleep.

By Wednesday he was packing his car. The twins were playing in their room.

"Rochelle is moving to Adelaide," he said. "I am going with her."

Chapter 8

He loaded boxes of long necks of home brewed beer into the station wagon, and garbage bags full of clothes and his things. In between loads we sat together on our bedroom floor as we split photographs.

"I just want it to be the way it was," I said.

"I just want the brass bed," he said.

My heart was broken and empty as I watched him back the fully laden car out of the driveway.

The inevitable end of our marriage, and the devastating loss of my only true love.

Later that week Kyralee came to my workplace with a little troll doll complete with crazy hair, that looked suspiciously like Clayton. It was accompanied by a packet of sewing pins in a range of colours.

There was an instruction sheet typed out. It was a guide to stick pins of various colour into the doll's orifices or body parts of my choice. Blue was for releasing pain, red was for expressing anger, green was to heal the heart, orange for betrayal and white to manage any perceived lack of self-worth.

Kyralee looked at me with a twinkle in her eye as she hugged me.

Sometimes when I am too full of pain to hear effectively, wisdom whispers through the guidance of my Goddess girlfriends. When in doubt, voodoo. And laugh.

Chapter 9

The night I first met Amy was unforgettable. I had planned to visit Kyralee, ready for a late-night shopping trip to Kmart. I was staying overnight in town at Mum and Dad's, who were caring for the children while I went out. Clayton was living in the city with Rochelle.

The separation was weighing heavy on me. I just wanted my marriage back and would have done anything to make it work. Distraction was good, and I was soothed by the promise of retail therapy with my best friend, who had unique ways of cheering me up, as we ravaged the stores for bargains or home improvement ideas.

After I had some dinner and settled the twins to sleep at my folks' place, I arrived at Kyralee's to discover that they had double booked, and any moment they had a vacuum cleaner salesperson coming to demonstrate their wares.

I was annoyed at the interruption to our plans. Kyralee attempted to placate me.

"I want to check this vacuum cleaner out," she said. "I have heard good things."

Kyralee is a clean freak and likes a tidy organised space. Their daughter suffered from severe asthma, so maintaining a dust free

Chapter 9

home was important for health reasons too. Kyralee is the total opposite to me. I live in the space and am surrounded by cluttered and delicious connections to special times. I usually clean in a stressed out frenzy just before visitors arrive.

"Let's just go to the shops and Richard can sort it out," I suggested.

Kyralee was wavering but was queen of her household and integral to any plans made.

Richard sat drinking an after dinner instant coffee.

"The demonstrator's name is Amy," he said, "Tell you what, if she is hot, you guys go shopping and if she is a dragon, you have to stay and protect me."

We laughed. I sighed and settled in to await the fate of my evening.

There was a knock at the door and two people were on the front verandah.

Matt was a good-looking guy who gave his name first and then introduced his colleague.

"This is Amy," he said. He stepped back as Amy moved forward into the light.

Amy was gorgeous. She had long tousled blond hair and blue eyes sparkling mischief. As she stepped into the room, breasts first, with a white linen shirt and tight jeans she was sexy, shapely, and overflowing with life.

"I'll be back after the demo to pick you up," said Matt to Amy cheerily, and he left us to it.

Richard turned to us both overjoyed with a sly grin.

"So, girls, you are off to the shops then?" his voice was knowing and cheeky.

"Sure," I said, getting to my feet. Kyralee stopped me with a long hard look and all-seeing eyes, her brows furrowed with an obvious rejection of that idea. She didn't have to say a word.

I scowled and settled onto the couch. We were staying put.

Richard grinned and offered Amy a drink. He disappeared into the kitchen, with a broad wink directed our way, as he left the room.

Amy bustled about getting out her equipment. The most expensive vacuum cleaner we would ever meet. Reportedly the most effective lifelong investment on the planet, that made every task as easy as pushing a button to power this multi-purpose cleaning machine about.

"Let's show you what this girl can do," Amy said. She indicated for me to move sideways as she vacuumed under me on the couch. Grime and dust disappeared in obvious lines where the cleaner moved along, sweeping up every protest I had in its path.

"Can I go up to your bedroom?" Amy winked at Richard as he jumped up to lead the way. Kyralee followed close behind. I groaned to myself at the blatant innuendo, and reluctantly followed them to the other end of the house.

Amy expertly whipped off the bedding and installed a black cloth as a filter into the suction fitting. She deftly demonstrated the amount of dead skin that will come off a mattress with the magic of her machine. There was a parade of white flecks of lifeless flesh stuck to the black cloth that Amy whipped in front of our faces with a flourish.

"Gross!" I said.

Richard's eyes brightened as Amy leaned over the bed, seductively wielding her magic wand. Making the shape of a body on the surface, she paid particular attention to where the nether regions rested at night, with an accompanying seductive giggle.

Her breasts touched the surface as she reached across the mattress. Richard was glued to the demonstration like a fat kid loves cake.

"It sucks so very effectively," she said. I rolled my eyes at Kyralee, but she was firmly keeping an eye on proceedings and missed my ironic observation.

"It is amazing," said Kyralee. "I had no idea that my cleaning routine was leaving so much behind. I feel sort of… dirty."

Chapter 9

Richard playfully grabbed Kyralee on the behind and gave her a squeeze. This vacuum had more turn-on than its instruction manual might promise.

Amy ran through the vast list of household tasks the vacuum cleaner could cover... floor buffing, sanding, shampooing, scrubbing, and even a fucking knife sharpener.

"Yes, but can it walk the dog?" I asked. It was ridiculous and fascinating all at the same time.

"Do you really think you can AFFORD a three-thousand-dollar vacuum cleaner?" I asked Kyralee, incredulous that our girl's night out had been hijacked by a buxom blonde selling a cleaning appliance, and that secretly I was enjoying myself.

"We have a very affordable five-year repayment plan," said Amy, "With a no obligation, three-month free trial of the equipment, before the first payment is taken."

My friends moved into conference mode, as I continued to define good reasons why the vacuum cleaner was too expensive, overrated, promised too much, and could never deliver. Amy rebuffed my every sales block.

"Can you even *SPELL* vacuum cleaner?" I asked Amy, disgust plain in my voice.

Kyralee and Richard ignored me as they focused only on Amy and her magic machine.

"Do *YOU* do the after sales service?" Richard asked, plainly ever hopeful to see this woman again.

Amy caught his eye, tousled her gorgeous hair, and giggled.

"Not USUALLY," she said full of promise, "But for my favourite country customers I could make the trip. We are loving it here in your town. Matt will be here shortly to pick me up. It'd be great to have your decision tonight so we can start the paperwork."

Richard and Kyralee conferred and then picked up the pen. I sank into the couch. It was after nine o'clock and the shops were shut. The deal was done.

They were still signing their inheritance away when there was a knock at the door.

I answered it.

There was Matt, this time in his Ugg boots and quite obviously looking like he had just partaken of a joint.

I was quick.

"Had some attitude adjustment, have we?" I teased. "You are looking VERY relaxed."

He caught my eye and laughed.

"Well, I had knocked off," he said. "You should come around to where we are staying, we are here for the rest of the week."

"I'll make you......," he hesitated in a tantalising moment that lasted longer than I dared breathe ever again, as I held and waited, "…..a coffee," he concluded the strip tease of my soul with the promise of heat.

In a drink.

His proposal surprised me. Separated woman who had only ever slept with one man, the man I married, fully immersed in my grief at the ending that I could not heal. I laughed awkwardly.

"Sure," I said. "What's the address? I'll bring you a present. Homegrown local."

"What's your number and I will text it to you?" he said. He winked, just between us, and in that instant, for the first time, I had given my number to a gorgeous man that asked for it.

Suddenly single, even when the demise is devastatingly slow and painful, separation still had a certain freedom etched in it. There was a feeling, like the meat hook embedded in my back, holding me at bay in the cold room of life after a sure execution, was swiftly removed, and in its place were wings.

I am alive. I am free. I will survive.

And I MAY even get laid another time in my life beyond my marriage, if a man might find me attractive enough to do so.

Chapter 9

Amy moved past me in the doorway, lugging her vacuum cleaner and folders of signed agreements, that locked my friends into long term friendly payment arrangements.

She gave me a wink. Salesperson speak for deal is done. Despite my protestations.

Matt and Amy loaded their gear into the car and disappeared into the night.

In the aftermath of a marriage the odour of unhappy woman permeates every room. It is understandable that people avoid being around failure and rejection. Over time the process of healing replaced the stench of sadness and happiness crept in. It has a sweetness about it, where new earth is turned ready for seeds to be planted.

Meeting new friends like Matt and Amy were part of that journey for me.

I got a text message from Matt the next day.

"Do you like it hot?"

I felt that squirmy, yummy feeling of secret delight.

He likes me! AND he got in contact. Matt sent me their address and reaffirmed his invitation for me to visit. The twins were being collected by their father for the weekend.

After the children had safely departed and I finished work that Friday I went to knock on my new beginning, and Matt answered the door. Coffee offers transformed to a beer, and we sat at the kitchen table of their short-term rental house, eyeing each other. Amy had breezed around us but went to her room to make a call.

"Amy is having an affair with our boss," Matt was matter of fact. "It's complicated, but they are in love."

He was short and sweet as if that explained everything.

"And he is married?" I knew the answer.

"Yeah. Like I said. COMPLICATED." Matt rolled his eyes.

"Affairs are painful all round in my experience," I said. "Heartbreaking."

"It's why I have never married," said Matt, "And probably never will."

In a micromovement he was next to me, stroking my shoulder.

"Did you want to come into my room? It's more private," he said.

"Sure," I said, before I could think clearly and talk myself out of it. I stood to follow him across the hallway. My stomach flipped but my legs were automatic.

As soon as he pushed the door shut and turned to face me, his lips were on mine. I closed my eyes and returned his kiss, falling deep into his arms, which enfolded me, assured, experienced and strong.

The years of pain and rejection floated away as our 'meet cute' was consummated in a flurry of hot sex, complete with screaming orgasms. A meet cute is described in the movie 'Holiday', about the moment in the script where two love interests connect in weird and wonderful ways. This was my very own movie show.

Amy knocked on the door laughing.

"Keep it down you two," she called out. "I am on the phone!"

Matt made a date for the next day. A date where we didn't go anywhere, apart from across the hall to celebrate in bed.

From there our short fling extended into a sexual healing encounter, that cleared my emotional body of the cobwebs that sad celibacy in a broken marriage had created.

Matt was experienced and gentle. I floated in our fantasy world of connection.

After a few weeks they packed up and headed back to the city, and Matt moved on to the list of women he cared for in his own unique way. Our fling was complete, and my heart was salved.

Amy and I became firm friends. She was fun and full of flirtation. Men flocked to her like bees to honey. She called me every time she came back to town to service her clients. I helped her find more opportunities to sell the most expensive vacuum cleaner in the entire world.

Chapter 9

Mostly to my family. It was a match made in heaven.

Chapter 10

After the separation, Clayton and I had an arrangement of shared custody, where he got every second weekend with our children. We drove the 120 kilometres each and met in the middle to exchange the children between cars.

Each fortnight I carefully packed the twins' bags, snacks, and favourite toys, and drove my precious Rachel and Thomas to meet their father. I hoped that his car would make the distance, that he would be sober, that Rochelle wouldn't be with him, and mostly that my beloved children would survive the weekend.

All the little things.

Communication was not Clayton's strong point. Every weekend my stomach churned as I waited to see his car come along the road, invariably late.

As a couple, while I was the main income earner, Clayton had spent his life dreaming of becoming a filmmaker without taking any real action to bring it to fruition. His life looked like home brewing production lines in the shed and hazy days that leaked into nights of joints and old music. Clayton loved to stroke his treasured antique tins, bottles and sundry items that brought back memories of days gone past.

Chapter 10

Before he was alive, even.

The welfare system wanted Clayton to get a job and as a single man in the city he was out of excuses. The implications of a job meant he was being followed up to pay minimal child support to assist in the care and education of the twins. His reality hit home. A campaign to avoid the need to job search, have me pay child support while he became the full-time carer of the children, commenced with a vengeance. His career goal became stay-at-home Dad.

Every second weekend while the children were with their father, was time I spent with my friends and family, playing sports, and gardening. I planted seeds of renewal in the dirt and wrote my journal, seeking to heal my broken heart, that I might trust again.

I taught the twins how to use the phone box so they could reverse charge call me in case of an emergency. We practiced on my landline and when we went to the post office.

One Sunday morning I was home alone, and the children were with Clayton in the city, when the phone rang.

It was the operator.

"Will you accept a reverse charge call from Thomas?" she was brisk.

My heart stopped.

"Yes! Of course," I said. Immediately she connected the call.

"Mum?" It was Thomas. My beloved son.

"Thomas? Yes love, where are you?" My heart was in my mouth.

"With Rachel Mum. We are walking the dog near the beach."

"With your dad?" I asked.

"No. Just us. And Maxie the dog. Dad wanted a sleep in." Thomas said.

Matter of fact and four years old.

Images of my precious children walking around in the big city dodging traffic, with strangers intent on abduction and murder on every corner, screamed in my head.

On the inside I was frantic. My voice stayed calm as my mind raced.

"Is the dog on a lead, Thomas?" A scene of my twins chasing a small dog into busy traffic flashed in my distraught mind.

"Yes, Mum," he said.

"Great," I said breathing out with relief. "Don't talk with anyone will you?"

Thomas spoke to his sister.

"Mum said don't talk with anyone!" he called to Rachel. I could imagine my darling daughter beside the phone box, holding tightly to the dog's lead in her still chubby hand. They were barely beyond toddlers.

"That's what Dad said!" he giggled.

My God, he LET them go walking by themselves aged four, in the city they barely know. They are babies!

"Can I talk with Rachel?" I asked.

"Sure, I will get her," he said. I heard the shuffle against the door of the phone box open and the traffic noise came through the phone as Rachel exchanged the dog lead for the phone.

"Mum?" she asked.

"Darling. How are you?" I said. I wanted the conversation to last forever, while I wished I could swoop in and save them from certain tragedy under their father's care.

"Good, Mum. We woke up and Dad wanted to sleep so we are taking Maxie for a walk," she said.

Oblivious to the threats imposed by strangers in hostels that frequented the suburb where their Dad lived. Places for alcoholics, men's homes, and mental health shelters.

"Rachel?" I was firm and clear.

"Go straight home. Use the lights at the corners, press the button, make sure the cars have stopped and you have a green light to walk, and go straight back to your father's place please. Right now! Don't talk to anyone at all. I love you both very much," I said.

Chapter 10

"Yes, Mum, we will. Love you!" She said and hung up the phone without waiting for my response. They were gone.

I sat with the Sunday morning sun streaming through the window and my imagination running wild. Sleazy men slobbering their ways along the streets, white vans of child snatchers ready to steal my innocent children from the road.

I prayed, and picked up the phone to call Clayton and ask what the hell he thought he was doing, letting two four-year old's walk the streets by themselves in a city they hardly knew, surrounded by strangers, with the responsibility for his dog.

Anything could happen.

I dialled and listened to the phone ringing his end.

There was no answer. The call rang out. Helpless and alone, I put my head in my hands and cried.

When I drove to collect the children later that afternoon, my mind was filled with all the things I would say to him. Eventually his car came around the corner with the twins straining over the dash to see me, waving happily.

He parked his car beside mine and gathered their bags from the back seat.

I spoke quietly.

"The twins called me this morning while they were out walking in the city," I said. "By themselves!"

He didn't meet my eyes and shrugged.

My question came out as a hiss.

"They are FOUR... what were you thinking?"

"I was thinking I needed more sleep. It was a big night," he said.

He handed me the bags and turned his attention to the twins, gathering them up for a hug.

"See you next fortnight, twinnies," he said, his nicotine yellowed fingers paused on their shoulders, then without looking back, he jumped into his car and was gone again.

I hugged the children and strapped them safely into the car. On the way home I listened to their happy chatter about their latest adventure. I thanked our lucky stars and the God who made them, because She was all I had to rely on to keep my children safe.

We had made it through another weekend. My children were still alive.

The marriage breakup proceeded on its inevitable path. After leaving home with his record albums, garbage bags of clothes and boxes of antique treasures to be with Rochelle in the city, Clayton returned so that we could sort through more things.

We sat on the carpet of our former shared bedroom at the base of our high brass bed with photos we had taken in our ten years together, spread in front of us. Evidence of happy times. Country drives, arty photos of me looking forlorn in our filthy rental, after the phone had been disconnected, due to our fiscal limitations.

Our dog Paisley rolling on the lawn in the sun, with a wide puppy grin.

The farm in Queensland where we lived after we married. Our people who had co-adventured with us through our lives: Penny, Gary, Nick, and our respective families alternately grinning, or looking slightly surprised by the camera flash they weren't expecting.

As a budding filmmaker Clayton always had a camera in his hand. He observed life through a lens. He preferred that to taking part.

Clayton and I sat next to each other like old times. The hours, days, months, years we had shared as best friends and lovers. Husband and wife. Mother and father to our beloved twins who were playing in the other room, coming in to check on us every now and then as four-year-old children do.

They could feel it.

The ending.

"I just want it to be like it always was," I began, with my hand on his leg.

Chapter 10

I held out a photo of us standing arm in arm at his mum's place, squinting into the sun.

He shrugged me away and shifted just out of reach.

"I want the Clarice Cliff pottery, the cassette tapes and the bed," he said. "Among other things. I have a list."

He reached into his pocket and started reviewing his inventory of goods and chattels.

"It is not about the things," I said. "I do not give a shit about any of the things. This is about our marriage. Our life that we share, our children and their stable home, their happiness."

"I'll take the coffee plunger, too," he said.

He got up to leave the room and I heard him put the kettle on for one last brew.

Spread in front of me were the images of other times, photos of the children as babies, eyes shining with new life. Yoghurt covered after they climbed into the fridge to deconstruct its contents. Our precious daughter and son who I had willed into existence despite my fertility challenges.

I started putting photos into two piles, silently thanking Kodak for double prints, and my own foresight in photo printing orders.

He re-entered the room.

"Take whatever you want," I said. "I don't care about the things. If we can't have our marriage back, I just want our kids and the house."

"Great," he said. Clayton started dismantling the bed. "Can I get a hand?" he said.

When he drove away this time, the car was overloaded with furniture and boxes. The precious porcelain on the brass bed was carefully wrapped before we placed it gently on his roof rack. Myriad antiques and collectables which had been our shared passion after he introduced me to clearing sales, were boxed up and packed into the station wagon.

I kept the wooden pepper grinder that I had moved into a mixed box in a clearing sale way back when, a purchase costing two dollars.

I love that pepper grinder.

I held the twins' hands as we waved their father goodbye from our home a second time. Watching as his car belched fumes in its wake, he turned the corner at the end of the road.

Thomas squeezed my hand.

"Love you, Mum," he said, so wise in his compassionate hug.

"I love you too, mate, I love you both SO much!" I said and bent to gather them in my arms.

"Want pancakes?" I asked.

We went back into our home, just the three of us and my mattress on the floor.

A few months later Amy was visiting. Clayton arrived to collect the children for his access visit. In a special twist of malice, he had arrived driving Rochelle's car.

I caught the admiring glance he sent Amy's way as he entered the house and realised I was not alone.

Amy didn't notice. She was busy giving the twins big hugs goodbye, as I made sure their bags and snacks were fully packed with everything they could need.

It was a quick turnaround. Clayton made to leave as soon as we were ready. I followed him out carrying Rachel. He strapped in Thomas and I strapped in Rachel, double checking to make sure their seatbelts were on firm and safe.

I gave them both long hugs and kisses and gently closed the car door.

I spoke to him quietly.

"Please don't let the children walk around in the city by themselves. It is scary enough for them dealing with our separation, without you putting them in direct danger when they visit," I said.

Chapter 10

"I no longer have to listen to your bullshit Andrea. When they are with me, I get to choose how it happens," poisonous venom oozed from his lips. "And THIS time you NEVER get to see them AGAIN."

He was striding to open the driver's door and got in. I opened the door of Rachel's side of the car and leaned in to speak to him as he settled into the seat.

"What do you mean? Never see them again?" I asked panic rising.

He wanted to take my children, so I couldn't see them again. What does this mean?

Adrenaline rushed, and in desperation I reached across Rachel, unlocking her seatbelt while simultaneously attempting to grab her back out of the car.

Clayton leaned over the back seat and punched me away, grabbing the door and slamming it closed, flicking down the lock at the same time he put the car in gear.

Stepping along the front of the car on the passenger side, I bashed the window.

"Let me hold my children! What are you doing?" I screamed.

He pulled his foot from the clutch and the car lurched forward.

I felt sick.

To avoid getting run over, I stepped back and kicked the door of the car in mute frustration, as gravel spun from under the wheels. The other woman's car lurched out of the driveway, taking my children away, as he turned the corner in a spray of rocks. They were gone in a cloud of fumes.

Holding my head in my hands, I sobbed as Amy came to me from outside the back door, where she had watched the drama unfold.

She held me close as I howled.

"How can this happen to us? I am so scared they are not safe. Oh my God..." I began to hyperventilate, having trouble breathing in my distress.

"You have done nothing wrong," she assured me. "The guy is a fucking maniac. What the fuck is he thinking…??"

My bare feet crunched on gravel as I limped towards the house leaning on her for support.

"He says he isn't bringing them back. They are my life!" I sobbed. Snot and tears congealed and streamed down my face.

Amy looked down.

"Look at your toe," she said.

Blood was streaming from my split toe caused by the swift barefoot kick to the car door.

He has an affair with a friend of mine, leaves to be with her in the city and then steals our children in her car. Did he stop to strap Rachel back in? How has this happened to us? What about the twins, seeing all that? Will I see them again? The unanswered questions crowded my mind. I howled louder.

Amy got me a plaster, washed and dressed my toe and put the kettle on.

I immediately called my mum.

Mum is my go-to Goddess.

As she soothed me on the other end of the phone, I could hear her uncertainty. She was experienced in the worst of life matters with her clients. Always held in the sanctum of silence, Mum's confidentiality was legendary.

"What are we going to do, Mum?" I was distraught.

"Let's see how it plays out," she said calmly. "I know it is hard to be calm when emotions are so high and you are worried about the children, especially what has happened on his weekends…" she trailed off.

"But let's be calm and you go to collect them Sunday, and if he is not there, we will follow it up from there."

"What if he…?" I couldn't speak it out loud. The absolute unspeakable. Desperate parents in a tussle over children who decide that NO-ONE ever will see those children again. EVER again.

Chapter 10

"He won't hurt them, Andrea. He loves them. He is just mixed up right now, he is confused, and he is taking it out on you. He has made stupid choices and has to live with those. I promise that the twins will be okay."

She paused.

"And if he doesn't bring them back, I have channels we can follow up." Mum was calm and clear. Like a fresh glass of cold water on the hell hottest day. I was parched of positive thoughts and fell into her suggestion.

"Okay, Mum," I said, "This freaks me right out. I spend each access weekend on constant alert praying they will come home safely and in one piece, and now he says they won't come home at all!"

My eyes started leaking.

Amy held my hand as Mum continued to talk me through to the other side.

There was a knock at the door. Amy got up to get it as I concluded the conversation with my mother.

"There's someone here," I said. "I will call you back."

I hung up and when I saw who was at the door my heart thrust itself into my mouth. It was a policeman.

"Oh my GOD!" I groaned as I leaned against the doorway for support.

"Are they alright, is everything alright?" I stammered as I searched the officer's eyes.

"Can I come in?" he said.

Amy stepped back to let him pass, and I led him through the kitchen where the morning sun soaked into the dining room. We sat down.

"I have received a report," he began.

"Yes? What… are my twins okay?" I pleaded.

"Your former husband arrived in person at the police station in town and has made a property report against you. You kicked his car?" He opened his pad of charge sheets and began to write.

"Can I confirm your full name and address?"

The reality of the situation began to sink in. My voice hardened.

"You mean his girlfriend's car?" I said pointedly. "For the record!"

Amy leapt into defensive action.

"I witnessed the whole thing," she said words tripping out of her mouth fast as bullets. "He was threatening and abusive, and said Andrea would never see the children again. As Andrea tried to get her daughter back out of the car, he punched her away and nearly ran her over as he took off."

She pointed at my foot.

"Anyway," she peered at him with her eyelashes fluttering winningly, "How could bare feet cause damage to an old wreck?"

Amy was charming with the policeman. Charm is Amy's superpower. He closed his notebook. He didn't take his eyes from her cleavage. She twinkled at him, brushing his arm as she passed him coffee.

I sat there in silent shock.

The sun was still shining, when the policeman informed me I was let off with a warning.

I stood up shaking as he prepared to make his leave.

"Don't let it happen again," he said without looking at me. The policemen only had eyes for Amy, as he dipped his hat and drove off into the day.

I grabbed the phone to call Mum back.

Chapter 11

On Sunday, I sat at our meeting place watching the sunlight dapple on the water, waiting for the children to arrive.

My whole life with Clayton felt like a journey of interminable waiting. There were poems I wrote when we first got together, detailing my anguish whether he'd take another breath.

Looking back, I was potentially a control freak, attempting to marshal some sense of calm harmony in our togetherness.

I had creative ways of processing the amount of time I invested waiting for him.

There was the time I was helping to put myself through University. I got a holiday job during the federal election at a suburban primary school in Adelaide. A place I hadn't visited before or since.

Clayton had dropped me off for my shift. I turned my attention to counting votes. Madonna polled well, as did depictions of dicks on the ballot papers, making those votes invalid, but notable.

After a very long day at the booth, we finished late and I had gone out into the dark to wait.

There was no way of getting in touch to see what the plan was. He knew that I finished at about nine.

I stood alone in the dark and I waited.

The night got darker and the streets were silent.

I waited.

I had no money for a taxi and no idea where a bus might be.

I waited.

I craned my ears at every sound of a car that may turn into the street. My eyes were glued to the corners of the block, awaiting the glimpse of lights that indicated I was safe, and could ensconce myself in the imaginary world of together forever, no matter how late my ride ever was.

Eventually after about four hours Clayton arrived, like nothing had happened.

I got into the car.

"Where WERE you?" I asked pointedly.

"I was hanging out with Nick and then I was on my way," he said.

And that was it.

The wait was complete. Like every other wait for him I experienced in our relationship together.

Five years later and separated, the waits were laced with much deeper anxiety. This love of my life who I had married and brought twins into the world with, had another woman, and a new life.

And every second weekend, our children.

I waited.

Other cars came and went, with single parents in each vehicle, getting their children and bags out and swapping to the other car, returning to their respective homes after access visits. Some of those people smiled at each other, and even hugged. I could see the respect flow between them.

I waited for four hours. Five. Six.

The sun was setting golden that Sunday when it sank in that he wasn't coming.

I called my mother, who called the police.

Chapter 11

The police went to visit my parent's place.

"Are there court orders in place?" they asked.

"No," said Mum. "He has brought them back every time before."

"Without court orders there is nothing we can do," they said, and left.

Mum called me back with the news. Turns out because I didn't have court orders, I had no rights.

My heart was in my mouth on the lonely drive back home.

When I arrived, the answering machine was flashing.

There was a message. Clayton's voice filled the room.

"The children live with me now, and you cannot see them ever again. Don't try to find me, I have moved," his voice was calm and clear.

The timing of his message meant I had already departed for the drive to collect the children at our agreed meeting place.

The wait had been for nothing.

My darling Rachel and Thomas were never coming home again.

I called Mum and Dad, my heart breaking, tears spilling down my face.

"What if he...?" I could not give the thought words.

"Andrea we will find them, and they are safe. He won't do anything stupid. I promise." My dad's voice was strong, with not a sign of the shaking uncertainty we were all feeling.

"Tomorrow we will drive to Adelaide together and we will not come home without the children," Mum said. "There is more than one way to skin a cat."

My shoulders were heaving with the fear and pain of it all.

Never seeing my children again.

"Have a shower, darling, and something to eat," Mum advised. "Have a good rest and come to us first thing in the morning. We will drive you to the city. Meantime, I have a few contacts that I will follow up."

What Wisdom Whispers

Mum's calm assured approach was ever admirable, but sleep was impossible. I tossed and turned, walking the house in the dark, tripping over toys, books, and the twins' shoes in the hallway.

Imagination was in overdrive.

I could not live without them.

How to locate one ex-husband and four-year old twins in a city of a million people?

Next morning, I called my work to explain the situation and drove to my folk's place.

They had also arranged days off from work with no return date.

We would search for as long as it took.

Greg, my brother, arrived.

"I'm coming with you," he announced.

On the way in the car, Mum revealed that she had managed to get the new address of Clayton's girlfriend.

"I have my ways," she said with no detail needed. Immediately there was hope riding in the car with us.

We arrived in the city and went straight to Rochelle's address. It was a little flat in a block of four or five single story units. There was no car in the drive, but playing on top of the carport was Rochelle's ten-year-old son Timmy.

I got out of the car and called to him.

"Is Mum home?" I called. He swung down from on top of the structure.

"No," he said, suspicious. We knew each other and shared a lot of time at family events together, meals, barbecues, swimming, but I imagined the propaganda shared since our respective separations made him wary. He'd be hurting too.

"We are looking for Clayton," I said. "Do you know where he is?"

"Not here," he said. "He has a new place."

His offering was the snippet of purpose I needed.

Chapter 11

I hesitated at the open front door, then with resolve, went into the unit. By the phone table there was an address book, and I quickly searched it for evidence of a new address of her lover, my husband, the father who had stolen his children.

Mum was calling me from the front door.

"Andrea, you shouldn't go in there, we don't want any trouble."

"No trouble, Mum, we don't want any trouble, just checking if Timmy knows where Clayton is, or if his address is written down anywhere," I called back while desperately flipping through the paperwork I could see on surfaces. Searching for signs of life. Signs of my missing children.

There was nothing.

I flung open the door and bent down to talk to Timmy.

"Where is your mum, mate?" I asked.

"At Clayton's," he said.

"Tell me where they are?" I asked. "I need to know. Or it might be that Clayton AND your mum are in BIG trouble."

He shook his head looking down at his shoes.

My Mum stood next to me shaking her head silently. I knew she disapproved but I was desperate.

"I don't know where they are," he said. "Clayton has a new place in Port Adelaide somewhere and Mum has gone to visit, but I don't know the actual address. I didn't want to go."

I looked at Timmy. His eyes were downcast, and his mouth was sad.

Ten and home alone. His mother is off with her lover. His dad is back at the family home. Alone.

He is a victim like the rest of us.

"Are you okay home alone like this?" I asked.

"Happens all the time," he shrugged.

"Thanks, mate," I said as I ruffled his hair with care.

Mum and I got in the car with Dad and my brother, completely deflated.

"I felt sure they'd be here," Mum said.

"Port Adelaide," I groaned, "Like a needle in a haystack."

Dad started to drive slowly away from the flats.

At that moment my phone rang.

It was Kyralee, asking how we were going.

"Shit," I announced. "He's not at her place, and apparently he is somewhere in Port Adelaide."

"Port Adelaide?" she queried. I could hear her thoughts churning.

"Isn't their new production studio in Port Adelaide?" she enquired.

We all snapped to attention. Kyralee was right.

"Dad the new production studio is in Port Adelaide. Kyralee just reminded me, maybe he is there?!" I spoke urgently, there was not a minute to waste.

Dad slammed on the brakes.

"Thanks, Kyras, you are a star!" I said feeling hope for the first time since the devastating discovery Clayton and the twins weren't at Rochelle's place.

"My pleasure, darling," she said, "Let me know how you get on." We finished the call.

"You and Mum wait here, in case they come back," Dad said, "Greg and I will drive over to the studio and see if they are there."

We leapt out of the car and stayed out of sight of the flat, not wanting to traumatise Timmy any more than he had been already, but with the view of the driveway, should Clayton or Rochelle return.

Dad and Greg took off.

Mum and I sat on the kerb, holding hands.

"It will be alright, Andrea," she soothed.

Chapter 11

After what seemed like an eternity, but was more like half an hour, Dad's car came swiftly around the corner. He turned into the driveway and put down his window. At the same time Greg opened the back door.

"We've got them!" Greg called.

And there they were.

My beautiful babies in their seatbelts.

Rachel with her beautiful long hair now cut to a bob, and Thomas's grubby face, smiling at me.

Mum and I jumped into the car and put on our seatbelts. Dad took off and we were away.

"What happened?" I asked, incredulous that they had successfully recovered my precious children so quickly.

"Great lead from Kyralee," Greg said. "We went to the new production studio and knocked at the door. Nick opened it and recognised me. I told him there had been a mix up, that we arranged to pick up the twins and thought that Clayton said to meet here."

Greg's face was flushed, and his words tumbled out quickly.

"Nick shook my hand and said that Clayton wasn't there, but his new place was very close by, and gave us the address."

Dad chimed in.

"We made a plan and when we got there, we found it was a shopfront," Dad said. "Rochelle was basking in the sun in the shop window, in a lounge chair and the door was open, so we entered and ran straight up the stairs before she could say anything."

"Clayton was at the top of the stairs looking surprised to see us," Dad laughed quietly. "I pushed him to one side and told him to get the children's things because the police were waiting outside."

"The police?" my eyes widened in surprise.

"I lied," said Dad.

Greg continued.

"I picked up Rachel and Dad picked up Thomas while Clayton packed their bags. Not sure we got everything, but we didn't want to wait around."

"And here we are," Dad was triumphant.

Mum and I laughed with joy and the twins giggled at the excitement of unexpected events.

I snuggled between the twins in the back seat and held them close.

"You got a haircut?" I asked Rachel.

"Dad cut it off himself," she said innocent of his attempts to change their appearance while he hid with them in the city.

"You look beautiful, darling," I said. "I love you both so much."

I held each child's hand and listened to the twins' stories of the weekend adventure.

Dad got on the highway and took us home. My first move was to call a lawyer and seek court orders for custody and assured access arrangements. It meant that bringing the children back to me was a legal requirement. One with which I could call the police and get some action.

That action commenced the ensuing twelve years of trauma in a Family Court drama for care and custody of the twins with their recalcitrant father. It was a battle we all eventually grew out of.

Chapter 12

My early career which was dedicated to working beside people with disabilities shaped me. My clients experienced a different range of abilities, and I was committed to their goals and dreams. Our team and ethos connected them to the possibilities and potential for their lives. It was a responsibility I took seriously, with deep passion for the people and the work.

Early in my career I had started working one on one with Philip, who had partial quadriplegia. Initially my role was taking him swimming and shopping, plus to a range of social events. Philip loved to get out and about, especially to the motocross and dirt circuit racing. His wheelchair was his access to the world and he could push it himself slowly and surely, while I would assist to position it at the door of my car, so he could stand, wobble, and transfer into the vehicle, lifting his legs into position beside me.

Philip's speech was slow and garbled as a result of his accident twenty years earlier.

"I ….. was….. just….. twenty….. one," saliva pooled at the corners of his mouth with the effort of long conversations, large sections of which he patiently repeated until I understood.

"I was….. out….. on…. the…. motorbike…. with….. " his head hung low and sideways with his eyes peering up at me across the broad strength of his face, hair flopping across one eye, his glasses fogged up while the explanation continued, "my….. best….. mate……. and…. we…. stopped…. on….. the…. shooooouuuuullldddeerrr,"

I leaned forward watching his lips to glean the message.

"Stopped on the what?…… ." I asked

"on…. the…. side…. of…. the…. road, we were….. right….. off….. the…. road….. and….. we….. were….. admiring…. our….. mean….. machines……," his grin was cheeky, if slightly awry, as he chuckled with the memory of the pride and joy he shared with his mate.

"A car….. passed….. another…. car….. against…. double…. lines….with….someone….. coming the…. other way….. and they ….. had to….. swerve…. to…. avoid…. a…. head…. on….collision," sweat beaded on Phil's top lip.

"He…. overcorrected….. and hit us… standing there…. by our bikes……. my….. mate…. had….. taken…. his…. helmet…. off….. and ….. we… were…. both… thrown….. metres….. "

I touched his shoulder, where he could feel my hand, as it was not much point touching Philip's knee, where sensation no longer lived.

"My….. mate….. was….. killed…. on…. impact….. I…. had…. my…. helmet…. still…. on…. I….. was…. the…. lucky…. one……," his deep guffaw belied the irony he knew his monotone could carry.

My companionable laugh masked the silent tears that rolled down my face.

Philip and his best mate were both 21, in the prime of their lives. In one instant, through one decision of one stupid impatient driver, their destinies merged and changed forever. Philip taught me compassion and patience, understanding and acceptance. He got angry, and sometimes cheeky, with his wobbling hands reaching across the car to clumsily brush against my leg, with a twinkle in his eye. His intentions were clear.

Chapter 12

"Phil! You touch me and I swear I will drag you out of this car by the side of the road, and leave you there without your chair, to contemplate your behaviour!" My mock anger set the limit on his lechery.

I worked with Philip for years, helping him get ready for swimming, taking him shopping with his list of chosen products, cooked some meals and made sure he got the dignity of choice.

I interviewed the revolving door of cleaners and personal carers who he pissed off with his abrasive style. After some years in that personal support work with a range of clients I got the role supporting people with disabilities in an employment program. I drove the region each week in a white van and picked up a vast range of amazing people. Then drove to the adult college where we ran accredited training, supporting people to get work experience and jobs, aligned with individual skills and interests.

The challenge sometimes was their parents, who just wanted their child on a disability pension, so that they'd be cared for in the system when they passed on. I chose staff who saw their individual gifts the same ways I did, and we shared the expectations their goals could be reached.

People would stop us in the street when we were on field trips to workplaces.

"Ohhhh....you are so wonderful!" they would gush." It must be so rewarding."

I never wanted any reward and found their exclamations exuding charity offensive. There was so much more to do to ensure that our clients had the dignity of choice, open employment opportunities the same as a job I might get, in line with my abilities and interests, coupled with the support they required to get and keep their chosen job. I became a sexuality and disability trainer to educate my clients about sex. I never looked at bananas or condoms quite the same way again. Mum's family planning suitcase set the scene early in my life for sure.

Then I had the bright idea of a social enterprise with recycling at its centre. Cardboard was commanding a good price and I envisaged that with a business approach we could create self-employment opportunities for the people we were working with.

I rang the head office of a random paper recycling business in the city that I found in the phonebook.

A man named Michael was on the line. His smooth baritone voice answered my call into the wild.

"Hi there, I am calling to talk about recycling cardboard, to look at business opportunities for the people with disabilities I work with," I explained.

Michael was affable, and suggested we meet next time he took a country trip. We made a meeting date for a few weeks hence.

"I'll buy you lunch," he said with a deep laugh and we hung up the phone.

The day of our meeting I was wearing my red cardigan and black slimline skirt. He followed me from the reception at the college to my classroom. He was huge. Six foot eight with sandy blonde hair and remnant freckles. Celtic powerhouse and former professional basketballer, then footballer.

I was in the midst of the muddle that was the end of married life, when I met Michael. At the time, I was caught in the illusion of specialness of marrying my first and only lover, legacy of integrity coupled with Christianity. The one and only man for me, then caring for our children together in the fairy tale of love forever.

Despite this, when I connected with Michael, there was an instant of recognition. Like we had been here before. His cheeky grin. Our conversations. The instant deep knowing of the other. I thought about Michael often. I contemplated the potential of him, but the thoughts were fleeting as things were unravelling at home by then. I was increasingly desperate to hold it together, for the kids' sake, for my sake, for the sake of our marriage.

Michael was abundant. Larger than life. A big man with a big job to do. We talked. Proper adult conversations that had long been lost to derision and disrespect in my relationship. And in his.

Chapter 12

My marriage woes intensified. By this time Clayton had moved deeper into apathy and ignorance and Rochelle and her husband were embedded in our lives.

It was a saving grace to meet Michael and we talked about ideas like anything was possible. He wanted to write a book. Like I did. He became a friend who cared for me just the way I was. Michael was my muse.

"I have known I am a writer since I was born just about," I confided. "But I never had much to write about. Too young to have any material to work with."

Michael gazed deeply into my eyes and nodded. The recycling project I proposed never got off the ground, but our friendship grew. Conversations and meetings grew more regular. Michael's country trips diverted my way and he became the State Manager of all things recycling, as well as delivering commentary for television football on weekends.

There were times I thought we'd be together forever. There were a couple of barriers. One being his wife. The other my husband.

When Clayton had left our marriage, I was devastated and broken. Michael was on the other end of the phone, reassuring me with encouragement and hope. I wrote him a letter, which he amended with notes all over it and posted back. He suggested next lunch we'd share lobster and chardonnay. When chardonnay was still fashionable.

"You will get through this Andrea, if anyone can, you will. I promise," Michael said as we finished a call full of my tears.

My resolve faltered after the end of my marriage. There was less reason to hold my muse at bay. He persisted, I resisted, then surrendered to the attention. We folded into each other's arms, for a brief consummation of lost integrity. It was incredible. We clung to each other.

One day we shared a drive back from a country meeting at sunset. Michael pulled over to the side of the road in the purple glow of the Flinders Ranges. His breath was hot on my face as he pulled me close.

We kissed.

He had a smell about him.

Off limits.

I pulled away from him. My conscience got the better of me, and I retreated into the grief of all I had lost. All that could never be.

"Call me when your wife dies," I said. After he dropped me off, I cut off all contact.

Six weeks later my phone rang. It was Michael.

"My wife has been diagnosed with breast cancer," he said, matter of fact.

I took a sharp intake of breath.

"Did I create this experience through my thought?" I gasped. "I feel responsible."

"So do I," he said.

His wife survived. He nursed her and the children through the process. He cooked and cleaned while he lived a busy corporate life, working to ease the guilt of our collective thought that had surely caused her affliction.

A vision of possible outcomes dissipated in a crumble of certainty. I was broken. I was angry. I was rejected. I told Michael the truth. We always told the truth.

"I cannot do this to another woman," I cried. I was resolute.

Michael kept in touch.

"I have told my wife I am leaving when the children finish school," he said. "Will you sail around the world with me?"

"No," I said. "I prefer to feel earth under my feet and follow my own destiny."

Michael stayed in his holding pattern. The waiting place of life. Taking responsibility for the impregnation on their first date that had evolved to marriage and four children.

He kept putting food on the table and his dreams in the scraps for the chooks.

Chapter 13

Clayton's lover attempted suicide by taking two packets of Panadol washed down with photographic fluid from the darkroom. She was admitted to the hospital fifteen kilometres away. By this time access visits had slipped into a routine of sorts I could rely on, where Clayton was often late, but he always brought the children back to me, just as the court had ordered.

Clayton drove up from the city to visit Rochelle. He was spotted by one of the mums from the twins' school at the hospital.

She called me with the news.

"Did Clayton come and see the kids on the weekend?" she asked, aware of the turmoil that was our separation.

"No, why?" I asked.

"Oh, I saw him up at the hospital visiting Rochelle. She tried to kill herself on Friday you know," she said.

"No, he didn't," I said, "It would have been nice for him to make the effort, seeing as he drove all the way up here."

I pondered Clayton's demonstrated inability to communicate effectively with me about anything, or maintain regular calls with the children.

The next time I saw Clayton I asked him about it.

"So, you came to see Rochelle in hospital but couldn't drive the extra ten minutes to see your children?" My question was rhetorical.

Clayton looked sheepish.

"How did you know?" he asked.

"It's a small town, Clayton, and people talk," I said crisply.

"It's a confusing time, and Rochelle is erratic. She visited me at my place and when I didn't answer the door, she climbed up two stories, threatening to throw herself off the roof if I didn't let her in…" Clayton's voice was plaintive.

Hope that we could ever salvage our broken marriage was over for me in that moment.

"I am sorry things aren't working out the way you planned. You know what? I think we are done here. How about you send me the paperwork?" I said.

My Dad was working interstate and I asked Clayton's permission to take the twins to visit. We had a wonderful week away catching trams, eating out, and enjoying all the sights and sounds of the city. It was nourishing to be in a different place, be anonymous and free.

On our arrival home, the neighbours met me in the backyard to hand over my mail.

"It was lovely to see Clayton while you were away," Dorothy said as she passed me a stack of letters.

I looked at her puzzled.

"Clayton was here?" I said. He still had a key but hadn't said anything about visiting and he knew we were away.

"Oh yes, I didn't recognise it was him because of the truck, but we brought him over coffee and toast for his breakfast in the morning," she said.

"A truck?" I said.

Chapter 13

"To pick up all his things. He struggled with the big antique cupboard out of the back shed, but he managed it in the end," Dorothy said.

"He has already taken all the things," I said looking around with new eyes.

"Oh, has he? Well he managed to fill another truck then," she said goodbye and walked slowly back across the road to her place.

I unbuckled the twins from their car seats, and we walked under the lean-to at the back of the house. As I got out my key to open the door, I spotted my thesaurus sitting on the washing machine.

Clayton had bought it for me. A gift for my eighteenth birthday to support my writing.

I flicked it open.

Under my birthday inscription from all those years earlier, Clayton had written a new date, and a note in red pen.

"Dear Andrea, Deep down I really do love you & think about you all the time."

I closed the book.

Inside it was obvious Clayton had been through the entire house. Arriving in the dead of the night with his rental truck, he took everything else he wanted.

I went out to the back shed. The antique cupboard had been part of the settlement of the house purchase. It was so large the shed had been built around it.

It was gone.

I shook my head sadly to myself. In the end, for Clayton, it was all about the things. If he got the goods and chattels he wanted, he could pretend to be happy and feel whole.

I went back into the house and picked up my thesaurus on the way. I put it back on the bookshelf and got the twins ready for their lunch. I made a mental note to change the locks.

It was a Friday afternoon when I opened the letterbox to find a large envelope with the unmistakable scrawl of Clayton's writing on the front. The man I married for love forever, created beautiful children with, and who had left with another woman, was writing to me. I considered what the envelope contained. A heartfelt letter explaining his reasons for unfaithfulness and why he moved away to be with Rochelle? An apology for the emotional torments of the previous ten years?

I stepped out the back into the garden and opened the envelope. I noticed the legal logo on the top right-hand corner of the document. There were no heartfelt letters here. Instead it was an application for divorce filled out by Clayton. Complete with every detail except my signature.

For a few moments I couldn't see, momentarily frozen in shock that he had actually sent me the paperwork. Just as I had requested.

All I had to do was sign on the dotted line and I was free from a marriage not active for over a year, and way too active on his behalf for at least the year before that.

It was not a huge consideration when I reflected on the experiences in the breakdown of the partnership, but still it panged my heart. In the trampling of my core I came to understand pangs. I experienced physical pain in my heart. The sharp stab in the initial discovery of betrayal which dulled to an ache for ages, then remained forever as a pang.

When a memory invaded, or when I lapsed and thought of the children and what they were missing out on through our separation, the pain deepened. As time progressed, I understood the children were happier, I was happier, and time shared together was devoted and quality.

The papers that signaled the completion of our marriage were in my hand. I shuffled through them and underneath Clayton had enclosed two pages of handwritten notes.

It was my handwriting. Not dated.

The first page was my name and his name written all over it, on both sides, scrawlings of our entwined names, writhing forever together.

The second page was a poem I wrote to Clayton years ago. Prose in observation, candour and prescience in every line.

It read:

You sit there darling
I'll stay right here.
As long as we don't have to
touch it will turn out.
But will it? You resent me.
I can feel it. I love you.
But can you feel that?
No I don't think so.
Maybe you are a plaything to me.
Something not someone.
I am the hunter. You are my prey.
Is that what you think?
You smile. Your mask shatters
into a thousand pieces.
Don't cry. Maybe this is the end,
the end of you, of me, of us.
Can we survive? The eternal
optimist in me says yes.
But can we really?
Maybe this is the end.
THE END

Clayton had scribbled the words of Jim Morrison, *The End* by the Doors, alongside my poem.

I could see that we were now at the same point. It was truly the end.

I signed the papers. There was no other decision, as opposition was futile, and my writing was a premonition that struck me with the truth from many years before.

I called Carol,

"Darling will you do me a favour?" I asked when she answered her phone.

"Anything for you, my sweet, what do you need?" she said.

"Will you witness my divorce papers and help me plan a post-nuptial party?" I said. "I can see the invitation now; *Celebrate the divorce of the decade with drink, decadence, and dancing! Scratch your seven-year itch for fun, with good company and a great night out. Child bride breaks loose and invites you to end the gloom, dump the groom and party!*"

Carol laughed hysterically.

"Bring your own wet stuff, chair, and your divorce jokes!" she added with flourish.

"Brilliant, let's set the date!" I said. And we did.

The post-nuptial party was amazing. All my close girlfriends from across the country made the effort, and joined me to toast the end, creating a new beginning in that precise moment. We drank champagne. The few men I had invited stood awkwardly in the back yard. They looked uncomfortable as my raucous tribe of mostly single women celebrated in style.

Carol pulled me aside.

"Let's go cloud surfing!" she said as she held my hand and guided me to the garden, grabbing Kyralee on the way. The tight circle of men stood sipping beer, looking at us sideways.

We stood by the flower garden and Carol linked arms with me and Kyralee. Slowly but surely, we slid down together until we laid on our backs among the petunias and chrysanthemums, giggling happily. The full moon lit up the clouds scudding across the night sky.

Nothing else mattered. It was just me, my precious children, and my girlfriends. I was free.

Chapter 13

My friendship with Michael continued across the distance of space and time. Over the years our attraction rendered through clear boundaries into a solid friendship. An ear to listen to the stories of life. His wife still treated him with contempt.

"Perhaps she is justified," I said, "I don't have to live with you. Maybe her dislike of herself just breaks out at the edges, overflowing you."

We pondered all the reasons. Still, I loved him.

He called me on his drives home from work in the city.

"Write your book," he said.

"Write your book," I responded.

We shared our secrets.

"The first time we met," he said, "I remember it so clearly, I was following you between the buildings and I was admiring your legs… Great legs."

"Thanks…. I think." I said.

"It was the first thing I noticed, after your eyes," he said.

I smiled to myself, but was still bewildered by any interest in me of the opposite gender variety. I was naïve and usually didn't notice, so it embarrassed me to have it pointed out.

We called each other when on the road, travelling nowhere. Having challenging conversations about choices, about creative urgings, about talent, about possibilities. We loved each other, but he remained married, while my life moved quietly on.

It was another year later. My lack of luck in love was legendary. Kyralee fondly called me a 'bum magnet'.

Luck that was about to change.

Forever.

It was in the corridor at the college I worked that I first saw him. Lucas was new in town, tall, Celtic, and handsome. He wore a suit every day, looking suave, as he smoked cigarettes in the courtyard outside the IT office of his new job.

I saw him as I walked in the back door, past his office to my classroom. I dipped my head and smiled.

"Hello," I said shyly.

He took a deep drag on his cigarette.

"Hey there, how's your day?" he offered.

"Great thanks, just getting started," I replied.

"You have a good one," he said, and his grin softened his face and crinkled his eyes.

A few weeks later I noticed a fax pinned to the staffroom wall announcing birthday greetings from his mum. Same age as me, same year, six months apart. Cute.

I composed an email.

"Happy 30th Birthday! Couldn't help but notice the love note from your mum in the staffroom. I am thirty this year too! Synchronicity much? Have a great day!" I pressed send as my stomach flipped over with anticipation.

It was then the communication started. We wrote often.

"Can I take you for dinner? I'd like to get to know you better, and being new in town, maybe you could show me around?" he wrote.

We shared the challenges and lessons of our marriages. His divorce from a long-term girlfriend had faded into isolation, with no children to bear the brunt of the separation. And mine, a soap opera continuing saga, with affidavits, and court orders thrown in. True love unfolded in dinner dates and deep conversations.

"My dad was a preacher. I was seven when my father abandoned Mum, my sister, and me. He left Australia for America to study and preach in the Pentecostal denomination. He never got in touch again." Sadness soaked Lucas's story.

"He raised his arms and his voice in the ecstasy of faith and promised forgiveness, to a congregation soaking in the euphoria of church rock and roll. He is blinded by love, lessons, and the acceptance of the one true God. But he never spoke to his children again."

Chapter 13

My heart broke for him. Another son of a preacher man.

His Mum Wendy did an incredible job raising her children on her own, juggling work and life to put food on the table, and give her children the best life she could create, full of care, compassion, and love. Her story sounded a lot like mine.

Lucas and I dated for two years. It was perfect. My whole family loved him. After Lucas moved in, we got a kitten and he and Rachel shared their love of felines, ever doting on the fluffy bundle of joy which played with abandon.

"I am going to learn guitar," Lucas announced and he started playing in a band, singing Powderfinger's *My Happiness*, like the angel he was.

I shared all my deepest secrets with Lucas. My family and friends were astounded at how Andrea had "fallen on her feet." Me, the poster girl for second chances at love and life. The children loved him, too. We bought Rachel a guitar and she sat on his lap adoring his attention and care.

Single working parent transformed into double income, two kids.

Our house had a vine growing up between the lean-to bathroom and the wall and we decided to renovate the house.

"I will organise it all on my Fridays off," I said and then I worked as owner/builder coordinating all the trades. We added on a new living area, huge modern kitchen, and an exquisite bathroom with love seat installed in the shower. There was a large outdoor pergola entertaining area which we paved and then put the pool table.

One evening after dinner, Lucas said he had an announcement to make. The children looked on with happy grins, their eyes sparkling with delicious delight.

"I have spoken with Rachel, Thomas, and your father, and they approve" Lucas said with a nervous grin. "Will you marry me?"

I threw myself into his arms. The twins smiled and we had a group hug. A blessed new beginning. This time it was all happening the right way.

Lucas proposed a second time and revealed the beautiful diamond ring, adorned with sapphires, that we had designed together and got made. It was an abundant fairy-tale reality. Cinderella made good.

Our wedding was an intimate gathering of thirteen at an exclusive winery and the guests consisted of Rachel and Thomas, our parents, my brothers and wives, his mother and sister and my best friend Penny from Queensland as our witness.

After a couple of blissful nights in a bed and breakfast, we arrived home to a beautiful gathering of one hundred and twenty friends and extended family in the backyard of our newly renovated home. As our guests smiled and shone in the sunlight, we cut cake and held each other in the promise of a future forever together.

We settled into the cosy routine of married couple, and Lucas enjoyed the ready-made family with my precious twins.

Lucas's mum Wendy and sister Kerryn doted on us with generous gifts, expensive shopping expeditions and scrumptious meals together. We shared lots of beautiful meals as a family, laughing, playing, and drinking good wine.

Lucas and I respected each other's privacy. As a writer all I asked was that he didn't read my work, or my journals, as they are sacred and private, and for my eyes only.

The family court matters with Clayton were still a hot topic, and there were regular trips to the city for court appearances, and precious time spent preparing affidavits and witness statements. Lucas took it all in his stride and was in full support.

He pulled me into his arms.

"Let's have a baby of our own," he murmured into my ear. "Let's make all that practice count for something!"

"Cheeky!" I swiped at him playfully. "You will need to get tested to make sure you aren't shooting blanks!"

Lucas got tested and with the news of his healthy sperm count we ordered the IVF drugs which waited at the chemist for Sue, my nurse friend, to administer the daily injections.

Chapter 13

A fresh start, a new beginning, with a baby born of love. The twins were excited, too.

"A little baby sister or brother," Rachel crooned, "I can't wait!" She hugged herself and then threw herself onto my lap to be enfolded in my arms.

Thomas giggled.

"Another boy I hope," he said. I hugged him close. After all the drama of the marriage breakdown with their father, I felt blessed to be in love again, feeling cared for and safe.

Wendy and Kerryn were stoked. The excitement and anticipation of her own grandchild was overwhelming. Wendy called me.

"Don't say anything to Lucas, but I have started shopping for the baby. Just neutral colours," she giggled.

"You are crazy!" I laughed, and after I got off the phone, I immediately told Lucas, because we had no secrets ever.

He laughed.

"Mum is crazy!" he agreed, and we held each other close.

At the same time, I was in a conflict at work. My colleagues had accused our boss of bullying, and in the process of advocacy, I had also been threatened. I was seeking professional advice and solace.

Every day at work was a new drama.

When I came home Lucas held me close.

"How about we make that baby?" he whispered in my ear.

The wisdom of my small voice declined his attractive offer.

"Not now, darling," I said. "When this conflict is resolved, we can move on that plan. I don't want to bring a child into the world when things are so unsettled at work. I want us to create a perfect space of calm love into which to introduce our child."

Lucas was convinced and hugged me harder.

Sharing a pleasant routine of harmony contributed to the happiness of the household. We were the perfect couple. I was ready to bring our dreams to reality with a child of our own only when the time was right.

Meanwhile the story at work became more complicated. Accusations were flying and my boss was out of control. Everyone was on edge.

I maintained my normal routine of sport and community involvement but at work it was a very challenging time. It seems as one area of life became balanced; another provided the drama I sought to avoid. All I wanted was a calm, peaceful life of joy and bliss. Was that too much to ask?

Chapter 14

Chapter 14

It was winter school holidays. Lucas was tucked away in his computer room, door firmly shut.

The twins were at their dad's place, like they were every half of all school holidays. I was watching my third Australian Football League match on television, when the thought crashed in like a bird hitting a clean window, shocked and reeling, stunned but alive.

I am alone in a marriage again. How did this happen?

The air in the hallway outside Lucas's computer room was colder away from the fireplace. My fingers halted before I went to tap lightly on his door.

The sound of killings techno style, were low and continuous beyond the closed door. His grunts of combat, commando thrusting, harmonised with the bass tones, broken only by the staccato clicks of the mouse or maybe his joystick. Lucas didn't hear me, and I realised his headphones crowded out the life beyond the monotonous sure deaths on his screen.

I didn't knock.

My footsteps were light on the floorboards as I crept back to the couch and snuggled myself into the corner, diving deep into the game on the screen, to shield myself from undisturbed rejection with the comfort of cushions.

Clayton had been late to pick up the children for the holidays. A whole day late. He had tried to change plans last minute, but we were already visiting with my parents overnight forty kilometres away.

The next morning his car was waiting out the front of our place.

I realised his car was full of people. A First Nations family from the desert lands, a mum, dad, and two kids who Clayton was giving a lift back to the city. They were standing by his car on the footpath out the front of the house. Their children were sitting on the kerb, tracing in the dirt with sticks, as we turned the corner to park in the driveway out the back.

Clayton approached the car as we pulled up.

"I have waited all night," he said, clearly frustrated.

"Clayton, you had arranged for Saturday morning pickup and we made plans, but you didn't explain you had other passengers. I still wasn't going to wake the children when you called so late last night to change the arrangement. Anyway, it wasn't safe for you to be driving so late," I said.

A quick assessment of the situation confirmed there were not enough seatbelts for the twins in the car. Clayton was driving his Mitsubishi Hatch five-seater and there were seven people on board.

I said as much.

Clayton was cantankerous with having to wait around and was short with me when I questioned the safety aspects of the trip.

"The twins will have seatbelts. Just get them ready to go," he paced around while we got bags and snacks packed.

Lucas hung in the background, keeping his distance from the negotiation.

I settled the twins in the car and the other children sat on the laps of their parents.

I leaned in to make sure everyone who could be strapped in, was.

Chapter 14

"Hold those kids tight," I smiled to the mum, who tightened her grip on her child, and settled back into the back seat next to the twins. The sweet sweaty odour of campfires in the desert filled the car.

I turned to Clayton as he opened the car door.

"I am not comfortable with this, Clayton," I began.

"Get fucked, Andrea, it's my time and I will make the decisions," He was tired and angry.

"At least call me when you get there, so I know you all arrived safely," It was a desperate mother's helpless plea to deaf ears.

He slammed the door and the car took off. I stood behind it, watching my children disappear, then noticed something on the road. It was our Saturday newspaper delivery, opened, and then discarded under the car.

Tears of frustration and fear filled my eyes. I felt helpless in the face of this fortnightly anxiety, ever heightened by the weird and never wonderful circumstances my children were in with their father.

Shoulders slumped, I watched as they turned the corner near the old jail and disappeared from view.

I prayed. It was all I had to offer.

Four days later, despite many attempts to make contact, I still hadn't heard they had arrived safely, and Clayton wasn't answering his phone. I rang a mutual friend in the city who hadn't seen them, and I scoured the news to no avail. My girlfriend Melissa was helping us repaint the renovated dining room when the phone rang late at night.

It was Clayton.

"Thomas has been admitted to hospital and they have no idea what is wrong. He has severe vomiting and diarrhea that has persisted for days," he sounded worried. "He is in the isolation ward in the Women's and Children's hospital, and they plan to operate, some sort of exploratory surgery to find out what is happening."

My heart dropped.

"How long since he was admitted?" I asked.

"Three days," he said. "Thought you should know as they are not sure what is wrong and well, maybe…"

He couldn't finish the sentence. As usual, vague on details.

Three whole days and you are calling now? I thought.

"Thanks for letting us know, we will get in the car and come straight down, so we can see him first thing in the morning. Don't let them operate until I get there," I commanded, taking charge and seeming calm, despite the shock to my screaming soul.

My darling son, alone and scared in hospital.

"It's out of my hands," Clayton said.

"How is Rachel? Is she okay? Can I speak with her?" My mind was racing.

The phone was silent. He had hung up. One of Clayton's afflictions, reported in his affidavits to the court, was his phone phobia. The reason he refused to call the children to connect at any time outside access visits. His modus operandi for being elusive and silent, never communicating any change of plans. Thomas being in hospital was a big emergency. Clayton was as worried as I.

I immediately rang the hospital to check on Thomas, let the nurses know that I had just been informed and I was on my way. I got an assurance that no operation would happen until my permission was granted, unless Thomas deteriorated any more.

When I hung up the phone, Lucas and Melissa gaped at me.

"I had a feeling something wasn't right," I said, "I could feel it in my gut."

Lucas held me close as the tears started to fall. Melissa washed out her roller and the tray.

"I will get home and leave you to it, best you sleep now so you can make an early start to the city," she said as she gave me a hug and headed to her car.

"Thanks, Melissa, for all your help and support," I said as I followed her out, "I really appreciate it.

Chapter 14

Lucas and I woke early for the drive to the city before the sun came up. Making our way into the Women's and Children's hospital I asked for the isolation paediatric ward.

As we pushed our way into the room, the only single bed was crumpled and empty.

"Thomas?" I called. My imagination went into meltdown. *Were we too late?*

"Mum?" a weak little voice emanated from the adjoining bathroom, and there was Thomas, naked, sitting on the toilet with his face in a bowl.

He was green.

"Darling boy," I ran to his side and felt his face. He was cold and clammy. Wiry and thin at the best of times, Thomas was now skin and bone.

"I can't keep anything down Mum, I feel SO BAD!" He dry retched into the bowl.

I got a flannel from the basin and soaked it in cool water.

"I am pooing blood, I am so empty," he groaned and put his face back into the bowl.

I smoothed his hair from his face.

"It's okay, darling, Mummy is here now. Lucas is with me. You will be okay," I crooned.

I turned to Lucas.

"Can you find a doctor or nurse and get them to come straight away?" I asked. "I can't believe he has been left alone."

Lucas left the room to search for help.

After the retching had eased, I wrapped my son gently in a clean towel and took him back to the bed. His soiled jocks were on the floor and there were no spares to be seen.

"Have you showered, love?" I asked.

"No, I feel like I am going to faint all the time," he replied.

I filled the basin with warm soapy water and got another fresh towel. Gently sponging his body, I dried him off as I went and wrapped him up, so he was cosy, clean, and warm.

Lucas reappeared with the doctor.

"Thomas, I am just going to speak with the doctor outside. I am right here okay?" I said and gestured to the doctor with my head. We stepped out of the room.

I introduced myself as Thomas's mother.

"Where have you been?" the doctor enquired, "He's been here VERY ILL for three days."

The admonishment was obvious.

"I am so sorry, I didn't know. The children spend school holidays with their father, and he only called me late last night to let me know Thomas had been admitted three days ago, or I would have been here. There are issues but I came as soon as I was informed," I said. "What is the story? What do you think is wrong?"

"We weren't sure, and it has been touch and go, he is a very sick little boy," the doctor said, "We have run some tests. His father was keen that we operate but that is our last resort. We finally just got the tests back. He has severe salmonella poisoning."

"Oh my God," I said. "Something he ate?"

"We did some tests on his first stools, and apparently one of their puppies died after eating the same meal of fish and chips. Dogs are very prone to salmonella poisoning. It affects them badly," the doctor was now a vet.

"And my son?" I asked pointedly.

"We will start another nutrition and hydration drip," he said. I had noticed the canular in Thomas's hand. "It should pass of its own accord, but it is very severe, and he might need to be here another week. I will write another script now we are clear on the diagnosis and send the nurse to administer it."

"Thank you," I said and went back into the room to hold Thomas's hand.

Lucas waited in the chair next to the bed.

Chapter 14

"We have a diagnosis," I said. "It is salmonella poisoning darling, food poisoning. From the fish and chips you ate for dinner."

"The puppy died in Rachel's arms," Thomas said as big full tears rolled down his face.

"It's very sad, darling, and I am sorry about the dog, but I am very worried about you. Your dad should have let me know what was going on earlier," I said, "I would have been straight here."

I called Mum and Dad who were also on their way to the city. They were relieved to hear we had some answers.

"Can you go and buy some pyjamas and underwear for Thomas please?" I asked, "There is nothing clean left here."

I went to the bathroom and threw the soiled jocks on the floor into the bin. I caught my face in the mirror. Sad, angry, frustrated, but here now. I sighed and went back into the hospital room as Clayton and Rachel walked in the door. I gave her a big hug. She folded into my arms.

"How's my boy today?" Clayton tickled Thomas's foot as he stood at the end of the bed. He was full of bluster and was using his extra fake happy voice. Clayton was scared, too.

"He's very ill," I said. "The doctor says the tests came back positive for salmonella. It's what the puppy died of." Clayton nodded his head slowly, eyes widening.

Rachel's face fell. I held her tightly and kept my voice light. Now was not the time for accusations and reprimands. I spoke to Rachel gently as I held her close.

"Grandma and Papa are on their way and will buy some pyjamas, undies, and supplies for Thomas, so we can get him warmly dressed and he can get better," I was calm and collected. Mama Bear in charge of her cubs. Keeping them safe from harm.

I replenished Thomas's cup with fresh water and a clean straw and held it to his lips.

"Have a drink, mate," I said, "We need to keep your fluids up so your body can flush through the poison and you can get better again."

Thomas drank deeply. Then began to heave. In one movement I had a bowl under his mouth and a flannel on his forehead. Lucas looked concerned.

Clayton stepped away from the bed.

"Righto then, I might go and get a coffee," he said. "Back soon."

We sat there together. Rachel, Lucas, Thomas, and I in the hospital room. Soothing Thomas as he retched while mopping his brow.

I rang the closest accommodation to book us into a room.

After four days, Thomas was improving and off the drip. He was starting to keep food down, and his colour had shifted from wan green, to pale and clammy light yellow. Clayton sat with him during the morning, and after lunch we would come in for the afternoon and evening shift. Mum, Dad, Lucas, Rachel, and I had a family motel room across the road from the hospital. Lucas was a pillar of support, making sure that everyone had lunches and cups of tea, while we cared for Thomas to bring him back to health.

Thomas was improving, but the doctor thought it might be another three days until we could take him home to rest.

Lucas went to the cafeteria for a coffee. On his return he pulled me aside into the hallway outside Thomas's room.

"It's been four days now, and Rachel is missing school, I am missing work. I am thinking I drive her back home, Rachel can go back to school, I can go to work, and you stay here with Thomas and your folks, until he is well enough to come home," he said.

We returned to the room where Mum, Dad, and Rachel sat beside Thomas, distracting him with a game of cards.

"Rachel, Lucas is thinking he will go home and back to work. Did you want to go with him or stay here with us?" I said. "It might be another three days or so."

It was pretty slow going, and not much to do in the hospital for a healthy child.

"I am happy to go home," Rachel said. "I can see our friends and let them know how Thomas is going."

Chapter 14

We went across to the motel to pack up their things and came back for them to hug Thomas goodbye.

Lucas kissed me and I hugged Rachel close.

"Drive safely," I said. "Precious cargo!"

We laughed and Lucas held Rachel's hand as they disappeared down the hall.

By the end of the week we were all home together. Thomas slowly recovered and regained weight, then finally went back to school. We fell back into our normal routine. Together. And alive.

Chapter 15

Six months later it was access visit weekend. Clayton arrived to collect the children, and was taking the twins' bags to his car, when Rachel ran to lock herself in the bathroom.

Rachel was crying loudly, the sound echoing off the tiles.

"I am NOT GOING! You CAN'T MAKE ME!" she yelled.

I was taken by surprise. Thomas looked on with tears welling in his eyes, as I spoke to his sister through the door.

"Come on, Rachel, your dad has driven here to see you; he looks forward to it," I said calmly.

Clayton had re-entered the house with thunder in his eyes. I could read his silent accusation that somehow, I had created this resistance.

"Rachel, the court orders say this is your dad's time with you. He loves you. You really do have to go," I rested my face against the cool fresh paint of the door frame, closing my eyes.

"Please?" I pleaded.

Her sobs came from just behind the locked door. She was sitting with her back to it as she spoke.

Chapter 15

"Mum, please don't make me go. I don't want to go, especially after the way he treated me last time. I don't feel SAFE!" She was howling.

Tears welled in my eyes too.

Rachel had told me the story about their last visit, when the twins had been left home alone, while Clayton and his latest girlfriend went out to party. They had arrived home late. Thomas had fallen asleep, but Rachel had steadfastly refused to rest, and waited for them to return, confronting the inebriated couple with the righteous anger of an innocent eight-year-old.

"I want to call Mum," she had said. "I want to go home NOW! You left us here home alone and said you would be back by MIDNIGHT," her voice was cold hard retribution. A parent already beyond her eight wise years.

Rachel told me she had grabbed the phone to call me, and Clayton pushed her away into an armchair close by.

Probably with more force than he intended, but he scared her, and then he sent her to bed, sobbing.

The constant battle in family court had been an ongoing nightmare since we separated. His attempts for sole custody, arguably to avoid anything remotely like paid employment, were obvious after he had abducted the twins, and hidden them in the city. I later discovered he had completed the sole parent payment application form at the welfare office in his planning, prior to taking and not returning the children that fateful weekend. All he needed was the children full time and he wouldn't have to work again, while I paid child support. Getting custody was his career choice and a life work.

It was confusing for the children, exhausting for all of us, and expensive for me. Because Clayton was unemployed, he got legal aid, while I paid barristers, lawyers, child representatives and fees at full tote odds. Funds I could have invested in the children, were instead spent on my campaign to keep them as safe and secure as possible, in my custody with a shared care arrangement, which I believed to be the best option for their upbringing.

Family court is steeped in sadness, toxic anger, and despair. Sticky blue cloth covered chairs are all bolted to the floor in miserable rows. It is a bald attempt to avoid any weaponry being available to warring factions, on either side of the debate, where whole loving families used to be.

There is a distinct odoriferous stench of sweaty toxic armpits. Tension exacerbated by the various camps on both sides, caught in an adversarial system huddled in corners of the waiting rooms, strategically designed so the parties can be invisible to each other until they get in front of the judge.

Waiting their turn to tell their sorry tale.

Family court relies on affidavits that outlines the sides of the story in an eternal parade of he said, she said, he did, she did, or didn't.

The stories are all the same. Documentaries of broken relationships where the fallout rains on the most innocent caught in the crossfire.

Children aren't normally present in the waiting room as it is not a place for young innocents. This is an adult world where shields of shame, fear and fiction mask the undeniable deep love every parent has for their child, no matter how twisted or disappointing the circumstance.

This scene would have me back in court.

I could imagine Clayton's affidavit already.

"The mother encouraged my daughter to run to the bathroom and she locked the door making sure that my daughter was standing across it, deliberately barring my way. The mother blatantly prevented my daughter from coming on the access visit with me as per the court order. The mother is breaching her court directed order. I had driven my broken-down car with dubious safety features for hours in the heat of the day, arriving later than scheduled for the pick-up, only to be denied direct access to my daughter your honour. Please find the mother in contempt for her spurious actions that thwart the aims of justice for single fathers!"

Fuck.

Chapter 15

Clayton would arrive wearing a newly purchased op shop shirt in some stunning shade of paisley, still smelling of camphor.

There was no honour at all, as he represented himself, glowing in his moment in the sun.

His voice would be strident and reprimanding all in one tone. In the rows behind there would be sad faced mums, dads, and grandparents. All waiting their turn to share their deluge of disobedience under the eyes of the law, and seek permission to transform hatred into more time with their most valued settlement feature.

Their children.

"Rachel?" I said gently. "Please?"

Clayton was beside me. His voice was practicing for his next court appearance.

Stern, loud, and plaintive.

"Rachel. Come out now. RIGHT NOW. I have driven all the way here to see you and it is MY weekend. I wait a fortnight to have you. Come out now and get in the car. Your brother is waiting. I am waiting. You are making me VERY SAD!" he yelled.

Lucas had faded into the background, waiting on the lounge. I wondered what he was thinking while we estranged parents stood shoulder to shoulder at the bathroom door, pleading with our upset, confused, beautiful daughter.

For just this moment with different reasons we were on the same team once again.

A scream came from beyond.

"I am NOT GOING! Just GO without me. I am not coming out until you are gone! I am never going with you AGAIN. NEVER! EVER!" Her sobs got louder.

I turned to Clayton and touched his arm, speaking softly.

"I will talk with her, but I think that today we are not going to get very far when Rachel feels like this. Perhaps you and Thomas go, and I will call you once she settles and I can talk with her. We can try for next fortnight. I will talk with her."

Thomas waited leaning on the wall, with tears welling in his eyes. I hugged him close.

At least when they are together, I know they can look out for each other, whatever their Dad gets up to.

"Rachel, I am VERY DISAPPOINTED in YOU!" Clayton yelled at the locked door.

He pushed past me roughly and grabbed Thomas's hand.

"Let's go and have SOME FUN!" he spat the words back at the shut door.

Rachel was silent beyond, holding her breath while the door remained firmly locked, a blank faced bastion, silent witness to the drama.

I gave Thomas another hug.

"You call me if you need me, Thomas. You call me when you get there please? I love you so very much," I breathed him in, a coppery sweet boy smell. I gently wiped the tears that had formed under his eyes, and held his quivering chin, looking deep into his face.

"It will be alright, mate. I love you and Rachel will be okay, she is just upset for now. You go and have a good weekend with your dad. He loves you both very much. We will see you Sunday," I said softly, deliberately maintaining my sense of calm.

"Mum?" Thomas whispered making sure his father couldn't hear.

"Yes, love?" I said.

"I am going to live with you until I am at least thirty-one years old," he said as he looked deeply into my eyes, with a serious frown on his innocent little face.

"Thank you, mate, I love you very much," I said and stifled a smile. I followed him out the front to make sure his belt was firmly fastened. I waved until the car disappeared, coughing fumes in a cloud of carbon monoxide floating behind them.

After they left, I went back to the bathroom door.

Chapter 15

"Rachel, they have gone now," I said. There was a rustle as she stood up from where she had been sitting, back to the door, and with a click, the door opened, and Rachel was in my arms sobbing.

"Mum, I just want to stay with you. I can't go anymore. Please don't make me go," she cried.

Court orders don't account for the human sacrifice of our children in the process. The judges aren't there to witness the heartbreaking scenes, where shattered marriages play out through the myriad of awkward childcare arrangements, between people who have forgotten how they loved each other, and why. Clouded by emotion, new relationships, old wounds festering, side conversations of vitriol and barely disguised hatred under the veneer of abandoned love that was supposed to have lasted forever.

The plan had been until death do us part, but this is death by a thousand cuts, mostly paper and exploded heart shards.

I wiped Rachel's tears, and Lucas got up from the couch. We all hugged and got ready for dinner.

Chapter 16

The next August in the depths of winter, Rachel had a cold and I was driving her home from the doctor's in the nearest town.

"Mum, can I tell you something?" she said.

"Sure love, what's up?" I said lightly, concentrating on the road in the dusk.

"You know when Thomas was in hospital that time?" she ventured.

"Yes love," I said. "I remember it well."

"Well……." she hesitated.

I turned to look at her smooth cheekbones reflected in the dying light outside. She is beautiful, I thought for the millionth time. I am so blessed to have such beautiful people as my children.

"Lucas touched me. Down there," she indicated between her legs. My heart stopped. My stomach dropped out of the floor of the car. My mind tried to make sense of what I was hearing.

I kept my voice even.

"He what?" I asked.

Chapter 16

"Lucas touched me," she reached out her hand to mine on the steering wheel.

"Like this." Rachel made a circular motion with her finger on the back of my hand.

I believed her. It was how Lucas touched me.

"When did that happen, Rachel?" I asked.

"He asked me if I wanted to sleep with him while you were at the hospital with Thomas. I woke up and he was touching me," she said.

My mind was racing.

"He should not have done that," I said. "That is very wrong. I am so sorry! I will talk with him when we get home and find out just what is going on!"

"Mum, I don't want to cause any trouble, but I thought you should know," Rachel said, tears forming in her eyes.

I held her hand tightly.

"You have done the right thing telling me and I will sort it out," I said. We drove home in the looming dark, holding hands.

My brain was overloaded with thoughts. He touched my daughter, while my son was sick in hospital.

I trusted him. We all trusted him.

When we got home, Rachel went straight to her room. I confronted Lucas in our bedroom.

He looked confused as my rage overflowed.

"Rachel has told me you touched her on her vagina, while I was at the hospital with Thomas! What the FUCK do you think you are doing?" I hissed, incensed.

Lucas looked deeply into my eyes. They didn't flicker.

"She is confused," Lucas said. "It didn't happen. There was a time when she was sitting on my lap and my hand brushed across her, but she is mistaken. There was no sleeping in the bed, no touching in the night. Rachel might be a bit traumatised with everything that has gone on with her father," he said.

He stood up and held me close.

"I would never ever hurt Rachel. I love her, I love Thomas, I love YOU!" he said.

I was confused. Could she have made a mistake? Lucas was a straight up sort of guy. There was no sign of anything out of the ordinary. He was a good provider who loved me and my children. The thought that he was a predator would not compute in my mind. He was a professional, kind and friendly guy, who wore a suit every day to work.

"I am not sure," I said, thinking back on the familiar circular motion Rachel had made on my hand.

"I am sure," he said. Let's talk to her together."

We crossed the dining room and knocked on the door of Rachel's room.

"Darling, can we come in? Lucas says it is some sort of mistake," I began.

"I am sorry, Rachel," Lucas said from behind me. "If there has been some sort of misunderstanding, I am very sorry. I would never hurt you. Any of you."

Rachel looked up at us with sad eyes.

"That's okay," she said. "I really don't want to talk about it anymore."

In that revelation and despite his pleas of innocence, everything shifted. On high alert for any changes in behaviour, I made sure that Rachel was never alone with Lucas, and the twins were always together.

Our life as a family seemed to be normal. I watched with eagle eyes to gather evidence of any transgression. Lucas was affectionate with both the kids and they returned his affection. Rachel often chose to sit on his lap rather than mine.

To keep myself accountable and get a second opinion I disclosed the incident to my closest friend Kate. Kate was on a driving holiday with her husband. I asked her to take me off the speaker in the car, then I told her what had happened.

Chapter 16

"The fucking bastard," Kate said. "Keep your eyes peeled for anything out of the ordinary. And if you like, I can talk with Rachel."

"No," I said, "I don't want to breach her trust any further. I feel sick. But he is adamant it didn't happen. Rachel said she didn't want to talk about it."

"Let's keep a close eye on things," she said. "When I get back let's talk it through properly."

My stomach churned as I hung up the phone. I felt out of my depth and decided we needed expert help.

I booked relationship counselling in Adelaide and we drove to the city as a family in Lucas's car, which was small and sporty.

Music was playing and the twins were laughing in the back seat. We sang songs together as we drove.

Lucas turned the music down.

"Hey, why don't we look at a new car?" he said. "Something the whole family can fit easily into. Maybe a station wagon for camping trips and the band equipment."

"YAY!" the children yelled in unison. "A new car! Let's do that Mum!"

I looked into Lucas's smiling kind eyes. The need for relationship counselling seemed far away from here. I turned back to the children laughing in the back seat, and relaxed, giggling in unison with them.

"Okay," I sighed. "A new car it is, and then we can drive it over to Wendy's place and surprise her!"

Lucas' mum Wendy loves a surprise and she is such a beautiful woman; kind, generous, and loving.

"YAY!! Show Wendy our new car!" the kids yelled.

In that moment relationship counselling felt unnecessary and so I cancelled the appointment. Not attending the appointment meant I didn't tell any professionals about what my daughter had revealed to me a few months earlier. Rachel hadn't mentioned it since and despite my repeated quiet questioning of her, she continued to seem comfortable in his presence, so Lucas' explanation had become the scenario most likely to have taken place.

We drove to a car yard and chose a brand-new midnight blue commodore station wagon. We signed the paperwork for a finance contract and traded Lucas's car in on a family car.

It was a new beginning. Wendy was very impressed and hugged Lucas close when we dropped in to show her our purchase.

"I am so proud of you, son," she said. I looked at them both and thought about our beautiful family with Lucas and his mother and sister, that we were blessed to be part of. An expansion of our loving connections in blended family.

Wendy made us a meal and we shared a group hug before we hit the road in our family car, to our newly renovated family home. Life was a sweet ride.

On June thirty, 2003, the twins were ten and Lucas was away for work. It was the first time in ages that he had gone on a work trip. His employers had asked him to go away on other occasions, but he had always chosen to stay home. Lucas said he preferred to be with us, and spend time on his hobbies like making music, and playing on his computer. We had been married nineteen months.

I loved to cook and was in the midst of preparing dinner on our new six burner gas stove. I was lost in the moment, enjoying the process, humming tunes to myself.

Thomas walked into the kitchen and stood next to me. He looked me straight in the eye.

"What is it, love?" I asked.

"Mum..." He took a deep breath. "I've been wanting to talk to you about something... I asked Rachel if it's okay to tell you. And she said yes."

I stopped stirring and looked at my beautiful son, so delicate but strong and growing up so fast.

There was a long pause. We looked into each other's eyes.

He blurted.

Chapter 16

"Lucas takes naked photographs of us every time you're away for work or a meeting. It is child abuse and I want it to stop."

Everything did stop.

My heart.

My mind.

The all-knowing insight awakened to brutal reality as my thoughts raced to make sense of what my son was telling me. I couldn't breathe.

My soul slowed to certain wisdom.

That new digital camera he had ordered months ago. How he was so excited when it arrived, he drove forty kilometres home to meet the post. A tiny little camera, such modern technology.

All that time he spends on his computer in the darkened top room.

The distance that had crept into our relationship. How I felt alone in a marriage again.

Rachel's disclosure the year before.

I knew Thomas was telling the truth.

For all to see we were in the perfect marriage, the perfect little family. A second chance at love, a father figure, so affectionate and caring. My best friend. Gentle, loving, and accepted into our family with compassion, as the children and I have been accepted into his.

All those people closest to me, astounded I had fallen among rainbows and fairy floss of true love this time around. The fresh start of happiness forever.

After the words were out of Thomas's mouth I was in complete shock. My breath flew from my body and my heart was pounding. A cold clammy sweat broke out across my face, and I felt weak as I leant back on the counter to avoid falling over in a dead faint. I grabbed the benchtop for support.

My voice softened, as I looked into the concerned eyes of my gorgeous son.

Rachel was still in the shower.

I knocked on the door, went in and spoke to her softly. Thomas followed behind me.

"Is it true? Is Lucas taking photographs when you are both home alone with him?" I was gentle.

She nodded.

Her eyes filled with tears.

"Why didn't you tell me before now?" I asked quietly. "I have been on the lookout for anything out of the ordinary. Since you talked with me last year, I have often asked you if there was anything happening you weren't comfortable with."

"When I told you before you didn't do anything about it," she said. "He threatened us and said he'd hurt us if we told you. Whenever you are around it is like everything is normal, but every time you go out......"

Rachel's tears mingled with the water flowing around her.

"Oh my God!" I leant against the door next to the shower and sank to the floor, head in my hands.

"You are so happy, Mum," she spluttered. "We wanted you to be happy and to have a new baby and just be happy".

"Darlings, I can never be happy when you are being hurt," I said, crying too. My heart was bursting inside me, and I took deep even breaths to avoid passing out. I had to hold it together.

I knelt down and Thomas folded into my arms. I turned off the water and wrapped my precious daughter in a towel and held her close.

Quietly, I asked for details. Information I wish I could erase from my knowing. Background that shattered trust into a million pieces, while my heart fragmented into searing pain that comes with total awareness of truth.

The whole world shifted on its axis.

Moments like these bring a certain clarity. A resolve that is superhuman and all senses align into immediate action. Drama in real life, except this was OUR REAL LIFE.

Chapter 16

He had groomed them. Tricked me. Threatened them. I had left them unsafe in their own home through my ignorance. I had handled it very badly, allowing myself to be lulled into complacency, and had put my children at risk.

As Rachel went to her room to dress, I went outside and screamed silently at the sky.

"Why us? Why them? Why me? Why? Why?" I cried into the darkness between the sobs that wracked my body.

There was silent stillness. Stars sparkled in their billions above me.

Then it was like the top of my head opened right up. A visceral feeling of complete alignment and total awareness. My mind exploded into the stars and channelled energy of light into the clear night above me.

The voice that answered from inside me was very loud and clear.

"Because you are strong enough to put this in its right place….."

It was a feeling of knowing that if I had thought life is a certain way and it clearly is not; it certainly and immediately is not……then potentially *ANYTHING IS POSSIBLE.*

I knew what I had to do.

I went inside and picked up the phone. My first call was to Lucas. He answered with his usual terms of endearment, but I cut him off. Incensed pure rage overflowed down the line.

"The children have told me you take photos of them in the shower when I am not home. Just what the FUCK do you think you are doing?" I spat with anger like bullets as I shot words his way. "You can NEVER come home here again." He took a deep breath and started to deny any wrongdoing. I hung up the phone.

I went to settle the children, holding them close.

"I love you and I will make this right. Lucas is never coming home again. Ever. You are safe. I promise. I am so sorry I have been blind to what has been happening," I hid my tears as I kissed their heads.

"We love you, Mum," they said in unison.

It's a twin thing.

I held my sobs silent until I closed their doors.

My nurse friend Sue and her daughter were on their way to visit. When they arrived, the children were in bed. I was completely rattled.

"Are you okay, Andrea?" Sue asked, pulling me aside.

I was all business as I attempted to pull myself together.

"Something has happened," I said. "Something I can't talk about yet, but as soon as I can, I will speak with you. Thanks for understanding."

Sue touched me on the shoulder.

"Of course, whatever you need, I am here," she squeezed.

"Thank you, Sue, I just need some time alone right now to work it through, and decide what to do," I said. "Thanks so much for always being here for me, Sue, you have no idea how important it is to me right now."

"Whatever it is, it will all be okay," Sue said as she squeezed my arm. They turned to go.

"I hope so," I said and hugged myself as I watched the safety of their headlights leave the yard.

As soon as they were gone, I went outside to phone my parents. They were in Adelaide waiting for my elderly uncle to come out of hospital after surgery so they could drive him home.

I hesitated before I dialled Mum's number.

How to tell my beloved parents our whole world was a lie? That I had failed as a mother and had invited a predator into our home.

I called them from the dark in the middle of the road where I couldn't be overheard. Mum and Dad listened in stunned silence. Stars sparkled, silent witnesses overhead.

I told them everything. The disclosure from Rachel ten months earlier. My close attention to any changes that might be happening, all the way to tonight, and the bombshell reason for my call.

Chapter 16

"He has been taking photographs of the children when I am not home. Naked photos. The children told me tonight. I have called Lucas and told him he is not able to ever come home again. It is done," it all fell out in a rush.

"Mum, Dad, I am so sorry…." I began…" I know you thought this was the perfect marriage, that I had finally got it together, and that I had chosen well," I paused.

There was silence. A deep hole of possibility into which I could tumble headfirst and be swallowed, never to see light again.

"Our marriage is over. Lucas is never coming home here. Ever." I was resolute.

"We need to wait until Uncle Les is out of recovery in the morning and then we will come straight to your place," Mum was practical. "How are the children?"

"Their faces, Mum, they are so sad. I asked why they hadn't told me, and they said that I was so happy, that they just wanted me to have Lucas's baby and be happy. If I was pregnant with his child, I'd have scraped it out!" My voice was cold hard, and full of hurt.

There was a sharp intake of breath at the other end of the line. Mum and Dad were in shock, too.

My anger was rising, threatening to take me over, while my parents attempted to take it all in.

I explained how it had unfolded, how Lucas was away for work, his first trip for ages, how he had avoided going away and this trip was mandatory. How the children had waited until they knew they were safe to tell me, how he had threatened them to keep them silent.

"It will be okay, Andrea, we will work it out together," Dad's clarity and strength overtook his devastation.

"What a fucking nightmare! I will see you tomorrow, drive safe, love you both and I am so SORRY," the words caught in my throat as the sobs flowed.

"We are right here, darling, you are not alone, and we will make it right," Mum said. As we hung up the night air closed in and I crossed the road to go back into the house.

The children were sleeping peacefully.

I was alone in my new reality.

My first move was to Lucas's computer room. His computer was always on. My technical skills are limited but I knew his password and clicked past the home screen. Once I got the internet fired up, I did a history search of the websites he had recently visited.

My eyes were wide, and my heart sank to the dark depths of my saddened soul.

Site after site of child pornography filled the screen. There were babies, children tied up, silent faces with big eyes that had seen too much. Thousands of them. I searched for over an hour.

Pain, abuse, and exploitation of innocence stared back at me. Images I could never unsee. There were no images of my children that I could find on these sites, but they were somebody's children. Children at risk, in despair, abandoned, and abused, for some pervert's pleasure. Some pervert that lives among us, who sleeps in my bed, whose rings I wear. Invited in by me.

I went to the bathroom and turned the shower on to searing hot. Tears and shock flowed freely into the plughole, as the life I had known drained out of me. Innocence, naivete, hope, and trust all shattered. The thought my children had carried this, broke me. I howled into the steady stream of the water. I was alone and had no idea what to do. Attempting to wash those images from my mind and soul was useless.

We were changed forever.

As I dried myself, I caught my eyes in the mirror.

What do I do with all of this? What can be done?

I looked at myself. A good hard look, right into the pain of this revelation, which mirrored my broken heart back out through my leaking eyes.

Chapter 16

"Can you live with this, Andrea? Can you live another day with this knowledge pushed down deep inside of you?" I interrogated my reflection.

The answer was easy.

No. Not another day. Not another moment. No. No. No.

That night was completely sleepless. Every sound resonated through my racing brain, as I played back the memories and moments where life shifted forever. I excavated my mind for signs I had missed. Chastised myself for not following through with authorities when Rachel had disclosed.

Birds shuffled themselves, chirping softly outside the window as they snuggled into branches to hold them while they slept.

Mountains of pillows taking up too much space in the wide empty bed, encroached on my hollow soul. My mind replayed accidents and incidents and rewound micro movements. I recalled conversations and moments in time. Searching for the answers of how it had gone so horribly wrong.

I rose before dawn to the start of a new financial year. I reflected on how the universe has neat ways of compartmentalising life into time pockets, to be accounted for and filed, audited, and reviewed.

Times for dues to be paid.

Snapping back to present time, my footsteps were light as I traversed the hallway to open the door, silently clicking it wide to breathe in my daughter's innocence while she slept. Light from the streetlight outside broke through the edges of her window blind, and her translucent skin glowed, long eyelashes framing her ten-year-old face, her cheeks flushed. Rachel was beautiful, wise, and serene. She rolled over and her arm dropped out of the covers. Gently I covered her and smoothed her silken hair.

"Mum?" she murmured.

"Yes, darling, I am right here. Sleep now, baby." I never wanted to leave her side.

I checked on Thomas who was snoring gently with hardly a quilt in sight, and covered him up, tucking the edges to keep him warm.

If only I could have kept them safe here in our own home, where people can usually run for shelter should a threat occur.

Back in bed, burying my head under the covers for protection from my own thoughts, my mind churned with the knowledge I would never sleep soundly again.

I can never let my guard down.

I will never love because I always lose, or worse still, choose losers. This loser tops the pops. How could I have been so oblivious?

I tossed and turned until eventually the light of dawn rose, pink beyond the curtains and the birds called again. Another day was here, and the strangeness of the night faded with the dark and burst into a stranger day.

There is a strange magic that happens when everything real is taken away with one piece of truth delivered with innocence. The fact that my family had been infiltrated, and our trust crushed into oblivion, was sinking in.

The morning blended into the night before. Sleepless eyes stared at me from the mirror with new knowing in the blur that was my life now. The sun rose over the horizon and the children woke from their sleep.

Daily routines were safe zones. Breakfast prepared, uniforms, school lunch packed. I breathed in their hair as I hugged them both close.

"I love you both so very much, and I will make sure you are safe. I am so sorry, but we will put this in its right place," My assurances felt too little, too late.

The children held my hands as we crossed the road to the horse track that led straight to their school.

"I will pick you up at the gate this afternoon. I am not going to work today. Love you both," I said.

Off they went, across the paddock to some semblance of normal life, to be children, innocent and free.

Chapter 16

I called Kate, my work colleague and best friend, to tell her I couldn't be at work and to confess the darkest secret I could never hold for fear it would break me apart.

"I am on my way," she dropped the phone and started the drive to our place.

As I spoke the little signs of dissonance pricked my conscience.

All the time he spent in his computer room in the dark. How he stopped coming to bed when I did, despite my pleas for intimacy. How he liked me to shave down there. How I felt alone again in a marriage. Whether I had chosen him, or he had chosen us, the complete package. How had that worked anyway? I strained to recall our first encounters and who made the first move on who.

How he had groomed my children while lulling me into a false sense of security. How he had lied. How scared my children must have felt every time I had a meeting or sport, and they were left alone with him.

A predator in our home.

The man I had married for love. Until death do us part.

The phone rang. It was Lucas. I couldn't believe his nerve!

"I am in at work, dropping off the work car at the depot. I am going to come out and get the car and my computer," he was cool and practical. "I will head to Mum's while we sort things out."

Sort things out? He was so remote from the gravity of the situation, it was like we had chosen different coloured tiles for the kitchen. My wise voice was whispering. There was no way he was getting his computer.

"You aren't coming here," I said, "EVER AGAIN. I will pack the car with some clothes and some of your personal items and send it into town with one of my staff. The practicalities can wait until later."

I called one of my team and gave scant details, a vague explanation about a family emergency, and asked if she could come out to leave me with the work vehicle, and drive our family car back into town to give to Lucas.

Half an hour later, as my staff member was leaving with the car packed with his clothes and some CDs, Kate arrived and we made a cup of tea, musing over a range of murderous plans. Kate is a very special friend, with a wonderful sense of humanity, justice, and humour. We worked together running the program for people with disabilities to support them win a job they loved.

When my children disclosed to me it was natural that Kate was who I talked to first.

Kate kept me accountable. There is no hiding from the knowing eyes of a best girlfriend, where we share our deepest secrets and honour and heal each other in the acceptance of truths given light. Sometimes we only know it to be true when we tell a friend. As we say it out loud, we realise that is what we know and believe.

"I want to see that fucking bastard opposite a detective, explaining just what the fuck he has been up to," she spat. The anger of ages fuelling her plan for Lucas's demise. This was an opportunity for him to have consequences. Repercussions that many other's attackers had never faced. A chance to protect innocent children and for him to face judgement.

I agreed. There was only one option.

The response of family and friends was like someone died. They rushed from the corners of Australia to be by my side.

The sound of a car outside broke the reverie. I put the kettle on again.

I met Mum and Dad in the backyard as they turned off their car. They were drawn and anxious

We had probably slept the same amount.

"Greg and Karen are on their way from Ceduna," Mum said. My brother and his wife lived over 500 kilometres away. "They will be here in time for dinner tonight."

Dad looked through the window and saw Kate at the kitchen table.

"What is Kate doing here?" Dad whispered. "This is our council of war."

Chapter 16

"Kate knows everything. We are going to the police to make a report. We have been waiting for you to arrive," I said.

Dad was stunned. After a long drive it was taking him time to process. Mum looked at me with eyebrows raised.

"But the police, Andrea? Just how far does this go?" Dad asked.

"Yes, Andrea, how far does this go?" Mum asked.

My mind flashed back to all the times around the dinner table that Dad was firm about us not talking at school about what happened at home. That our family life was private. Perhaps because he knew his daughter was a chronic oversharer, but for no other reason, as our relatively wholesome existence didn't bear sharing in the school yard. There were no destructive secrets to be held.

There was a clarity in moments after the disclosure that brought my warrior woman to the fore. It was like being possessed by another entity, a force of nature and knowing.

A mother protecting her children.

My response closed the conversation.

"I don't know how far this goes, I really don't, but that is not my job," I said.

As we went inside the kettle soothed us with its burbling promise of peace.

Chapter 17

The phone beckoned with the opportunity to begin to set things right. After I made cups of tea for my folks, I looked up and dialled the number of the local police station.

The phone was answered by a policewoman I played tennis with on Wednesdays.

Small town connections.

"Hi, Tracy," I said, "Where is Dale?"

"He's on holidays," she said, "I am holding the fort."

"Lucky you," I said, but was hesitant.

How far does this go?

"I have ten-year-old twins, Thomas and Rachel," I said. "My son told me last night my husband is taking naked photos of my children when I have not been at home. He is not their father. He is my second husband. It has happened over ten times. I found a vast quantity of child pornography on his computer. He was away for work. The computer is here. I want to make a report," I said.

Dad and Kate sat next to me in the kitchen hugging hot cups while I talked. Mum came over to touch my shoulder, standing close.

I recalled the night before when I had gone outside to ask the sky

Chapter 17

"Why Us? Why Me? Why Now? Why Why Why??!"

The quiet clear calm voice had said *"because you are strong enough to put this in its right place."*

The images of innocent children I had found in the picture history search on his computer the night before flooded my mind. Babies, toddlers, children, gaffer tape, and chairs. Pictures of pain burned into my mind. None of my children. Thousands of images of other mother's children from all over the world. Sad eyes caught in horror and fear, the ultimate betrayal of trust and innocence. Images of lives twisted by depravity forever.

I was in a trance when I showered, sobbing, washing the disgust from my skin which was crawling with alarm. Everything changed in one instant, with one piece of information. *What do I do with this overload of horror, the betrayal of my children's trust, of my trust?*

I am totally alone.

It is one thing to be hurt in a marriage, it is another thing entirely for my children to be hurt. After showering, my eyes had locked on my face in the mirror. Deep in my eyes was confusion and sorrow. *Can I live with this? Can this secret be put anywhere safe?* The answer was clear. It had already devoured my children for God knows how long, and it was eating me alive.

I snapped into the present at the sound of the policewoman's voice.

"I have a P Plate appointment," the copper said crisply. "Someone is booked in to get their driver's license."

"Oh," I said. Deflated, I wondered what I should do next.

"Leave it with me and I will get back to you," she said.

I gave her my number and hung up. I turned to the others, empty.

The phone rang. It was Lucas's mother, Wendy. We were close. Wendy loved the twins. She and her daughter Kerryn bought the children gifts at every opportunity. We loved sharing lunches and dinners together, spending quality family time. They were the whole package, Lucas, his mother, and sister. We loved them so much, and they loved us. It was perfect.

"What is happening?" Wendy asked shrilly. There was fear in her voice, she was breathing heavily as she verged on hysteria. "Lucas has called me and said he is on his way through to my place, that he is not welcome at home, what has happened? Tell me the truth…."

I was gentle. Softly I launched that grenade of truth, shrapnel that would tear us apart.

"Wendy, the twins have told me Lucas has been taking naked photographs of them when I have been out at sport or meetings. It is child abuse. He can never come home here again," I said my shoulders slumping as I awaited her response.

The howls of a wounded animal built in volume and filled my ears. Another mother bear helpless in pain and fear. I held the phone away from my ear as her inhuman cries filled the room.

We were both sobbing.

"I am so sorry, Wendy, I love you…." I whispered and I handed my mother the phone.

Mum's social work tone took over as she spoke soothing platitudes into the receiver. Telling Wendy that we didn't know what happens next, we were just working it out.

All the practicalities.

I was shaking, tears filled my eyes. This was the result. Moment by moment the world was tilting more violently on its axis, threatening to tip us right off into oblivion.

Mum completed the call, hugged me and we sat down, bewildered, to discuss what had happened. We couldn't tell Wendy that we were making the report. It would break her heart, and we could breach an investigation.

Everything was different now.

We were on different sides of the same story.

The phone rang again. It was Tracy the policewoman. She was back on track.

"I have cancelled the P Plate appointment and have a detective driving over to come to the house now, will that be okay?" she asked sounding unsure.

Chapter 17

"Sure, of course," I said, wiping my tears, "We are all here waiting for you".

Kate folded her arms, resolute and strong beside me. Mum and Dad exchanged looks of despair and I put the kettle back on to boil.

We busied ourselves with meal plans and morning tea. Normal things that keep life in focus.

There was a solid knock on the front door.

As I opened the door the detective was immediately familiar. Her stocky legs, dark bobbed hair and angular features blocked out the light.

"Call me Anne," she said. She shook my hand, firm and strong. Anne was a hockey player in our archrival team.

As the game reporter each week I wrote up the fixtures and results for the local paper. Anne was new in town this season, but a force to be reckoned with on the forward line, scoring sneaky goals every single week in a very short skirt. I started writing the column for next week in my head, about Anne flashing her badge in the goal circle, as one does when life as we know it is over.

"Ahhh, so this is what you do?" I smiled innocently as I invited them in. "On the weekends you carry a big stick, and during the week you carry a gun!"

The bulge on her hip was unmistakable. Anne was accompanied by Tracy in uniform as they entered the hallway.

"I cancelled the P Plate appointment," said Tracy, "I am so sorry. Your phone call was unexpected on a quiet shift in this small town. To say the least."

"It's okay," I said, "It has taken me by surprise too, not at all what I was expecting.

I paused.

"And I wish it wasn't true."

We stood for a moment on the hearth of our home. It was like we shared a collective breath into our souls as we stepped into an alternate reality.

I took them straight to Lucas's computer room. I opened the blinds to let light into the dark cold space. The sun shifted its foreboding sense of secrecy to the appearance of administrative order.

They both snapped on gloves.

"To protect the integrity of the evidence," Anne said quietly.

We got on with the task at hand.

"Lucas has taken the car and has been in touch to ask for his computer," I explained, "I told him we can sort out the practicalities later...." my voice trailed off.

So many practicalities.

A happy marriage all a lie. Our brand-new home extension now a crime scene. The idyllic life we had created together shattered by secrets. My children who tried to protect me to keep me happy. My darling children.

I shoved down the tears with a gulp.

"Great work, we will be taking the hard drive for examination by our specialist forensic IT team. He won't be seeing that again anytime soon," Anne was all business, and the sudden shift from loving husband to cold calculating criminal, was complete.

I snapped back into reality with a sharp focus on the present.

"We have trust in our relationship, and our one rule was that we don't look at each other's computers. I am a writer and I like to have privacy with my creative expression," I explained wanly.

The irony wasn't lost on me.

I had returned the favour, by never asking what took up so much of his time in the dark, ensconced in the computer room. I assumed it was computer games as he had all the joysticks and online games in the world, shooting things in nether regions, interacting with faceless people across the planet.

"He bought a mini-digital camera. I can't find it. He must have it with him. The children said he was using that to take their photos," I said.

Chapter 17

The women looked around the room. I took it in through their eyes. A fireplace full of used tissues and a stained computer chair. A computer forever on. Hundreds of disks in piles on the desk.

I clicked into the history search, and showed them the thousands of images I found of other parents' children, positioned in helplessness, by people they have no choice but to trust.

I averted my eyes, as one viewing was enough.

"We will get you to come in to make a statement, Andrea, and we have expert child liaison officers who will work with the children to get theirs," Anne said as her gloved hand clicked through images with the mouse, while Tracy took photos of the browser addresses.

The list continued, medical examinations, forensic investigation of hard drives, crime scene photography, interviews with witnesses for their statements.

"Where will he go?" she asked.

"His mother's. That is the only place he has. He only has one best friend, apart from the band, and his mother called to confirm he was heading to her place," I said.

I gave the address and imagined next steps. The sanctuary concrete courtyard between tidy units, little garden beds of flowers, security screen doors in the suburbs that keep good people safe in quaint little lives, about to be exploded by the boys in blue.

"His mother called me this morning, and I told her bare bones of what has happened, but not that I am reporting it to police. She is devastated, as we are," I said. I felt protective of Wendy. She didn't deserve this. We didn't deserve this. No one in the whole wide world deserves any of this.

"Full name? Address? Phone number?" questions like bullets. I responded rapid fire.

"Does Wendy work? Where? What is your car registration number?"

"We have officers on standby ready to pick him up," Anne said. The manhunt was underway as we spoke. For my husband.

For my former husband.

Tracy shut down the computer. An electronic sigh filled the room, as his window on the world closed its eyes in relief. Even the appliance had a burden too large to carry on its bandwidth.

She unplugged the hard drive from the wall and the monitor and put it by the door.

"Do the children keep a diary? Are there any pictures they have drawn? What about their schoolbooks, writing exercises, poetry, art?" Anne was thorough.

The investigation had moved offline. My heart skipped. Had there been signs I missed that my children were at risk? We searched their room, flipping through their pictures, homemade cards on mantelpieces, notes in their books, all their creative colourings.

My heart stopped. Turning to Anne I sat on the single bed, butterflies floating on its cover.

"There was this one time when Rachel told me Lucas had touched her, when I was with Thomas who was very sick in hospital in Adelaide, and Lucas took Rachel back home for school," I began. The incident came flooding back to be recorded as part of my statement. "When I confronted Lucas, he said she was sitting on his lap, that she had clothes on, that nothing had really happened. Rachel seemed to agree with his version of events and shut down, she didn't want to talk with me about it again... oh my God.... he apologised to her. They have been close since, like nothing changed in their relationship, I have been asking her if she is okay, if anything else had happened since……"

"When was this?" Her notebook flipped opened to record the details.

I recalled when it happened. I started to shake.

"I trusted him and that he was telling me the truth," I stammered.

"August last year". Ten whole months he had been sneaking around, now abusing my son as well as my daughter. Rachel was only nine when she disclosed to me. It was my responsibility to

Chapter 17

listen, hear, believe and act. My responsibility to be focused solely on the wellbeing of my children and to keep them safe.

I had believed her, but I had failed, thinking somehow, I could keep them safe by being wary, and watching for any aberration.

I died inside.

I told the detective everything. How I had tricked myself with believing his deceit and lies. How everything had appeared so normal despite me being on high alert. That he had threatened to hurt the children if they told me.

"As I said, we will need you to come in to make a full recorded statement," Anne said. "We will make appointments for the children to see our investigators in the city."

"We have a team that specialises in these cases, because the risk of harm to perpetrators on their way through the system means our chances of a conviction are reduced," she paused, "If I had my way….." Her hand touched her gun, unconscious but sure.

They gathered up their evidence and wrote a receipt. Cards that Rachel had written Lucas, notes and drawings once innocent, now had a sinister undertow. The list included his hard drive, all CDs and floppy disks, and the charger and box for the digital camera he was so excited about.

Within 18 hours, the whole world had turned a pasty grey hue, where criminals lurk in plain sight, as part of happy families. Where husbands treat children as possessions and not cherished treasures of humanity to be protected. Where faithful wives have blind trust ripped from their hearts and eyes opened wide with abhorrent deliberate acts of betrayal.

Lucas had groomed and abused our beloved children under my nose.

Anne and Tracy were on their way out the door.

"Don't worry, we'll get him," Anne said. And they were gone.

Chapter 18

The phone rang.

"Andrea?" the woman asked.

"Yes, Anne, Andrea here," I assured her. It was Detective Anne. It was only an hour since the police had left the house. Mum, Dad and Kate held their breath as one, frozen and silenced when I addressed her by name.

"We've got him," she stated, blunt.

"You've got him," I repeated numbly and sank down on the couch next to the phone.

They got him.

My criminal husband on the run. My mind's eye tuned in on imagined siege scenes with dark uniformed Star Squad Officers, fully fitted with bullet proof vests, and communication helmets that shielded their eyes as they converged on the suburban unit, guns drawn ready. The scenario played through my head like a scene from a Hollywood blockbuster.

"He was at the doctor's," Anne went on. "His mum sent him straight to a psychologist, and you were right, he had the camera with him."

Chapter 18

"He came quietly, no fuss. Meek as a lamb. Wearing his suit," she hesitated, "Seems a nice enough guy….." she paused. Now that they had him, the incongruity of it all was sinking in for her too.

"Of course, we know better," her voice hardened with resolve and we were back to business.

The phone was clenched tightly in my hand, my ear pressed hard against the receiver. Mum came over to rest her hands on my shoulders. Dad and Kate sat at the kitchen table listening to my side of the conversation.

"The psychologist had made a mandatory report after he had disclosed what he had been up to. He called in the report immediately, while he left him waiting in his office, and we were already on our way, after speaking with Wendy at her unit."

"We have taken him for questioning. We'd like you to come in now to make those statements."

It was a gentle command, no question. The practicalities of putting a criminal away.

The siege scene disintegrated, into the reality of my unwitting desperate husband, laying back on a shrink's couch, putting voice to his abhorrent behaviour. Owning up, in an effort to create a diagnosis of crazy for his defence.

Dressed in his usual grey suit, smelling vaguely of the fresh cigarette he'd had half of before the appointment. Drawing on reserves of courage going up in smoke. Reclined, innocently sipping a black tea, as his specialist left him to phone police from another room.

"Now? You want me to come in now?" Town was 40 kilometres away, I was yet to shower, and the children were at school.

"We can make a time after lunch. Bring the children, as we have a specialist investigator coming up from the city to speak with them and get their statements too. She will be here in a few hours," Anne was officious, with gentle at the edges.

"Do I stay with them when they speak to the investigator?" I asked.

"Yes, for some of the time, and you can bring your mum or family member if you like for support.... okay? Make it 1.30pm."

"Sure, we'll be there," I hesitated, "Thank you, Anne," I said and placed the phone softly on the receiver.

I rose, gave the update, and announced I was collecting the twins from school after recess. Mum, Dad, and Kate got set to go.

"I will meet you in town and come to the police station with you," Mum said and hugged me goodbye. As Kate hugged me tight, my eyes started to leak.

"You've got this, and we are right beside you all the way," she said.

Dad silently held me, then ruffled my hair like he did when I was a kid. Except I wasn't a kid anymore. I was a fully-fledged grown up, making my way and making a complete hash of it as I went along.

I thanked them and waved goodbye.

After a shower I walked over to the school to sign the twins out. As we walked home, I explained that we had some meetings and people to talk to at the police station.

"All we do is tell the truth, just like you have always done. I am so sorry Rachel and Thomas, I have let you down," I said.

"What will happen to Lucas?" asked Rachel.

The question hung there unanswered.

State Parliament had just passed stronger laws about child pornography. The timing of our allegations and any convictions for his charges meant that Lucas would pay the price. It was the law of the land. Lucas was gone. The Premier was calling for long sentences to punish those who compromised the innocence of children.

Children like mine.

The whole thing was unthinkable and playing out in regional Australia, in our own home.

Chapter 18

"Lucas has done the wrong thing, darling. What happens is not our job. All we need to do is answer the questions and tell the truth. That is our job now. Just tell the truth and support each other."

I hugged her close.

"Mum?" Thomas said. "He said he would hurt us if we told you anything at all. He told us it was our secret."

"You are so brave and amazing, both of you. Thomas for telling me what was still going on, and you, Rachel, for being so wise and honest. That is all we need to do, just be honest, just as you are."

"It's okay, Mum," said Thomas, "We've got this."

"Lucas is never coming home again," I said. The twins looked at each other and smiled. An open grin of pure relief. We linked hands as we walked in our front gate together.

That same day, Penny was traversing the wide brown land, to start a new life with her girlfriend in Perth. Her uterus, the affectionate name we have for her ute, unexpectedly rolled into the yard. Penny parked under the hills hoist while we were having another cup of tea.

The twins raced out to meet her and she enfolded them in her arms. Penny had brought gifts, which the children held like precious gems, as they made their way past me on the verandah. Racing back into the house to rip them open, squeals of laughter were emanating.

Friendly familiar eyes locked on mine, as Penny grabbed both sides of my face and looked deeply into my heart. She planted a big kiss on the lips and a hug that lasted forever. Biting back tears, I sighed and released my tightly held shoulders.

"I just kept driving after you told me the news when I called," she said. "Dodged all the roos like a good uterus and here I am. Who wants a night at Broken Hill anyway?"

We laughed.

Life snapped into semblance of normal.

"Coffee?" I offered, as we grabbed Penny's bags and headed into the house, dropping them with a thud in my bedroom. I had changed the sheets and scrubbed surfaces in vain attempts to clean up my soiled life.

We always slept in the same bed, as girlfriends do. Talking deep into the night, laughing, and telling stories and secrets. Other secrets we had shared through our letter writing habit for over a decade, keeping in touch while our creative juices flowed onto the paper. I sent Penny dozens of longhand letters, describing the marriage breakdown with Clayton. Cathartic tomes of descriptive vitriol as I attempted to hide from myself the sure knowledge, he was having an affair.

Letters about lives full of people so crazy, they didn't even need embellishment.

"I reckon I have topped the pops with my latest foray into unfortunate events," I jibed.

"I reckon you have," she said, and we continued the conversation, with vocabulary lifted into metaphor and mystery, so that the children were unscathed as they played.

After the twins went up to their bedrooms to try out the kaleidoscopes Penny had brought, her tone remained light, but her voice lowered a notch.

"Of course, I know people who could have the fucker killed," she said, as if she had asked for an extra sugar in her coffee. "They'd come and get him and take him somewhere dark and just cut his balls off, so he bleeds out. He wouldn't know what had hit him."

She stirred thoughtfully, with relish.

Similar thoughts had crossed my mind.

"I guess my wise self just says that is not my job," I countered. "My job is to put this in its right place, which I have done, and from there the consequences will play out. My job is to ensure the children are cared for and they get counselling and support. My job is to maintain the normal as much as possible after marrying a……" I stopped.

I couldn't say the word hanging in the air waiting to be truthed…..
Paedophile.

Chapter 18

Penny's hand reached across the table and covered mine. She was the official witness to our wedding and a witness to my life. She knew the word I couldn't say out loud. My breath caught in a sob half expressed.

"My job is to remain sane and stay clear when this shit is so cloudy it stinks, and could turn into bitter twisted hatred. My job….." I trailed off and the tears began to flow.

Penny rose, and came around the table to hold me.

Thomas padded down the hall and put his arms around my shoulders as I heaved hot guilty tears onto the table. Snot flowing freely. Rachel slowly edged her way into our huddle, and we all held each other close.

"Group hug!" said Thomas triumphant, as my tears mingled into his hair. I breathed him in. We are safe and the worst is over.

Our children are incredible. They are survivors.

"What about I cook dinner while you guys go to your appointment?" Penny said, as she opened the fridge to see what was on offer.

I looked at her. Gratitude filled my eyes.

"Thanks, Penny, that'd be great," I said.

"I don't know about *great*, but it'll be nourishing," she said and buried her face behind the fridge door, so the twins didn't see her tears falling.

Chapter 19

I held the twins' hands as Mum pushed open the heavy glass door to the police station in town.

The front foyer was cold and white, sharpened in focus by fluorescent lighting. Glowing like it could be washed out with a gurney gun, that removed all stains on the consciences of perpetrators.

If only there were enough years in a life sentence.

I felt calm and present, but surreal, a deep knowing that we had a right to be heard. That the process looked after itself. It's a strange sense of relief to know that the police are on your side, working on your team, when so often I have seen them as the enemy incarnated, sent out into the world to chase us, fine us, catch us, lock us up.

The children were wide eyed innocents, and saw the boys and girls in blue as their saviours, the one they could run to for help should they be threatened by a stranger. Understandable for cherubs so young, having not yet learned to drive, or all the other rites of passage I had straddled the boundaries of, mostly in my youth while hanging out with their father.

Chapter 19

Except now, I knew it was not the stranger we needed to be wary of, or watch with suspicion, but the man I loved and trusted with my most precious responsibility.

He had groomed my children, sworn them to secrecy, threatened them with harm if they said anything to me. He had slipped under the radar and through my defence shields, deep into my heart, straight into our lives. Invited by me.

This guy was a clever bastard. We were living in what I thought was a normal life. Until it wasn't.

The policeman behind the counter came out with perpetual quizzical written on his face. An expression that goes with the front counter job.

"Can I help you?" He asked the question like a saint who could save us from a speeding bullet or leap from tall buildings in a single bound. Thomas was looking up at him with something resembling awe, while Rachel pulled close by my side.

"We are here to see Detective Anne," I said, "To give our statements."

Important business, where the weight of words creates a reality that firms up the past, and determines the future.

"I will just find her for you." He pushed away from the counter to find Anne because this is HER job. I wondered whether they talk about cases over coffee like we might discuss students or situations, and suddenly felt exposed. Hot shame flooded throughout my body flushing my face, despite the fact I had done nothing wrong.

There was nowhere to sit.

Mum stood behind us like a sentry on guard from the rear.

Pamphlets were stacked in dispensers and posters of missing persons were stuck to the walls. I read through the details quickly, just in case we could help solve more cases than ours sometime soon.

Always on the lookout for opportunities to leap into action and rescue someone, I peered into the eyes of those missing people, and pondered their loved ones in limbo. Left ever wondering when they might walk through the door or answer a knock from a sombre police person announcing sad news.

Life is like that it seems. Changes futures in an instant.

The side door beside the counter burst open and Anne stood solid and smiling.

"Andrea, Rachel, Thomas, hello there," she said warmly. Anne nodded at Mum.

First name basis made it feel more familiar, like a coffee visit with a friend.

"Come in," she stood aside for us to enter the inner sanctum of behind the scenes policing. I held the children's hands as we moved through the open office area where a couple of police people worked at their desks.

She took us to an interview room and introduced us to a friendly looking blonde lady. Amanda was the expert child interviewer. The tissue box on the table was cold comfort, but excellent preparation for the session to come.

Amanda needed them.

Everything seems clear cut under fluoro lights. That cold blue fringe on it all, clinical somehow as our story unfolded, excavated by a series of questions. Digging into the daily life of us.

Factual and kind, Amanda brought what happened and when to light, talking directly to the children.

"When did Lucas take photos? Did he touch you? What did he say? Where was Mum when this happened?" all was noted in Amanda's swift neat handwriting.

"We will type up your statement, and you get to read it to check it and then sign it when you are satisfied it says what you told us," Anne explained.

I touched my diary with my hand, intermittently checking entries for sport and meetings so that the times and dates I was away from home could be firmly established. I keep a written diary every year,

Chapter 19

plus my journals. Ever the writer, I had always written everything down.

The voice recorder whirred on the table, catching it all. Anne wrote in her own notepad, discreetly taking side notes, interjecting with a few questions of her own.

The children relaxed after a few moments and answered clearly. After a while Anne shuffled and stood up.

"Andrea, Rosalie, could we talk with the twins alone, so their evidence could be further explored, where they can talk freely?" I hugged my children and nodded to them. My babies now ten looked at me with the wise knowing of eyes that have seen too much.

"Just tell the truth. That's our job," I said.

Thomas and Rachel hugged me, a group hug where we held on hard. I breathed in their hair as I kissed their heads. Anne took my arm and guided me into the hall, and Mum got up to join us.

Anne shut the door firmly behind her. Her voice was quiet and soothing.

"We won't show you the photos, Andrea, you don't need to see them, and you won't see their statements, as it is in their words, and you don't need to know. You don't need the pictures in your head. I can tell you," she trailed off.

I thought back to only two nights ago when I had searched Lucas's history internet file, and then CDs, searching for evidence myself in his office, after seeing the harrowing images of child pornography on his computer.

I recalled the day Australia Post had notified to say the digital camera had arrived and Lucas had driven 80 kilometres round trip at lunchtime to unwrap it and put it on charge. So excited about his purchase. My best friend, my lover, my husband, beloved and trusted with my full heart, to share our lives. The man who the twins loved, who had shown him only acceptance and affection.

So much trust with my most precious purpose in life; healthy, happy children.

"We are booking the children in to our specialist investigative team in the city and we'd like them to see a doctor. Can you drive them there next week sometime?" Anne asked.

Arrangements continued to be made and I made notes in my diary, addresses, doctor's name and numbers, thinking logistics in my head. The city was a few hours drive away.

I had to notify work for time off, and keep the circumstances from my boss, who was still on his workplace rampage. Recently exposed in a long-term affair we all knew was happening, but ignored as part of the furniture, he was on cover-up duties. He was not going down without a fight. His poor behaviour and treatment of staff was under the investigation of the board after several complaints. Many of the board members were his mates. As one of those in the firing line, work had become untenable, and my doctor was advising me to take time off for mental health reasons.

It was the worst kept secret at work, but when it came out, his vendetta to protect himself went into overdrive. There were mediation sessions and psychological warfare playing out in equal ferocity.

"Just take yourselves off for half an hour. We will call you when we finish," Anne opened the front glass door of the station and thrust us into a world never the same again.

"Come on, love, let's get a hot drink", Mum held my hand and we walked to the golden arches on the corner, to some more fluoro lights illuminating the unkept promise of nutritious nurturing.

Just like my marriage.

Twisted on its axis. Out of shape forever. Cut off at the core.

The whispers of wisdom had been on my side again when the fertility drugs prescribed by my specialist had arrived. Medicine that created a life-long tie to my husband sat waiting at the chemist for the simple administration of a daily injection. Sue was ready to give me my daily jab to prod my ovaries into production of precious eggs. Any time I wanted. Lucas had pushed me to start the treatment as he was supposedly deeply in love with me. He wanted to join our lives together in the forever of children.

Chapter 19

My wise voice whispered that to bring a child into the maelstrom of that moment was not the best idea.

I had held Lucas off, explaining that the conflict at work was not conducive to healthy fertilisation or gestation, and growing a baby is one of the most special things we do. I rang the local chemist and let them know to keep those drugs refrigerated and fresh because any time now we'd be happy to use them. Once the storm blew over at work.

Before we got that chance, our whole world had changed. A twisted tornado had torn our home apart.

I mentally put it on the long list of things to tidy up the bomb blast that was the instant end of our marriage. To ring the chemist and let her know to send those fertility drugs safely back to the pharmacy in the city, that some other hopeful couple could make their dreams come true.

In the midst of our nightmare yet fully unknown, clarity came calling. Over time those loose ends would be tied up, one by one, to put order across a disaster. A patch on a severed artery, gushing life force on the ground.

Chapter 20

We settled at the cafe after ordering cups of tea.

"You know I will have to tell him, Mum." The thought of having to share our heartbreak with Clayton was a stark reality.

Clayton had to be told, but how would he take the news?

Mum's voice brought me back to the present.

"Yes, you will have to tell him. He is their father and has a right to know."

"I know, and he loves them," I said.

"I know," said Mum.

I put my hands across my face as I wept crushing tears for our children, for their father, for me. For the dysfunction of it. The conflict. The separation. The tension.

All the years during every single access visit that I worried about the welfare of my children with their father. With no communication, he did nothing to allay my fears. I worked to maintain a sanctuary of wholesome home life, and was doing my very best to keep them safe, cared for, educated, fed and clothed.

"I invited the monster into our own home, Mum. My God!" My head dropped onto my arms as I cried.

Chapter 20

"Darling, it will be okay, the children are safe, and we will work through the process together. One day at a time. We are here for you all." She touched my hair, smoothing curls away from my face.

We finished our tea in silence and made our way back to the police station to meet the children with Detective Anne. The doors to the inner sanctum of the police station opened and the lights of my life fell into my arms in one big group hug.

"They have done really well, Andrea. REALLY well," Anne held my shoulder as we turned to go.

"We will be in touch about next steps and the medicals, make a plan to travel next week and I will confirm appointment times."

"Thanks," I said. I was truly grateful.

"Now kids, shall we go and get some ice cream and take it to the playground?"

"Yes!" they said in unison with eyes shining. "Let's GO!"

I took one hand each and we opened the heavy door together, bursting into the sunshine beyond.

That evening my brother Greg and his girlfriend Karen arrived. They had met while in similar roles in child protection, and had driven across the state to join the family rallying in the face of our crisis.

As they walked into the kitchen, Greg opened his arms wide.

I fell against his chest and he wrapped me in a comforting hug. Karen wrapped her arms around me from the other side. Tears started to fall. I wiped my eyes on the back of my hand and gently pulled away.

"Did you want a drink?" I offered.

"I'll get it," said Karen and went to the fridge.

The twins were playing in their rooms. Penny was bustling around the kitchen preparing dinner. Mum and Dad were on their way joined by my brother Sean, arriving soon after. Everyone hugged hello. Undisguised shock was clear on everyone's faces.

"I'll need some more chairs," I said, and I went up to the office to round up extra seats for dinner.

I entered the office. Lucas's office. The space where he hid in his fantasy world. I hadn't been in here since the police had been to gather and bag evidence.

I reflected on how everything changed throughout our short marriage. Lucas changed from an attentive lover to staying up late, never coming to bed at the same time as me.

He had articulated a strong aversion to masturbation, which I had considered a hangover from a puritan upbringing, and very strange for a man. I thought playing with ourselves was normal. The disgust he expressed when we discussed pornography.

Now I saw it was all a ploy to distract me from his true intentions.

I grabbed his office chair and turned to go. In the fireplace there was the pile of discarded tissues. As I pushed the chair on its wheels in front of me, I again noticed the triangular stain on the seat.

It clicked.

Laughing, I called to my brothers.

"Look at this chair! What do you think he has been up to in there?" I stage whispered. I knew it was common to supplant laughter in a situation where only tears mattered, because of the overwhelming hysteria that huge life changing shocks deliver.

Sean looked at the chair and his eyes grew wide.

"Oh no! That is SO WRONG!" he exclaimed and started to roar in hysterics.

I pushed the chair into the light of the dining room and Mum, Dad, Penny, Greg, Karen, and Sean all looked at the stained evidence on the office chair. Clear remnants of regular self-pleasuring in front of the computer screen.

I laughed loudly. I sounded manic. Everyone's eyes switched to mine. They smiled, confused and not sure how to react.

Thoughts screamed in my head. *How could I have not seen? How could I have trusted so deeply?*

Chapter 20

My laughter became hysterical. I couldn't stop the outburst. Just as suddenly, my laughing transformed to howling cries. My heart broke in a million pieces on the floor, in front of my family and my oldest friend.

My brothers and Karen rushed to me and gathered me in their arms. Mum, Dad, and Penny joined them, and we stood in a human huddle of soul searing grief as I wailed. Uncontrolled distressed body shaking sobs. My heart was pounding so hard I couldn't breathe. I gasped for air in between wracking cries of excruciating anguish.

As a group they led me to the lounge chair and gently lowered me onto it. Sean broke free and quietly pushed the offending office chair straight out the back door into the night.

Eventually Penny returned to the stove to check on the meal. Greg and Karen stepped back wiping silent tears from their eyes. They hugged each other.

Hearing the commotion, the twins came out of their rooms.

"What's wrong with Mum?" Rachel asked her grandmother. Mum held the twins close in a big hug.

"Mum will be alright, darling; it's been a big shock. You and Thomas have done so well, and we are all so proud of you both," she said.

My breath started to even out and I opened my arms. The twins piled onto my lap and we held each other tight.

"I am okay, darlings. Just a bit sad, but it will all be okay. I love you both so much!" I nuzzled into their shoulders as their arms entangled around my neck.

I looked around at my family, two social workers: one specialising in child protection, a youth worker, a manager, and an IT specialist. Lucas had chosen the wrong people to mess with. How it would turn out was anyone's guess, but as a family we could tackle anything, and we would stick together to support each other and survive.

Penny called from the stove.

"Let's sit at the table, dinner is ready," she said.

Sean came back with another chair and we all sat down together to eat.

Early the next week I had to be in city for work. The board of management were attempting to get my boss to participate in mediation. He was having none of it.

Mum and Dad took their caravan down to the beachside tourist park and set up a home away from home. Anne hadn't gotten back with any details, and so the children stayed home to attend school with my friend Sue and her daughter caring for them. We kept everything as normal as possible. Safe in routine.

After my meeting with the board about the treatment by my manager, I went out to meet with Mum and Dad. We were driving to have lunch when Mum dropped a bombshell.

"The Advertiser newspaper journalist dropped past us at the caravan park," she said.

"What?" I exclaimed, immediately suspicious, "What the fuck did they want?"

I was astounded. How could they know? Where was the sneaking informant who had given information? Was nothing sacred? Everything is just a story to some people, another snippet of tragic mayhem to feed the readership. How can we protect the children if a journalist gets hold of this juicy story? Our lives had completely unravelled in an instant. How DARE THEY??

"They wanted a photo and our story," Mum said lightly, sneaking a sideways look at me with a twinkle in her eye. "It was about regional people holidaying in the same state."

"Your HOLIDAY adventures?!?" Reality sank in.

Mum was taking the piss.

"You are a bitch, Rosalie," Dad said with the greatest affection.

They were the first to laugh.

I was still in complete shock.

Chapter 20

"Mum that was uncalled for. Mean, nasty, and uncalled for!" My heart was still in my mouth.

Jokes are the currency in my family. If we like you, we tease you. If something hurts, we make a joke. At funerals Dad holds back the giggles. A totally inappropriate response mechanism to most things in almost every circumstance.

Dad parked the car at the cafe, and we went in to order. As I studied the menu, my eyes started to blur with tears that seemed ready to fall in an instant most days. Mum went to place our orders at the counter and Dad looked over at me. Silent salty tears ran down my cheeks.

He put his hand on my shoulder.

"You have to keep trusting, Andrea. This is awful, bloody awful, I can't imagine what you are going through. But you must continue to trust. We have to be able to trust people. You must trust," he patted my hand comforting me, while his glasses blurred up and his voice choked.

There was a pause.

"But your mother?" he intoned quietly. "She is still a bitch."

Through our tears we started to laugh. Salt went flying from our faces onto the table, and as Mum came back, we looked up at her, blurry, wet, and snotty and laughed even louder.

"What?" she said. "You two are nuts."

My phone rang. It was Detective Anne.

"Where are you?" she queried.

"At Henley Beach Café with Mum and Dad," I replied.

"Late notice, but I got the kids in to see the special investigations team, first thing in the morning. Can you get them here?" she asked.

"Sure, it is earlier than we thought but I can call a friend to pick them up from school and bring them to town," I said.

"See you then," Anne said, "And in the afternoon you need to take Rachel to Yarrow Place for a medical examination."

Yarrow Place is a specialist medical trauma response centre for females. My beautiful daughter. A survivor. I started to cry again.

Mum came and sat beside me.

"We will get through this, Andrea, together," she said. I rang Kate to arrange for her to collect the children after school and meet us later, ready for appointments the next day.

After we had finished lunch we went back to Mum and Dad's caravan. My phone rang.

As I answered an official deep voice queried me.

"Is this Andrea? Andrea Broadfoot?" the unfamiliar voice questioned.

"Yes?" I said.

"It's Detective Darren Harmond from Port Adelaide Investigations Unit, and we are responding to a mandatory report from a psychiatrist about your husband Lucas," he said.

"Oh, of course," I said. "The regional team are already on the investigation. You can speak with Detective Anne. I made an immediate report locally. They have picked Lucas up for questioning already."

"Where are you now?" he asked. His voice had the undertone of suspicion. Like I was a criminal on the run.

"At the Shores Caravan Park with my folks at the moment," I said.

"Okay, we will just make a few calls our end, and then pop past and confirm your location and other details in person. Stay there and we will be there within the hour," he said.

There was no arguing with him. He sounded pissed off they had been pipped at the post by the regional team.

"Sure," I said. As I hung up the phone Mum and Dad were looking at me with questions in their eyes.

"It's the Port Adelaide Special Investigations Unit," I said turning to Mum.

"Coming to arrest you for your shocking jokes!"

Chapter 20

We sat in deck chairs outside the annex watching the world go by. Families on holidays, children playing on the swings, kids on bikes riding around on the little roads, blissfully oblivious to the darkness that can creep under the covers of family life without warning. How an ordinary day can turn into a nightmare in an instant. I was envious.

An hour later a dark sedan slowly trawled the caravan park searching for our site. They stuck out like the proverbial. I waved to them. Detective Darren and his colleague got out of the car and we all shook hands to introduce ourselves.

"Come in," I said and led the way into the caravan to maximise privacy.

The two burly men hunched down to get through the door then struggled to sit in the tiny bench seats at the table in the small space. We watched their progress with interest, exchanging bemused looks. The caravan was suddenly very full.

"So, Andrea, can we confirm your full name, date of birth and home address?" Detective Darren flipped out his notebook.

I answered all their questions and suggested they liaise with Detective Anne to check progress of the investigation.

"The children are meeting with the specialist investigation team tomorrow, and we have medical appointments booked," I explained. "Detective Anne has been amazing and is right onto it. We are in good hands."

Detective Darren shut his notebook.

"How are you faring with all this going on?" he asked.

"I haven't slept since we found out, and it all plays through my head constantly, but we have excellent support and the evidence is incontrovertible. We are hopeful of a clear outcome," I said. "I know of cases where people have been unable to lay charges, and I feel grateful to my children for trusting me and telling me what was going on. As things go, we are in a good position for Lucas to have significant consequences for his actions."

Detective Darren nodded his head, watching my face.

"Thanks for asking," I said. "It is not how I thought my marriage would end, that's for sure."

Our life felt like an episode of NCIS. From the questions the investigators ask which clarified the smallest details to cross reference them with diary entries, our account of events, witness statements and other evidence. It was clear the goal was to create a watertight case, and the best-case scenario was a guilty plea, so the children were protected from giving evidence at any trial.

"Okay we have what we need to close the case file our end and will pass on the psychiatrist's reporting statement to Detective Anne and her team," Detective Darren said.

Extracting themselves from the caravan kitchen took a lot of wiggling and shuffling. Mum, Dad, and I got out of their way and waited outside the door for them to emerge.

I extended my hand.

"Thanks for coming, and for following up, we really appreciate it," I said.

After they left, I turned to Mum and Dad.

"There's something I need to do. Will you give me a ride to Clayton's place?" I asked. I sent a message to Clayton to check he was home and available. He messaged back that he was. My stomach started to churn.

"Sure," Dad said. "We'll come in with you to see him."

"I couldn't tell him over the phone, it needs to be face to face. No matter how differently we parent, he loves our kids as much as I do," I said, steeling myself for the visit and his reaction.

It was a short drive to Clayton's rented house. We entered the yard through the driveway at the rear. He was in a new relationship these days, after Rochelle's deteriorated mental health and constant threat of suicide took their toll and ended their bond.

Clayton answered the door and invited us in. He looked at us all and his face switched to an expression of deep concern.

Chapter 20

"Is everything alright?" he asked. I sat down at the kitchen table and looked him in the eyes.

"The twins are safe, and at school today, but I need to tell you some distressing news," I began.

I inhaled a large lungful of breath.

"Thomas and Rachel have told me that Lucas has been taking naked photographs of them when I have been out for work meetings or sport. There has been some touching. An incident that Rachel told me about last year, and now it seems he progressed to involving both children. I found a large quantity of child pornography on his computer. I immediately informed Lucas he could never come home again. He went straight to a psychiatrist in an attempt to create a case for crazy. A report has been made to the police and a specialist investigation team is assigned to our case. Lucas has been picked up and interviewed and as details are firmed up, charges will be laid." After it all fell out of my mouth, silent tears started to fall down my cheeks.

Clayton stood beside me, watching my face crumple.

He put his hand on my shoulder.

"My God, Andrea, you must feel so deceived!" he said, sounding shocked.

In that moment it was like he also acknowledged the deceit he had inflicted throughout our marriage. There was a glimpse of humanity and understanding.

We were two parents who loved our children, both blindsided by betrayal. Me for the second time, but this was eternally worse.

"I am so sorry, Clayton, to have to share this news with you. I am always focused on the children's health, safety and wellbeing and this has come as a complete shock," I said holding back sobs.

"How are Rachel and Thomas going?" he asked.

I wiped my eyes and smiled.

"They are incredible. So strong, and clear; they are doing a great job. I am following up counselling and therapy options for them both. It's really important that they share only what they choose with us, and we don't pump them for information," I said. Clayton's response had been very understanding but noting the content of his family court affidavits, he and his new girlfriend loved drama, and that's the last approach the children needed.

"If you are okay with it, I can give Detective Anne your number and she can update you on the investigation side of things, so you can ask any questions you want," I offered.

"Thanks that would be good, I think," he said.

"It's a lot to take in, and I needed to wait until Lucas had been arrested to let you know. Detective Anne was keen not to breach the investigation in any way. It can be challenging to get charges to stick all the way through a trial and sentencing, hence the specialist team," I said.

"Thanks for letting me know. I appreciate it. Please tell the kids I love them very much," he said.

"I will, Clayton. I will tell them that we came to see you and let you know what is going on, and that you love them very much," I said as I stood up from the table.

Clayton opened his arms and we hugged.

Mum and Dad stepped forward and Dad shook Clayton's hand while Mum gave him a hug.

"Andrea is doing an amazing job with it all, Clayton, it is a big shock for everyone, and the twins are so strong, they are incredible, you can be very proud of them," Dad said.

"I am proud, and yes, horrible news, but thanks for letting me know," Clayton said.

As we left, I felt just a little bit lighter. It could have gone very badly.

Later it all came up in Clayton's affidavits in reinvigorated efforts to get sole custody. He included hysterical witness statements from his girlfriend and applied for court orders to prevent the twins and me relocating to a new hometown for a fresh start. By then Clayton was back to his old manipulative tricks, but on that day in

Chapter 20

that awful revelation, we stood together for our children. It was a glimpse of hope I could cling to.

Kate called to let me know she had picked up the children from school as we had arranged, and they were on their way to the city. The next morning Mum and Dad drove us around as we juggled between detectives taking more statements individually, specialist child interviewing teams, and then the medical appointments.

Dad, Rachel, and I were walking in the city mall between meetings, on our way to meet Mum, who waited while Thomas was still being interviewed.

Across the crowd of shoppers, I spotted an unmistakably familiar man in a suit, walking with his long gait. He was just across from us, only metres away.

It was Lucas.

He hadn't seen us.

Yet.

I flicked my head at Dad and gestured across the mall, my eyes desperate to avoid Lucas's, as I gently steered Rachel's arm away for some instant window shopping. I blocked her from view with my body, as I also turned towards the shop. Dad grabbed my hand; I took Rachel's and we quick marched in the opposite direction.

Dad stopped at the flower stand and bought a long-stemmed red rose. He handed it gently to Rachel.

"There you go, love," he said, "You are very brave, and it is all going to be alright. We are so very proud of you."

Rachel held her rose tightly as we headed back to the police station to meet Mum and Thomas.

It was the last time I ever saw my former husband.

Apart from at criminal court for his trial.

Chapter 21

When the sky opens up and explodes into a shower of stars, in the same meteoric catastrophe, it can be a challenge to discern the darkness from the light in the fall out. Epiphanies can bring more questions than answers.

A month later I called my mother, ever glad she was there for me.

"Mum??" She could sense my confusion and moved into soothing social worker matriarch mode.

"Darling. I'm here, What's up?"

"I think I need legal advice," I explained. "Everything is in joint names, the bank accounts, the mortgage, our car loan…." the list of practicalities mounts.

So many fucking practicalities.

This marriage I had taken my husband's name, a name now stained forever by his crimes. His surname was the same as my first ever love. Chris was a student teacher, our family friend who boarded with our family. I adored Chris. When I ambushed him in his bedroom one morning and professed my undying love, he promised he would wait for me.

I was four.

Chapter 21

When Chris married Julie, I was seven, and devastated.

The first betrayal.

My love runs deep and started young.

It was the first wedding of my short life. I cried throughout the service, inconsolable. It took some years and lots of work on Julie's part including scrumptious cakes and cooking lessons every summer holiday, for her to win me over.

Sweets have a language all their own.

Two and a half decades later when I met Lucas, I thought it was a sign. I got to have his surname at last. I had kept my own surname the first time I married at Clayton's suggestion.

For a whole nineteen months I had become someone different. A Missus. In the end it doesn't really matter, it is some bloke's name.

So, I changed it back again. I learned that a woman's maiden name is always her name. She gets to choose. I fell back into being myself by name and by nature.

How to explain the situation to the uninitiated?

"He's been charged. I am a witness. There can be no contact...." I stopped speaking mid-sentence.

Not that I wanted any contact. I never wanted to see him again. I wished he had never been born, that I had never seen his handsome profile in the hall that day. That I had ignored the cute birthday message his Mum had faxed through to the college staff room notice board when he turned thirty... the SIGN that our souls were connected.

Imagine... newly minted hunk of spunk joins the staff and is turning thirty the exact same year as me? It was a conversation starter and eternal love spring for sure. I gagged at the thought.

Mum was speaking to me.

"Good idea, love, it will help you get your affairs in order without breaching the investigation. We want to make sure nothing gets in the way of the best outcome for the children, and for you,"

Mum trailed off too. She didn't say we were hoping for a definitive jail term. That we wanted him to rot in the hell of his own making.

We did that a lot, then. Sentences finished midstream as we paused to muse and consider all alternate possible endings. It happens when life is out of control. A true choose-your-own-ending mystery adventure tale.

How was I supposed to conduct my business when my whole life was inextricably entwined with my husband? The husband who had touched my daughter. The husband I had discovered had a penchant for child pornography. The husband who had immediately sought psychiatric interventions to avert the impending consequence of criminal charges.

The husband I had trusted with my whole heart, and my children who are my life. The husband until just days before was perfect in every way. Well, in most ways. He had stopped coming to bed when I went to bed. Our intimacy had changed over the past year, from the honeymoon rush of first love and discovery in bed, to the slower, more relaxed knowing of each other.

Except I didn't know a fucking thing about him.

His whole world was a secret shielded from me.

If he wasn't working anymore, how would we pay the mortgage on the house, including the money Penny had lent us to start the renovations when the home didn't have enough equity for borrowing against? With everything in joint names, including bank accounts, it got suddenly complicated.

Sharing money through the same bank account was a big step of trust for me.

In my first marriage, after Clayton left, I put my wages into a new bank account but left the family allowance for the children going into our joint account. Because I had the children most of the time, I was sure he'd honour those funds and leave it to pay the childcare and the clothes, shoes and food that the funds bought each fortnight.

Until he didn't.

Chapter 21

It was a calm sunny morning with a clear blue sky the day I went to the ATM to withdraw money from the account and my card didn't work. There were no funds and the bank account didn't exist.

I put the card in again and tried the numbers, but the error message telling me to contact my bank flashed up again, and then a third time. It was a weekend and we struggled through without any funds.

When the bank opened, I contacted them to ask the question, only to discover all the money had been taken out by Clayton and the account had been closed, without any notification to me.

Men can do this without a signature from the woman on the account. The same way that banks address mail for joint accounts to the man on the account, they make changes to the account on the man's say so.

After I finished talking with Mum, I called the bank.

"Can I speak with the manager please?" I asked, tremulous.

"Catherine here," she was assured, a solid blonde Goddess always helpful.

"Catherine, I find myself in a delicate situation and need your absolute discretion," I began.

"Excuse me while I shut my office door," her chair wheels squeaked as she moved to create privacy in the bright lights of profitable money lending.

"We have an unforeseen family situation that has come up," I said, "I need to ensure my finances are protected and move some funds into my own account for the mortgage to be paid. We have separated. Quite suddenly. And charges have been laid." I took a sharp breath in and thought about what I had just disclosed.

"Against him," I hurried to clarify.

I continued to outline the situation.

"I can't have any contact. I am a witness for the prosecution. He has the car and will take responsibility for the loan on that. I have assurances from his Mum, but if there is anything he needs to sign,

I can give her details to you for you to make contact. I will need to sort out the house mortgage until further notice."

"Sure, Andrea, we can manage that for you," Catherine said, unruffled and clear. "I will create another account for you today, you have your wages put into that, we will then take the mortgage payments from there. Did you need respite from the payments for three months?"

Tears started to flow silently down my cheeks.

"We have that ability when there are natural disasters or….." she paused.

A sob caught in my throat.

"….when extenuating personal circumstances arise." Catherine sounded less like a banking terms and conditions pamphlet and more like an angel with every word she spoke.

"I can send him a statutory declaration form pertaining to the car loan and get his details for repayments. Did you have his mother's current postal address? We can send it registered mail to ensure we know it is delivered."

"Thank you," I said quietly, "Three months grace is amazing, just while I sort out what is happening."

"We will take care of it our end here, Andrea, and your privacy is assured. It will all be okay. Andrea, I just hope that you and the children are okay?" she finished.

I left the gentle question unanswered. We'd be okay, eventually.

"Thank you, Catherine, so deeply appreciated." I said and reached for a tissue.

We said goodbye like sisters in an unexpected storm, heading in different directions with only one umbrella. I stood alone in the pouring rain.

After so much bad luck in love, and in possession of an old fridge covered in stickers, I used to joke to my girlfriends that all I wanted was a man with white goods and a job.

The universe is a very specific place, and despite the fact I had gotten tired of waiting and bought us a new fridge, when Lucas

Chapter 21

moved in, he was fully laden with a full set of brand-new white goods and a full time job.

We sold his fridge as we didn't need two.

I forgot to stipulate pure intentions and integrity, honesty and a distinct lack of criminal tendency which could ruin life as we know it forever.

So how does one navigate through such a morass while in deep howling pain expressed alone late each night, no sleep, broken hearted and in shock to the core?

One seeks legal advice.

It was time for me to call a lawyer.

Chapter 22

I waited in the calming blue room at the community legal service for my appointment.

When I was called into the office the lawyer stood to greet me.

My mother taught me to shake hands correctly from a young age, firm from the beginning, and I have since run exercises on how to shake hands. It can tell us a lot about a person. Shaking hands originated in medieval times, when bows and arrows were tools of war. It was hard to shoot someone when you needed two hands to load your weapon, so shaking hands is an indication of peaceful intentions.

With a warm firm grip, the lawyer held my hand just a moment longer than required.

Long enough for me to notice.

He had a friendly crinkle around his sparkling brown eyes, crowned with a receding hairline.

"My name is Paolo Kay," he said. "Call me Paolo."

Settling back into the chair, I felt safe.

Chapter 22

The light from the windows behind Paolo silhouetted him as he scrawled on his yellow notepad, firing queries that seemed innocuous, but brought up more questions than answers.

"Full name?" he said, suddenly officious.

I was stumped at his first question.

Who was I?

My married self or my own person?

Was I married anymore?

I chose to give my maiden name. My father's surname which I resolved in that moment to return to.

"Date of Birth?"

This was easier.

"Twelve, twelve, sixty-nine. The end of a very good year," I quipped while Paolo twinkled.

We ran through the details, address, contact phone, circumstances.

The grubby reason I was here at a community legal service I didn't even know existed until I needed them.

"My husband has been charged with serious criminal offences against my children, and I cannot have contact with him. All our business is in both names. I need advice on how I manage from here," I explained.

"It was a sign," I told Paolo. "The fact our marriage concluded bang on June 30 when we run a small business is so tidy my accountant is in awe!"

"The universe is an interesting place," Paolo mused in agreement.

Yes, I thought, *a very interesting place.*

Paolo was older than me, and handsome. Olive clear skin and dark hair with a sure manner, and brilliant vocabulary. We slipped into an easy conversation as I laid out the facts that I knew to be true. I relaxed and made quips designed to make him smile, because it was all too serious to be taken too seriously. He hesitated a couple of times, then began to laugh more easily at my incredulous take on the tawdry particulars of my sudden separation, the investigation and pending legal charges against my former husband. As I laid out the gory details it all seemed far away, like it was happening to someone else.

When in doubt, laugh. It is a family trait imbued by our father. At moments of extreme distress Dad can break the tension with a succinct joke or turn of phrase. I am sure he was the reason Dad jokes came into popular vernacular.

My brothers and I followed suit. It is a form of light to share laughter.

I was probably not the appointment Paolo expected last thing on a Wednesday afternoon.

The irony, I thought, as I looked at my hand with my engagement and wedding ring still in place. I twisted them off and put them on my right hand, resolving to remove them and bury them in a drawer when I got home.

Paolo asked questions and took notes. Exploring my work, my hobbies and life, including the children.

"You can separate your bank accounts and make sure that he continues to contribute to the mortgage if he is able to," he said, "Keep notes on everything, dates, times, any arrangements that are made through his mother as the communication channel."

He paused.

"You are strong, you will get through this," he said.

As I stood to leave, I felt lighter. It felt good to explain it all to a stranger, and to get things in order. Sorting out the practicalities.

"You know, I am renting a house out near your place." Paolo said. "Beautiful little hamlet."

"I know. The hills and valleys are so green and lush this time of the year," I agreed, "It's a lovely part of the world……."

"When your house is not a crime scene…" I trailed off.

We shared a dark laugh in the face of the stark reality which brought me back to earth with a crash.

Chapter 22

He stood and came around the desk to shake my hand again.

"So lovely to meet you, Andrea," he said.

This time when his hand held mine, his other hand cradled our coupling gently.

We stood in the light of the window for a second longer before I moved back out into the world.

I made the drive home and collected the twins from family day care. A roast dinner was commenced, and the potatoes were baking when the phone rang.

"Andrea?" A man's voice queried, he sounded slightly unsure.

I was puzzled. I recognised the voice but couldn't place it.

"It's Paolo. From the legal service?" he was hesitant, maybe regretful.

"Ahhh yes," I said, "Did I leave something out?"

"No not at all," he said. "I was just thinking that as I live out your way, we could perhaps share a coffee sometime, or a drink? As..... neighbours? It is not totally regular, but I had your number from my notes...... and on a whim....." he concluded lamely.

"Sure," I said. It was out of my mouth before I could stop it. "Did you want to pop in on your way home?"

I figured if I liked his company he could stay for a roast. I was starved for adult company since before the marriage ended, and anyway, he had to be twenty years older than me.

"Tonight? Great. I will be half an hour," he said.

As an afterthought he said, "I have your address."

Then he hung up.

One of my foibles was that I had absolutely no idea when someone is interested in me. Perhaps it was the tomboy hobbies of my childhood, the fact puberty never visited, or my extreme secret contempt for myself which disguises any pickup line ever delivered. They washed over me like snowflakes in a desert.

Paolo arrived and I put the kettle on. We shared peppermint tea and then I offered a pre-dinner drink. The twins did their homework, and we all chatted and laughed.

At fifty-six, Paolo was twenty-two years older than me. He explained he was having sessions with an intuitional psychologist. I never asked why he was seeking such specialist treatment. Apparently, his psychologist was into numerology and he had advised Paolo that he needed a strong "four" in his life.

After I left his office that first afternoon, he had worked out my numerology using my birthdate.

Twelve, twelve, nineteen sixty-nine computes to a four.

$1+2+1+2+1+9+6+9 = 31$ then $3+1 = 4$.

"Did you want to stay for dinner?" I asked.

Suddenly there we were, deep in conversation that felt like it had no end. That night began a transformational friendship, that progressed to a healing interaction, where Paolo introduced me to ancient spiritual teachings, and wise insights, many of which were new to me.

Michael and I remained good friends. He called me when his sister died. They had grown up in a haze of agricultural chemicals that controlled the bugs in their family apple orchard. She had contracted a rare type of cancer and fought hard and long. Her friends gathered from all over the world for her farewell service.

"It was a peaceful transition," he sobbed on the phone. "She was so young. My parents are shattered."

He soothed them while holding it all together then grieved openly with me on the other end of the phone. I listened to his heart break. I whispered words of support but felt useless so far away.

"I am planning a trip to the west coast to surf and stare at the waves," Michael said. "Will you join me?"

I was torn. I was free to choose, but with the intimacy unfolding with Paolo, I was confused and had always been faithful in relationship. I told Michael about my friendship with Paolo, and how I wasn't sure where it would go.

Chapter 22

"Life is too short, Andrea," Michael was philosophical. "We can travel as friends if it makes you comfortable, and I will keep my hands to myself."

"Let me think about it," I said. "I will let you know. I am so sorry about your sister Michael, so very sorry for your loss."

His voice started to break again as we said goodbye. I called him straight back and promised I would join him on the trip. I had loved Michael forever, and we could travel as friends.

In the time that passed up until the scheduled trip with Michael, Paolo and I became lovers. It was a connection that was helping me to heal. I met Michael on the side of the highway at the service station, as he made his way through from the city to the west coast. Until the day before, my plan had been to join him, but with the changing relationship with Paolo, I couldn't reconcile it in my heart.

I sat in Michael's car and explained the situation.

"I can't come away with you on the trip and be in integrity with myself," I said. "I trust you understand." I looked over at Michael's face, reflected in the glow of the setting sun over the ocean in the distance, far across the saltbush flats. His eyes glistened as he nodded and held my hand.

"I understand completely. I wish you weren't so pure of heart, but I understand and accept your decision," Michael said, as he slowly lifted my hand to his lips and kissed me gently on each fingertip.

I brushed my hand through his hair, and cupped his cheek, where tears rolled down his face and wet my fingers.

"You know I love you Michael," I said softly as I took my hand back into my lap, then prepared to get out of the car into the fading light.

"I know, and I love you too," Michael said. "I will miss you. I was looking forward to time together."

"So was I, but I can't go with you, and live with myself, so go forth and have some quality time for you on your trip away," I said. "And take good care."

He leaned over to kiss me and I nearly faltered, but my wisdom whispered its truth.

It was time for him to go.

I stood by the road and watched as he indicated to enter the highway. I was perfectly still and present as the sun set into the sea, and the taillights of Michael's car receded into the expanse of space between the ranges and the ocean. I got in my car and headed home to pick up the twins from after school care.

Paolo shared the wisdom of his years with me and drank from the fountain of my youth. On the weekends the twins were with their Dad, he stayed over, and we made love all night.

"I have found my strong four," he whispered as he nuzzled my neck.

He took me camping and we wrote poetry under the stars. My heart opened to love again. We studied the spiritual arts and he introduced me to writers and teachers, while I presented my learnings to him. He bought me books and shared musical inspiration. Profound text messages and emails of soul communion flew across the cosmos between us.

Paolo lived with a fellow female lawyer named Ingrid in the city but continued working in the country while he rented a home in the community just down the road from me.

As he planned a trip overseas with his housemate to visit her ailing father, he assured me their relationship was platonic.

They were just good friends.

The conflict situation at work had continued to deteriorate. My boss was unassailable, and everyone was looking for other employment. Kate had found an amazing role to apply for which was coordinating employment programs through project management with the State Government.

Chapter 22

A statewide recruitment process was initiated, and Kate asked me for a reference and to help with her application. I looked at the job specification and saw that it was also a perfect role for me.

I decided then and there not to apply and put any thought of an application myself out of mind. It was Kate's job.

Despite my protests because of the situation at home, my doctor wrote me a sick certificate, saying the position at work had become so toxic that it was psychologically unsafe for me to be at work.

Our doctor made referrals to counselling and psychological assessments for the children as part of the healing from the trauma they had experienced. There were waiting lists that he managed to shortcut so that treatment could commence immediately. We were put in touch with the Victims of Crime service which had a counselling service, and also took up counselling with available and suitable opportunities over time.

All the counsellors were women and it was compelling that at every one of our appointments, the counsellor always commenced with the drama and trauma of her own life.

I wasn't sure if they were setting the scene for us, as we never really got to delve deeply into our drama or trauma, so I counselled them. I listened carefully to her worries and concerns and left long silent spaces for her to express her fears. The children did their activities and had various individual appointments as well.

There was the counsellor who had been caught in a rip at the beach on the weekend, and thought she was going to drown in front of her children, before being rescued. The Victims of Crime worker with the dysfunctional relationship with her mother. The art therapist with a nervous tic and myriad nervous reactions. Everyone, it seemed, had issues.

I sought out spiritual healing for the children and me. We travelled to a spiritual healer for regular sessions. It was Marilyn who told me that eagles were my totem, and one day I saw the unmistakable outline of Mother Mary in the room behind Rachel as she lay on the bed. She was glowing gold with wings in the dim light of the darkened room, while Marilyn's hands hovered over Rachel.

Marilyn waved her hands about extracting and shifting dark energy from her body, replacing it with golden healing light and peace.

Diana lent me *You Can Heal Your Life* by Louise Hay, which I consumed with an ever-increasing awareness of Spirit with a plan. Not a Christian God, but the energy of Love that suffuses everything. In a healing my Native American male spirit guide appeared, and Marilyn gently passed on his messages of wisdom and guidance.

My doctor referred me to Workcover, the system for people injured at work in Australia that provided back to work support, psychological assessments, and rehabilitation.

I was distraught and protested his recommendation for Workcover as my sick leave had run out.

"I can't go on Workcover!" I cried, "What will happen if my boss finds out what has happened at home?"

"Andrea, it is psychologically unsafe for you to be at work. Your boss is out of line, is not agreeing to mediation, and until it is resolved you CANNOT be at work," he said.

My boss was still interrogating all the staff, putting into place disciplinary arrangements and performance management reviews. My work colleagues and staff were in regular contact to keep me updated with developments.

I counselled them, too.

Kate wrote her job application which I edited and then provided her a glowing reference. Even if one of us got out, that was a good thing. I had been working for the disability employment organisation for nine years and had supported its expansion across regional South Australia, inducting many new staff, while managing several sites and staff.

The employment success for our clients was over ninety percent, beyond best practice for the industry.

All I wanted to do was go back to work, to normal. To support my children, my clients, and my team, and be in the purpose and service of my life.

My doctor was resolute.

Chapter 22

"Andrea, this is everything to do with your work and does not relate to your home situation. The referral to Workcover will be assessed and you will receive eighty percent of your current income while that happens," he was clear and firm as he signed the sick certificate and referral. "You need to take my advice on this please. You cannot be at work. It is not safe."

My doctor referred me for a psychological assessment as part of the Workcover process.

And that was that.

My observation was that all the systems we were immersed in including Workcover, Victims of Crime, and family court, perpetuate victimhood and keep us stuck in the story. Receipt of services was based on how sick I was, how unsafe the children and I felt, how abused, violent, undermined, bullied, and traumatised we were. There was limited focus on healing, strength, moving forward, letting go, forgiveness, and self-care. There was no celebration of survivors or encouragement to move beyond, as all of the supports relied on what was missing, instead of how we healed and moved on.

I received a brief stealthy call from a colleague at head office in the city.

"He knows," he whispered. "About everything, and he will fight this Workcover claim to the death. Of YOU!"

"What do you mean he knows?" I asked, mind racing. I had been betrayed. A colleague wanting to distract our boss from the attack on him had revealed my personal situation. Everything was getting very mixed up. It was every man and woman for themselves.

I started applying for jobs. Any job. Something to change my future and get me out of this toxic helpless situation. I won interviews and answered the questions with well-researched insights about the role and organisation.

The head of one panel was a close colleague, who rang after the interview to tell me how brilliantly I had come across, but that the final candidate of the day had experience with the same program interstate. She won the job over me.

"I'm sorry, Andrea, we will keep your resume on file for future positions, bad luck this time," he said as he hung up.

I missed out on every single job I applied for.

I was stuck. Suddenly single, in a double income household and unemployed, on Workcover at eighty percent of my wage.

Things couldn't get any worse.

As I drove to the city for my scheduled psychological assessment to determine my fitness for work, I reviewed my life.

Kate had progressed to an electronic test in the next stage of recruitment for the new statewide roles.

I was incredibly happy for her. My other colleagues in the organisation were winning new jobs. It was a sinking ship and they deserved so much better.

There was no farewell for me. I was static and hid out at home. I cared for my children and was home every day when they finished school. I cooked biscuits and cakes for their recess, and we planted a garden, reading stories snuggled together on the couch. We continued to attend counselling and accessed therapeutic supports to assist the healing process.

When the children were asleep, I cried, alone and exhausted.

The court case against Lucas was glacially slow. Perpetually adjourned to a new date a few months hence.

I arrived at the specialist clinic in the suburbs to see the shrink that Workcover had prescribed. The psychiatrist was a rotund, greying man, with a big beard, who looked over his glasses at me.

I smiled and extended my hand.

"So, Andrea, tell me your story about why you are unsafe to be at work?" After we got through the pleasantries he launched straight into his interrogation.

I rattled off the details, dates and times, complaints, conversations, and feedback received, the angst of my colleagues, the impact on me personally, the refusal of my manager to undertake independent mediation, my distress and grief after a long established and loyal productive career with the organisation.

Chapter 22

I was positive about how it could be resolved, and how I could return to work. If only we could talk it through face to face, my manager and I, and bring some understanding to each other's perspectives. Some mediation. Some honesty. The psychiatrist peered over his glasses and leaned forward in his chair.

"And when did you discover your husband was abusing your children?" he asked. Matter of fact.

"That has nothing to do with my Workcover claim, or what is happening at work. The situation at work has been ongoing for over 12 months. I have made official complaints to the board, and despite their call for mediation my manager refuses to engage," I said.

He sat there taking notes.

His questions dug deeper into our home situation and I answered honestly.

"We are undertaking separate counselling and processes for that, and it has no relevance to my work. Nothing to do with it at all," I said.

That was that. It had been four long months off work. Nothing was resolved.

Throughout, Paolo was a great support when we caught up, and then he went away on his trip to Europe with Ingrid, his housemate whose father was dying.

He wrote me long loving emails from abroad.

I was in the city for work and he was in contact immediately the plane touched down. We arranged to meet, and he gave instructions for finding his house.

"Come in the back way along the service alley," he said.

He opened the door and gave me a beautiful strand of large smooth wooden mala beads. I fell into his arms.

I was insatiable in the dark of his cosy flat at the back of the house, as we made passionate love by candlelight. I drowned in the passion of him. It was like we had known each other for lifetimes before this one.

There were times he was forlorn, and I salved his broken spirit with reassurance and compassion. It was like there was a deeper force within him. Old pain and sadness that I attempted to touch away from his beautiful soul so that he could be free. He seemed to bury a hidden sorrow that I couldn't reach no matter how loving I was.

It was a match made in heaven. For sure, I mean, there were signs!

Four weeks later the psychologist's report landed in my letterbox. He had detailed my bright and breezy approach to the situation, my recall of dates, times and details, my competent and confident attitude, and the fact that my former husband was facing charges for crimes against my children.

His finding was final.

The Workcover Claim is rejected, and payments will cease forthwith.

My heart sank into my stomach when I read the last line.

I was single, unemployed, with a double income setup, and no safety net.

I rang Centrelink to arrange an application for the single parenting payment and called my parents to tell them the news.

Things apparently, could get worse. Much worse.

Chapter 23

The phone rang.

It was Kyralee, who had moved to Western Australia some years earlier. Kyralee is always full of amazing ideas and plans borne from her love and compassion for all people everywhere. She is my kindred spirit, fellow Sagittarian and is an expert rescuer at her core. Some rescues were simple, and some unfolded as complex logistical exercises disguised as plans that take a tribe to enact, or at a minimum, me or someone like me, doing some sensitive crucial tasks for it all to work out.

There was the time she called concerning a young woman she had met who was in a family violence crisis.

"Andrea, he is threatening to kill her. YOU know what it is like to be in a custody battle...." Kyralee paused waiting just a moment for the reality of my shared experience and inherent empathy to kick in.

All those sleepless nights, and then the interminable hours spent in the car park at Port Wakefield, waiting to catch a glimpse of their father's exhaust fumes which heralded the safe delivery of our children back to me.

"ALL you have to do is drive her to the house," she went on, "Because her partner won't know your car, then you keep watch out for him while I help her pack."

"AND then she can stay with her son at your place overnight, because you live so far out of town and he will NEVER find her there, until she can catch the bus to the city tomorrow and get away from him forever," she caught her breath and delivered the final plea. "Then, they will be safe."

I reluctantly agreed.

Her friend's unit was in a block of seven with a shared cement car park in the centre. Units that I had never really noticed despite growing up in the town.

I pulled in, turned around for easy escape and parked.

Kyralee and her new friend entered the unit with an armful of large blue, white, and red striped zip up bags.

I waited near the car, tapping my feet.

A man pulled up and slipped into the car park in front of the unit. He looked at me, a bit puzzled.

I smiled congenially, like I wasn't part of the biggest shock he was going to get for a while.

Instincts kicked in and I engaged him in conversation to create a delay for Kyralee and her friend inside.

"So? How's your day?" I asked as I glanced sideways at the front door, willing the women to get the hell out of there, so we could make the getaway and be safe.

"Alright. And YOU are...?" he was momentarily distracted.

"Just a friend," I assured him with all the diplomatic muster of a B grade heroine.

I heard the shuffling about happening inside as I continued to calm him with platitudes.

After an eternity, and just as he moved to open the front screen door, Kyralee and her friend shuffled carefully past him, arms full

Chapter 23

of bags and heads turned away so as not to meet his eyes. He looked at them confused for a second.

We pushed the bags into the boot of my car, and I leaned on it, as it clicked firmly shut.

The women leapt into my car, and locked the doors, strapping in the small boy ready to be driven to safety.

"What the fuck…..?" His realisation hit home as I got into the driver's seat.

The mother of his son opened the window a crack.

"I will call you to make arrangements," she said. "For you to see Troy."

As I put the car in gear, he stood there, forlorn somehow. The little boy turned to wave out the back window at his Dad and giggled with the excitement of it all.

Kyralee and her friend hugged each other, then slumped in their seats and looked ahead. There was a collective sigh of relief despite the adrenaline rush, and we simultaneously burst into shared giggles of laughter at the great escape gone well.

It was never a dull moment with Kyralee.

I answered Kyralee's bright greeting on the phone that night with a wary hello in return. I love my friend dearly, but I have learned hesitance can be a good place to start.

"Andrea, I have an idea," Kyralee began in a rush.

I braced myself.

Sitting down was easier.

"Yessss???" I plopped into the nearest chair.

"I am thinking we have a sluts and trollops weekend at the beach. We get all the girls, bring our attitude adjustments, and share some time together and….. Paarrtttyyyyyy!!!!

Can you ask Diana if her shack is free, maybe the long weekend in October?"

There it was. My part in the plan.

"Once we set dates, I can book my flights."

"I can do that," I said, glad it wasn't more complicated. "I'll call Di and ask the question and get back to you."

"Great, then I can book flights and let the girls know. I was thinking my sister, Carol, of course, you ask Sue, Heather, Chantelle, you, me, Di, and whoever else…." she was deep in thought. I imagined her furrowed brow.

The plan was cooked.

There were a core group of women, soul sisters who were connected to each of us, and with each other. We stood by our girlfriends in the thick of it, we laughed until we cried and at times partied like there was no tomorrow.

A group of unanointed Goddesses in our lives who listen, accept, support and care whatever the drama.

We hung up. I called Diana.

"Di, it's Andrea. How are you?"

"Heyyyyy, how are you? Long time, no hear…..," Diana was warm and grounded.

"Yeah well there's been a bit going on." I launched in as we do.

Full disclosure in a synopsis of circumstance. How my marriage had evaporated in an instant with the shocking disclosure of the twins. How charges had been laid, and that we were in the midst of counselling, appointments and witness statements, while our house was a crime scene, and our lives were turned upside down and inside out.

"Upshot is Kyralee wants to have a sluts and trollops retreat at your shack at the beach. Invite all the girls, she'll fly over and we all hang out for the long weekend, and I thought that could be a good distraction plus fun hey?" I concluded my download.

"Hmmmmm, well we have had a bit going on here too, and I can't do sluts and trollops I am sorry," Diana paused.

"Is everything okay?" I asked.

Diana sighed. A long slow exhale of breath.

Chapter 23

"After what you have shared, you might understand. You see, for years I couldn't work out why I couldn't close my eyes in the shower. I started screaming. It was horrendous. And then recently I started having flashbacks to when I was young, stuff I had shoved very deep." Diana's story poured out of her.

Diana's flashbacks had led her to speak with her sister who also had vague memories of feeling ashamed, exposed and then stark memories of vile abuse started to become clear.

The sisters collected their shattered memories into glimpses of reality so dark they had buried it deep in their subconscious. Together they uncovered the fact they had both been abused by a family role model.

"As it stands there can be no charges, physical evidence had long since healed. It is too daunting a task to bring any true justice." Diana said.

"How are YOU?" I asked, horrified.

"We are working through it. It is shit really Andrea. I think we all would benefit from a healing and pampering weekend," Diana concluded. "My sister has studied kinesiology and we can bring our angel cards."

Tears rolled down my cheeks at the horror of the revelation Diana shared with me. I felt lucky. In our circumstance the children had told me, evidence was gathered, and charges were laid. The cycle of violation had been halted which may take lifetimes to heal, but at least we might see consequences for Lucas's actions and eventually closure.

I wanted to hold Diana close, and then call the police.

But in her case that wasn't my job.

The plan was struck and a group of ten women with our tents, drinks, life lessons, pain and joy got together at the beach shack. Thomas was with his Dad and Rachel spent the weekend with my folks.

Throughout the weekend we alternately laughed until we cried, cried until we laughed and drank wine by the fire under the stars, taking turns to cook up delicious and nutritious meals.

We did our angel cards.

Every time I pulled a card, I got Archangel Michael – protector of the children.

We danced around the fire pit and held each other's hands. We meditated while we walked on the beach. I took a fishing rod and stood in the sunset, waiting to feel a bite, as the orange fire sank on the horizon over the sea.

On our final day, Chantelle offered kinesiology sessions in the small lounge room of the shack. Each woman took their turn.

I sat out the back in the sun and watched my soul sisters go into the room one by one. They came out crying with joy and relief. I listened to their stories of insight and release.

Sue was best friends with Carol and adopted me as a friend when Carol left town. There was an informal handover of daily friendship that took a while to warm up. But we persisted and cemented our connection through daily support for each other, wine, cheese, and the invaluable nursing expertise Sue generously provided to me and the twins for every medical emergency. Sue saved me countless trips to the hospital and her friendship was a salve to my soul.

After her session with Chantelle, Sue burst out of the back door, which slammed shut behind her with a shudder. Sue stood in front of me with tears in her eyes.

She opened her arms wide.

"She told me to hug a tree," Sue said as she enfolded me in her arms and held me tight.

I felt roots curling from the bottom of my feet extending deep into the earth.

I was bound there, providing solid comfort, rooted to the spot.

Time stopped.

"She said hug a TREE, not ME!" I cried and held Sue firmly for a long time and then wiped away her tears.

Chapter 23

Finally, it was my turn.

I was last.

The golden light of the afternoon was sweeping up the dust motes like fairies in the air.

I laid on the floor. Diana sat at the table silently observing each session.

Chantelle didn't touch me but hovered her hands over my body. Her voice was flat and calm as she channelled the messages for me. It was like she was speaking from another place.

She explained she was providing a balancing healing for my emotional body.

Her hands hovered over my lower belly. I felt a tingling warmth although there was no physical contact.

"You have a beautiful huge white light in your soul," she intoned. "You are a lightworker. You are chosen for a divine purpose. You need to claim the fact you are a beautiful earth angel. Everything is perfect. All that has happened for you and the children is perfect. You have a cheer squad in your blue chakra saying, "Go Girl, you are doing well!" Everything is for a reason, a divine purpose. The children and you.... you will be okay. It is all in perfect plan."

Lightworker? What the fuck is a lightworker? My thought was so loud I was sure they had overheard.

She smiled.

"It is all perfect, you need to live in the white light, surround yourself and pray for the highest good, not your own. You deserve good things, beautiful things to happen. It is all perfect," she said again and with a brisk shake of her hands, it was done.

The floating feeling eased, and I came back into the room feeling lighter and oh so calm.

I was a lightworker? Here to learn, to grow, to be a resource for others and our collective highest good, to create as part of my divine purpose.

I felt an immediate irresistible urge to put my hands on Diana. It was like an ancient familiar otherworld feeling. Something experienced from lifetimes before.

"Di, I feel like I want to put my hands on you," I said.

"Well, you had best do it then," she said, and lay down on the couch where the sun's rays caught her hair.

I intuitively and gently placed my hands on her head, her tummy, and her feet. Holding there for long minutes until I felt like it was time to move on. I could feel the warm healing glow of love flowing from the ether through my head and hands into her body. I imagined old stale energy moving out and cleansing settling in its place.

When I felt the energy healing was complete, I lifted my hands.

Diana was still. She looked worried.

"I can't move!" she said. "I am stuck. I physically cannot move a muscle."

Chantelle moved to her sister and caressed her forehead, smoothing her hair gently.

"Just rest here now, sister," she said, "It is all perfect."

I stepped back and looked at my hands.

"I must need training to manage this gift," I said.

"Do your Reiki training," Chantelle suggested quietly. "It will help you channel the light energy effectively and protect you from taking on the pain of others. It is all about the healing. It is all light."

Diana started to stir on the couch, and we supported her to sit up and lean back on a cushion. She closed her eyes again. I got her a glass of water and stroked her hair.

"Powerful lightwork, Andrea, thank you," she said.

I went outside into the sunset. The girls had gathered around the firepit and were gazing into the flames, deep in individual thoughts.

Carol lifted her head and looked at me, questioning.

"How did you go?"

Chapter 23

"Apparently I am a lightworker, and Diana has just started to move after being immobilised on the couch after I shared a healing session," I explained, slightly confused.

Carol furrowed her brow as she leaned her head to the side, taking in this new development.

"I will get myself some training...," I reassured her.

"Awesome!" Carol exclaimed as she jumped up. "Can you do me next?"

Throughout my friendships with the women in my life we have shared our stories of lovers, motherhood, family, healing and lessons as only women do. We have shared our deepest secrets as we excavate our bottomless wells of experiences and perspectives. We clarify and build an understanding of what we think as we express it aloud and we support each other in our pain and renewal.

There are intense connections with people I have just met, hearts wide open and bleeding pure wisdom via shared humanity as we work to answer the big questions. Some of those people stuck around and others moved on into the flow. It was all perfect.

I sat down at the campfire and reflected on the days immediately after our own revelation at home a few months earlier. I recalled the gift from Edie, one of Lucas's band members who also worked with us at the college. Edie had visited the house to share her shock, and as she left gave me a hug and a gift.

It was a brown paper bag containing a joint and Doreen Virtue's Angel Guide.

In the book Doreen described our children as our teachers.

This profound thought struck me in the middle of the heart.

After the twins were born, I reflected on the reasons I chose to have children, seeing as my primary goals were to get a degree and go to Europe. I didn't envisage myself as the mothering type. Is there a type? Married at 19, I gave birth to our twins when I was just 23. Beautiful children who have taught me so much about myself and others, and the whole spectrum of sacred life this time around. I couldn't imagine my life without them.

All the lessons made sudden sense in that cocoon of clarity with my sisters at the beach shack. We are here to learn love, hope, trust, and forgiveness, and most importantly love, trust, and forgiveness of ourselves. This is our life work.

Before I poured my wine, I pulled an angel card.

There he was again.

Archangel Michael. The protector of the children. I looked up and a sea eagle flew overhead.

Symbolic reminders, that I am supported by the gifts of courage, which help to release the effects of fear, and stay true to myself in trying times. To use my voice and powers for good.

The girls were gathering around the fire, with chairs and stories of our revelatory day.

The wine glistened golden as the sunset caught the surface and I sipped in a silent celebration.

I toasted the trauma and tragedy and warmly welcomed the triumph that must surely follow.

A few weeks later I travelled back to the peninsula to study my Reiki Level One with Marilyn.

We shared a magical weekend. I learnt the history and techniques of the incredible hands on healing modality. Rediscovering that "old feeling" that moved through me when putting my hands on Diana in our spontaneous healing session at the shack. I learned to channel healing energy while I consciously protected my own. Our responsibility is to heal ourselves.

As I drove home in the twilight evening of Sunday, the car flew through the golden light, my favourite time of the day.

I thought about the weekend, when the voice in my heart was suddenly clear and strident.

Wisdom was whispering.

"Paolo is not telling you the whole truth. He has something he needs to share." It was a knowing, an almost silent sense which was the distinctive voice of clarity.

Chapter 23

I picked up speed and headed straight for Paolo's place. He was just alighting from his car in the driveway after a weekend in the city.

"You have something...." I began.

He cut me off but wasn't meeting my eyes.

'I have something I need to tell you," he hesitated.

Heavily laden with bags and boxes from his trip he led me inside. I sat down at the kitchen table as he continued to avoid my eyes.

"You start," I instructed.

"I went to my intuitional psychologist again on the weekend," he explained.

My arms crossed instinctively over my chest to protect my heart as I waited. I watched him fumble for words.

"He told me I must tell you the truth, that you are Earth Mother and you deserve the truth."

"I don't know about Earth Mother, but I do deserve the truth," I assured him.

"I am not sure how to say this to you," he faltered.

I gazed at him.

Nothing surprised me anymore.

"Ingrid my housemate and I are in a relationship. Have been for twenty years," he said. "I have betrayed you."

There are things which prepare us for betrayal. The verbal and emotional abuse of my first marriage, with a punch to the face thrown in. That feeling of never being safe or secure. Always having to be in charge, to take control, to be the grown up and make life happen.

Those initial experiences of deep pain inflicted on me through deceit, affairs, abuse, and lies, pale in comparison with the distressed betrayal I carried after my children disclosed the abuse in my second marriage. Put at risk by my choice of husband, blinded by love, and betrayed by his broken moral compass which showed up as criminal behaviour in the sanctuary of our home.

Home where my children should be safe. In the firing line of my lack of self-worth, through which I have measured myself. An illusory prism of acceptance by another in relationship, no matter how dysfunctional.

Paolo was just another chapter in a dramatic life story of disappointments.

"Paolo...."

I was soothing despite myself. I knew the quiet insight from my heart in the car on the way home had prepared me for this conversation.

In that moment I understood how grown men can still be boys. I pondered how I continued to attract them, no matter which decade they were born in.

I stood up to leave. Paolo rose from his chair too.

He held my upper arms, attempting to pull me into his chest, to hold me in his embrace.

I pulled away.

"I have to go home and feed the cat," I said.

The inanity of purposeful cat feeding made me giggle on the inside.

I turned and walked out into the dark.

Alone.

The night sky twinkled its perfection as I drove to our sanctuary of home where the ever-faithful cat waited purring.

It was only as the food hit its plate that my tears began to fall.

Chapter 24

Lucas pleaded not guilty on all charges pending a psychiatric assessment. This ploy by his lawyer delayed the inevitable jail term, and Lucas avoided being taken into immediate custody.

Detective Anne rang to tell me the news.

"I am disappointed. I wanted to send a message to all my colleagues to tell them he had pleaded guilty on all counts!" Anne seemed to forget the incredible emotional toll on us, and reported the facts from her own perspective, like I was part of her prosecution team.

"This way," she explained, "They buy some time, but the few extra months he has out of jail will equate to a few extra years inside. Just because he has put us through this."

All that Lucas has put us through. I felt my solar plexus seize up with the thought.

The job hunting continued. I applied for anything and everything.

I got a job interview doing energy audits, and news from the Developing Potential Company that I was in the top 50 of 300 applicants. They planned to interview 25 people at a time.

I told the guy good luck with his process. He asked my strengths as a trainer.

"Instant rapport building, developing and working with the strengths of the group, having a laugh and learning at the speed of light," I replied.

I understood the need to let go and trust. I desperately needed a job. Mum and Dad provided me with a fortnightly allowance on top of the single parenting payment which helped me to cover the house payment, so I could keep our roof over our heads.

My inner whisper was calm.

Let go. Let the legal system deal with Lucas.

The charges were listed on the internet if you knew where to look. No names were used because of the age of the children. The children's father looked up the information. I knew he had, because he had attached it to his latest series of affidavits tabled in family court, as he continued to fight for custody of just Thomas. He had given up on fighting for Rachel since she stopped going on access visits.

I saw a stark image of the inevitability of the water draining out once the plug is removed.

Letting go.

Kate didn't progress in the candidate selection process for the statewide project manager role I had supported her with. At the electronic test stage she wasn't informed by the facilitator that each section was time limited. The assessment timed out partway through and made her ineligible, knocking her out of the process.

I advised her to give feedback and request a second chance at the test. She declined and then won a management position at a leading community service organisation. Getting out of the trauma of our work situation was imperative, and I was happy for her. She deserved a new adventure in her career, with so much to offer the world, and true dedication to the vulnerable people she served through her work she would be amazing in her new job.

Chapter 24

Another court date for Lucas loomed, but the psychiatric assessment was not ready. An adjournment looked likely.

My days were spent looking at job advertisements, sharing time with the kids and cooking treats for them to eat when they came home from school. I focused on my self-healing practice and tended the garden. I gave myself Reiki most days and sometimes offered healings for others.

Some days I wept. For the pain and incongruity of it all. Single parent, unemployed, custody battles, criminal for husband, lack of finances, low self-worth, grief, loss, and pain were key ingredients in my life. Michael kept in touch, his soothing voice echoing across the distance between us. Our friendship was firm and sure. His dysfunctional marriage continued, and his children were growing older, appreciating having him cook their meals after he got home from long days in the office.

Sue, apart from being an award-winning nurse practitioner and midwife, was a football trainer. She invited me out to training night to help supercharge the team. Sue massaged and I gave Reiki, soothing tired torn muscles to send the players back onto the field with renewed vigour. At the end of the season they won their first A grade premiership in decades.

It was lovely to be home when the children got home, a luxury I hadn't experienced unless I was off work sick. The days were calm and relaxed. Despite the tight financial situation, and both former husbands in court.

I did have an early calling as a lawyer. It's a good lesson in being careful what we set our intentions for!

I played sport, tended our herbs and picked produce from the abundant earth. The year marched on. I practiced gratitude. I made lists of elements in my life I was thankful for. I journaled my intentions. I meditated. I let go. The days stretched into weeks which morphed into months.

One Saturday I woke very early and picked up the newspaper from the dewy lawn out the front. As I read the career section an advertisement caught my eye. Statewide Project Manager for

Yorke and Mid North regions. The role that Kate had entered the selection process for was being readvertised as a single regional position.

The selection criteria suited me perfectly, as it had in my first reading six months earlier. I sat down to write my application aligned to the job and person specification. I took my time. Time was the precious commodity I was gifted with right then.

A few weeks later I received a phone call inviting me to an interview being held in a small town about ninety minutes away. I researched, read, and prepared my answers to set questions. I arrived early, used the bathroom to freshen up and took my seat in the waiting room.

A grey-haired man came to call me into the interview room.

"Andrea Broadfoot?"

"Yes sir, that's me," I stood to shake his hand. Firm and sure like Mum taught me.

As I entered the room I took in the panel, three men and one woman. One was the CEO of the development board; one was the project coordinator located regionally and the other man and woman represented the department.

I introduced myself.

"My name is Andrea Broadfoot, and THIS is MY job. I am not leaving this room until it IS my job!"

The panel members looked at me wide eyed, looked at each other, and then laughed.

The interview proceeded. I gave them my presentation on the region, its unemployed population, skills gaps, employment demands and strategies for connecting people to work. I answered all their questions from my heart. I knew exactly how it feels to be unemployed.

Supporting people to reach their potential is my job, so that I might reach mine.

I made them laugh and felt good about the experience. As I drove home, I knew I couldn't have done anything more.

Chapter 24

My inner voice counselled me. If I keep my promise to myself to never marry anyone's potential ever again, maybe I will get another chance at learning to love myself.

The next week a phone call from the leader of the interview panel offered me the position. I could start in the new financial year, only two weeks away.

One full year since our revelation at home that changed everything forever.

There was a new car with the role, and it paid thirty thousand dollars a year more than my previous job.

The universe was smiling on me. The universe is an interesting place if we trust it and take the actions required to collaborate and heal ourselves.

I made a gratitude list of services with all my unpaid bills on it. Within weeks I was able to fix them all up and started paying Mum and Dad back, as well as Penny, who generously loaned Lucas and I funds for the house renovation. Repayments that had stalled in the meantime. We were on our way back into the black, and we still had our home.

I felt very blessed as I journeyed out into the light of the other side, forged by fire.

I did an online search in the family court website and downloaded a divorce application form, so I could officially unplug from Lucas.

It was time for a new beginning.

A seminar was advertised with Dr Freda Briggs, who was a somewhat controversial Australian academic, author, and child protection advocate. Dr Briggs started her career with the London Metropolitan Police and then did further study to become a teacher where she realised an innate ability to identify an abused child at three hundred paces. She discovered that children who are being abused often don't draw themselves with arms, and if they are keeping a secret, they may draw themselves without a mouth.

Mum and I booked in to attend.

Dr Freda Briggs' research work has been overtaken with more updated findings, but the information she shared at the time was peer reviewed and accepted. She found that the vast majority of mothers whose children disclose abuse happening in the home or by people they know, do not leave the situation. Forty four percent of children with learning disabilities experience abuse and they are seven hundred percent more likely to experience abuse than other children.

Children under the age of eight don't conceptualise strangers. As soon as you say hello to a child, you are their friend. Stranger danger does not work. I continued my research on the topic after the session.

There was a one hundred percent correlation between exposure to pornography and abuse. The ways pornography shrinks the brain, neural pathways can be altered and that translates to challenges in forming relationships. This is how intergenerational abuse can perpetuate itself. Some victims can become offenders because that is the expression of love and acceptance they know, or they are so hurt that they continue the cycle.

Eighty percent of children think secrets must be kept.

Ensuring children are aware of their rights and body autonomy is important. Teaching children to set boundaries and then maintain them with our support and respect is vital.

There were only a couple of good children's books on the market at that stage, including one on secret touching, which advocated that children are educated to report ANY touching that they are told to keep a secret. Grandpa washing you in the bath is not secret touching, unless the child is told to keep the touch secret, then it is a good idea to tell someone the child trusts straight away.

All the things I wished I had known.

The other thing our experience brought up was the number of my best friends, acquaintances, and family members who have survived abuse in their lives. Their disclosures staggered and distressed me.

Chapter 24

Countless secrets carried for so long. Corrosive betrayals that seared souls and robbed lifetimes of focused work to heal. It impacts us all, across our lineages.

My brother Sean called me to see how I was going, and confessed to being traumatised himself, by our experience.

"I will never look at nappy ads on the television the same way again. Some perve is getting off on that shit!" he said with dismay.

"I know," I responded. "It changes everything. A friend had a wise saying once: 'Paranoia is not a sickness. It is a state of total awareness!' I look sideways at everyone's interaction with children now, I cannot help myself."

"I love you, Andrea, and wish I could take this all away, so you and the twins didn't have to go through it," Sean said.

"That's okay," I said, my mind flashing back to the Bible verse that I relied on when doing my final year of school. We are never tested beyond our ability to remain firm, so providing our way out.

Wise words. My colleague James had shared that insight at the beach, the day way back when I confided in him that my marriage to the Clayton was suddenly and irrevocably over.

The way out is through. All the way to the other side. Forged by fire. Healed by love. Renewed by forgiveness. Of others, but mostly, of ourselves.

A few months later my new manager visited me for my probation review in my project manager role. We sat at a café sipping tea, discussing the projects I was working on with the community and local employers, when my phone rang.

Some weeks earlier I had attended court to read my victim impact statement for the judge to consider in the case against Lucas. Lucas had changed his plea to guilty on all counts and the prosecution had dropped the child pornography possession charges. Mum and I saw Lucas's mother Wendy and sister Kerryn in the hall outside the court. We caught each other's eyes which were red and flooded with silent tears. We could not embrace. The feelings were too raw and real, and we were at the pointy end of an exceptionally long and painful process.

The sentencing hearing was being held that day. Lucas, their son and brother, my former husband, was to learn his fate.

It was Detective Anne on the phone.

"Excuse me, I must take this call," I said to my manager, and stepped outside into the sunshine on the footpath.

"Hi Anne," I said as I pressed the button to take the call.

"Andrea? He got fourteen years head sentence, reduced to ten years and eight months for the early guilty plea that avoided you and the children having to testify in court," Anne said. "He was taken away in handcuffs into custody, to commence his sentence immediately." My heart sank.

"It doesn't feel like a win," I said.

How does one win these things? The criminal acts of an individual we trusted, who in return delivered trauma and pain. No sentence in jail will ever fix that. What process is in place to rehabilitate people who make abhorrent choices? That they are safe to come and live next door to unsuspecting neighbours some decade in the future? It was a well-known fact that rock spiders are a target in jail.

"I understand, Andrea, but it is a good result. It is a very strong message to perpetrators in our community that if they do the crime, they will do the time," Anne said. "You and the children have done an amazing job throughout the process. You have put this in the right place. Thank you for being so strong."

"Thanks Anne, for all you and the team have done to get us to here, I have really appreciated your support for me and the kids," I said. "I will see you on the hockey pitch flashing your badge!"

We laughed with mirth but devoid of joy.

I finished the call and looked up to the sky. The sun was still shining, and a gentle breeze blew through the trees. Wisdom whispered; *May your healing continue.*

This part of our story was over.

The twins and I needed a new place to live. Our house was a crime scene. There was no blue and white police tape scaring the

Chapter 24

neighbourhood because the crime was more silent and brutal than that. Questions raged through me. *Why us? Did I invite him in through my lack of worthiness and desire to be in relationship? What is the lesson?*

Thomas and Rachel had talked to their friends at school about what was happening at home, before they told me. Not one of those children disclosed anything to their parents. The Advertiser ran a front-page story on Lucas's sentencing and listed his crimes. They mentioned no names but did state the subjects were twins, a boy and a girl and their age.

We lived in a small town in a small state.

My best friend Carol called me, horrified.

"Andrea, I read the paper, I had no idea it was that bad," she said.

I was silent. We needed a fresh start.

My throat was taut just thinking about it. *Who can ever tell how it goes from here?* Mum was sure I was heading for an emotional breakdown. I didn't think so. I was calm. There was nothing worse that could happen. I was clawing my way, without fingernails, up the side of the abyss. The dark pit of lies that held my children and I captive for a year finally had some light streaming into it.

Our next move is to the beach, I thought. *It'd be great if the Eyre region job came up.*

Our annual family summer holiday tradition was shared in Tumby Bay, an idyllic beachside sanctuary teeming with succulent fish, and it rested on the remote, pristine Eyre Peninsula. Our familiar and nourishing town on the west coast of South Australia would be an ideal location to heal. It was where Michael had invited me to travel with him.

The next day at work I got an email. My colleague in the Eyre region had resigned. His role was on offer.

I looked up to the sky.

"That was quick!" I said and then hesitated.

How could I have manifested what I wanted, what we needed, with only one thought?

I didn't put my hand up for the role.

The department appointed someone. Two months passed. That person didn't work out within the probationary period, and then they interviewed again. Their preferred candidate withdrew from the process. Six months passed.

I made a friend online through a dating site. Derek lived in Eyre region over four hundred kilometres away. Our communication was regular and we went on a few dates. It was January 2005 and he was visiting my place.

I was at work ninety kilometres from home when he called.

"There is an out of control bushfire on the Eyre Peninsula, heading right for my block," he said.

"I will call my boss and let her know there is an emergency, and we can drive straight over there," I said.

I cancelled all meetings and jumped into the car for a frantic drive home. Thomas was at his father's place for half of the school holidays and I collected Rachel from her friend's place on the way.

Derek, Rachel, and I got into his car to drive over to Eyre Peninsula. The day was a searing forty-five degrees Celsius. As we got close the sky was blazing orange, smoke blocking out the sun. It was a firestorm.

Phones were not working, and we halted where emergency services had closed the road forty-five kilometres out. The radio blared incessant warnings. It was too late to leave, people in the path of the fire needed to bunker down, protect themselves from radiant heat and hope for the best.

Cars and trucks pulled over to the side of the highway. Country Fire Service volunteers and State Emergency Services flooded the roads, stopping drivers getting too close. The fire had started some forty kilometres away, fanned by strong winds and after coming through the forest, it had the momentum to burn all the way to the beach.

Some deaths had already been reported, and people in the small town between us and our destination fled to the jetty. They were standing in the ocean as embers rained around them. Mum and Dad were on holidays on the west coast and had travelled into Port

Chapter 24

Lincoln, using the main road which was now blocked. They were sitting at a foreshore café watching with horror as the hills burned all the way down to the beach.

It was unbearably hot. The sky was angry, filled with red and swirling black smoke.

We sat waiting for the road to open, and when it finally did, fire was still burning the trees on the sides of the road. The small town we drove through was decimated, like a bomb had gone off.

The radio reported that a woman had died there sheltering in her bathtub filled with water, discovered by her frantic husband after the fire front had gone through.

Derek's phone rang. It was his housemate Col, who had gone up to the block as soon as the roads were open. Derek listened intently.

"Thanks, Col, thanks mate, be safe and don't put yourself at risk. We will be there as quickly as we can get through," Derek said, and he finished the call.

He turned to me.

"It's all gone. Everything is destroyed. My sheds, motorbikes, pumps, tanks and all my furniture in storage, all my woodwork, everything is gone," he said.

"Are you insured?" I asked gently.

"No," he said. His eyes filled with tears.

I held his hand as we drove through the smoke and burning roadsides.

Rachel sat silently in the back seat.

Derek was lucky.

His neighbours lost their precious children and mother who was babysitting them when the fire came through. She attempted to flee with them in the car, only to be overtaken by flames. Her husband had raced out to find them in the burnt-out car, already gone, and got burnt himself, shielding himself under the vehicle. That was where his daughter and mother of the children found him after she convinced a guy in a ute at the roadblock to take her into the fire zone. They put on gloves to protect their hands, and cut fences as they drove across paddocks, working their way to the property. Derek's neighbour was tragically too late for her mother and children, but they managed to save her father who was huddled under the car on the side of the burning driveway.

It was a tragedy. Twelve people died that day. Mothers and children, grandmothers, fathers, brothers, sisters, husbands, and wives. Black Tuesday is forever commemorated in the community and those lost are honoured.

The smell of smoke puts the whole region on edge. Derek survived because he was at my place. He'd have certainly headed for the block and into the face of the firestorm, raining embers kilometres ahead of the front.

After the bushfire, the Eyre region job was still available. I transferred into the role to work on projects that supported rebuilding and recovery of the affected communities, ensuring people had training and jobs.

After the fatal fires, new growth sprang up in the weirdest places. Native lilies never seen sprouted, and yakkas grew green shoots in the days immediately following the disaster. Eucalyptus trees burst into fresh growth of green at their base. Some species of trees only send out seeds after a fire, it is the catalyst for renewal of their species. The way out is through.

From our experience I received a new insight and understanding of the process. Once stripped back and burned to the core, there is a clean space to start again, for the only option is acceptance, healing, and growth.

That's how we came to live near the beach.

The children started at a new school and made new friends. They chose to go to different high schools and flourished in their own individual ways through their education, community, and sport.

Some of our shadows followed us, as there were still lessons to learn, and mistakes to be made.

How else do we learn? Apparently, my path was the hard way.

Chapter 25

I awakened, inhaling sharply.

My dream was real. I was pulling Amy through menacing grey clouds of writhing vapour. Dressed in pure blue, I dragged her by the hand along golden red passages of time. There were sharp claws grasping at us from dark fiery voids. Into the light.

The sunlight was bursting through the curtains in my room as my eyes opened wide.

I became aware of my breathing, desperate panting, fast and shallow. I hadn't heard from Amy in years. Our beautiful golden girl who turned heads of both men and women with her alluring aura.

The dream startled me awake. It was so vivid. Amy was calling my name desperate to reach me. She was on a path in the forest, dark, damp, and totally lost. I held a candle in front of me. I could hear her voice but was not able to get to her. She was just around the next bend, but then she wasn't. Maybe the next?

Amy's calls were loud and clear, but I couldn't find her in the dark.

I woke up in a cold sweat.

A dream so real commanded action. The morning light was coming through the window in bright shafts as I reached for my mobile phone to see if I still had her number. I called and it was disconnected.

I got up and shuffled into the kitchen. I flicked on the kettle to make a cup of tea, while I dialled her Mum's number in the city.

Anna answered on the fifth ring. She was hesitant.

"Hello?" she said quietly.

"Anna? It is Andrea. Amy's friend," I said.

She recognised my voice and relaxed.

"I haven't heard from you in so long," Anna whispered in a rush.

"I had a dream about Amy. Is she okay?" I asked with urgency. The dream was so real.

"A dream? Really? Can I call you back? I am not sure about this line. What is your number?" Anna wrote it down and hung up.

I waited.

When the phone rang it was not Anna on the line but Amy.

"Darling, you found me!" she exclaimed.

"Amy? Are you okay?"

"I asked for an angel, and here you are!" she was bursting with joy.

"What is happening?" I asked.

She seemed furtive and hesitated.

"I am in trouble. The other night people I thought were my friends gave me some drugs. They drugged me!" she said, urgent and afraid.

My heart asked the question. *What scene are you into?*

My voice was silent. I listened to her talk.

"They drugged me. I passed out. I was sleeping so deeply," Amy was in the reverie of recall.

"Where are you living?" I asked.

Chapter 25

"I have a big house at the bay. In the early hours, some friends came and woke me. I was groggy. They took me to a bar. We had a couple of drinks. I was tired and wanted to go home," she said reviewing the experience.

"When we got home, my place was exploding, fully ablaze. Fire engines were screaming. I was hysterical. My dog.... Buddy.... was in there. The police held me back. Then they grabbed me to take a statement. Buddy came running out of the embers that used to be my home. After that I called Mum. I am at her place, and we are alive," she paused.

"Andrea, they wanted me to be in there. I should be dead," Amy was serious.

The words struck home like stone.

I recalled years earlier I had stayed with her while attending a film and television script writing course in the city. Her friends had pin-prick pupils and intense conversations. They didn't eat. They didn't sleep. Her boyfriend showed me how he had hidden a handgun to get into a nightclub.

That was long ago and after that first rush of friendship and different choices we had drifted apart, me to the coast with my kids. Where we were safe and made new friends in a wholesome welcoming community. We reinvented ourselves in our move, the children were doing well, and I felt safer to be me.

My children kept me focused on the healing required to love. Old souls in young bodies taught me to trust life as we healed together from our various experiences of trauma. Perhaps one day, to love again.

Amy's story continued on the other end of the phone.

"Andrea, I need a safe place to be. No-one knows you. Can I come to your place?" she asked.

I thought of the dream. What could I say? It was a sign.

We created a plan. Her mother would bring her out of the city. We'd meet in the town halfway. They knew to make sure they weren't followed.

Amy's life, and now ours, depended on it.

Suddenly, my life was embroiled in a drama not of my making. But the dream was a calling. A sign. I believed in angels that walk among us and dreams that come true. All lessons of love actioned through choices.

As I drove to the meeting place, I recalled how I first met Amy at Kyralee's place. When Richard wanted us to go to Kmart so he could stay home with the hot vacuum cleaner salesgirl. How Amy had been there for me in the breakup of my first marriage with the father of my children.

So much more had been broken since then. Surely and slowly I was weaving the pieces back together. Back into a healthy, happy life.

I parked in KFC. A white Ford pulled up alongside my car. Amy leapt out and I got out to hug her. Buddy jumped out and leaped up at me, barking madly. As we transferred the luggage I reassured Anna we'd be careful. Amy was safe with me.

We were cared for by angels.

The effusive energy that emanated from Amy filled the car on the way home. Her soap opera was spectacle in real life, full colour, full on.

"Mum snuck me out of the city in the boot of her car. We took all sorts of back ways to make sure we weren't followed," she said.

I looked sideways at my friend while she took in the scenery flashing past. She was so enamoured with this drama she soaked in. Amy caught my eye and we giggled.

Thelma and Louise on another amazing adventure.

I stopped at a toilet on the way. She went to the boot of the car to get her handbag from her backpack. I caught a glimpse of a huge pile of cash. Back in the car she pulled a glass pipe from her handbag.

She lit the powder in the bowl. The water bubbled as she drew deep on the fumes. Buddy looked on with sad eyes. I looked straight ahead and opened my window to breathe fresh air.

Chapter 25

"Want some?" she asked.

"No way, sister, not my thing," I said. "Not judging your choices but seriously, blow that shit out of your window. I want no part of it." I started having second thoughts, but her charm was irresistible. She made smoking methamphetamine in the car on the highway seem normal. Amy explained her whole story.

Amy had made a connection with a shady overseas businessperson in Asia, where she was the exclusive contact that they trusted. She had been working with them to import the key pharmaceutical ingredient in the manufacture of crystal methamphetamine.

"It's been going really well," she gushed. "But I hadn't realised the bikers in the tattoo shop across from my house had watched trade grow. They wanted a piece of the action, and my contact, but I refused."

She was proud of her staunch approach to the renegade takeover bid.

"I had a feeling, something wasn't right," she went on in full disclosure mode. By this time, it was impossible to stop the story flowing from her lips, crisp, clear and bubbling, like the water in her meth pipe.

"I built up $250,000 cash and stashed it at my grandmother's house. But in the past week I felt edgy so I went over to see Grandma, and while she put the kettle on for a cup of tea I grabbed the cash, put it in my backpack and brought it back to the safe at my place."

I kept my eyes on the road, so she couldn't see how wide they were getting. *What the fuck was I doing with a meth head in my car, a woman who had put her Grandma at risk, taking her back to my place?*

"I've got a sports car and my place was full of art, antiques, jewellery and all the brand names of luxury a girl could fill up on," Amy was pensive. "My house was so full of furniture; I couldn't move freely in the space. Big time hoarder, I could buy anything I wanted. And yet, I still feel empty."

When the house burned to the ground Amy lost everything. Illegally gained, it could not be insured.

"In a strange way, I feel free," she reflected and put her hand on my leg.

"And you have saved me. They will never find me with you, good clean-living girl you are!" she laughed.

Yep me, with the government job, two kids I strive to protect in an ongoing custody battle, healing from the second disastrous marriage, supporting the twins in regular counselling, making our way in our fresh start, with a new city to live in.

Listening to Amy, I felt lucky.

The whole conversation was surreal. It was a clear sunny day. We drove alongside open fields and through bushland. The cleansing sea sparkled on the horizon, stretching forever. I was awestruck by this clever, beautiful woman sucking a glass pipe next to me, high on her sordid tale full of intrigue and survival.

To me, life is a series of choices. There are forks in the road. So many options we can take. There are priorities and distractions. Side roads, dark alleys and dead ends. A map of life. We choose where we put our feet. Our choices are our own responsibility.

"Remember when we first met?" I asked her. "You pissed me off so much that night. I just wanted to go shopping with Kyralee and this blonde bombshell waltzes in, and we weren't going ANYWHERE!"

"I pissed YOU off?" she chortled and snorted. "You blocked all my best closes."

We laughed and the landscape rushed by in a blaze of fresh colour and life.

When we got home the twins rushed out the front to greet us. As Amy opened the door, Buddy flew out to jump into their arms.

Thomas patted his head and Amy grabbed him in a big bear hug.

"How's my gorgeous twinnies? Long time, no see," she clutched at Rachel who stood back, guarded with her affection and cautious with any interruption to routine. As we walked in the door, Amy held out her hand behind her and Rachel grabbed it, following her inside.

Chapter 25

Life with Amy was full throttle, and sometimes half cooked, as she grappled with the close escape from certain death the bad guys had evidently planned for her.

Amy's room was a detached hut outside of our home. I was insistent that she kept any drugs from the children, her eyes behind dark glasses. I never saw her take them again after that day in the car, but I knew their insidious hold was ongoing.

She bought our dog a new bed. She purchased a sander to renovate the coffee table. She planted new flowers in the garden. Dinner was cooked when I got home from work.

It was like having a wife.

We joked about it. My loving faithful wife Amy.

Suddenly I was visible to men too. Periphery friends immediately planned a visit after they knew Amy was sharing my home. There were cookoffs and game nights, laughter and light filled conversations. Part of my process was the exploration of my spiritual healing. I shared insights and Reiki with Amy, which she loved, pampering me in return.

Amy's ideas flashed up and disappeared just as quickly. I noticed that the sander was left out in the rain to ruin and the paint brushes were never washed out after a project.

Everything was half finished in the rush for instant pleasure.

Despite my efforts, the children were wise. At fourteen they knew that all was not as it seemed, and they started to express their disapproval.

"We want our house back, and just you with us, Mum," they said as I drove them to school.

"I know cherubs, but Mum is helping Amy out, just for a while," I said. It couldn't last forever.

I realised Amy's happiness veneer was a thin brittle disguise for deep despair, buried in an unspoken sense of foreboding. She needed healing. We were halfway to nowhere.

It was a sunny afternoon when Amy answered the home phone. She listened, eyes widening, and handed the phone to me in silence.

"Andrea?" An unfamiliar man's voice called me by name.

"Yes, this is Andrea," I confirmed, professional and clear.

"Detective Brown here. We want to speak to Amy in relation to a range of matters. We believe her life to be in danger. Can you both meet us at the Seafront Hotel, room eleven to discuss the situation? In an hour?" It wasn't a question, more a command.

"How can I be sure you are who you say you are?" I countered. My mind raced. He gave me the number of the drug squad headquarters and his badge details. He instructed me to call to confirm his authenticity. Then meet at the hotel room as requested. He gave a mobile number for me to contact if anything changed.

Amy was frozen in her seat, hair lank and greasy, she had been living on coffee and cigarettes. I called the drug squad head office and confirmed the detective's identity. As I put down the phone I turned to Amy, grabbing her by the shoulders I looked her straight in the eyes.

"Have a shower Amy," I said, "Let's go see what they want."

Amy took her time and put on layers of makeup. She dried her hair and dressed in her usual short tight skirt and cleavage revealing top, ready for anything.

With Amy, every experience was a party that just didn't know it yet.

While I waited, I sipped chamomile tea in an attempt to settle my exploding brain.

How had they known where she was? How long had we been watched? Who else knew where she was? Were my family in danger?

Amy came out of the back room.

"Let's go face the music," she said and led the way to the car.

It was a silent drive to the main street where we met the two detectives in dingy room eleven at the old Seafront Hotel. They showed their credentials and introduced themselves by their first names.

Mark and Luke.

Chapter 25

Like a Bible story, I thought.

Casually dressed in jeans, there were guns barely hidden in holsters under their sports jackets. There was a tiny round table in their motel room with two chairs.

"Have a seat, ladies," Mark said.

Amy sat down at the table and I perched on the edge of the bed, my eye on the door.

"We have had you under surveillance for a while," Luke said. "We have been tapping your phones...."

Fuck, I thought, *this shit is real!*

Strangely, it was comforting.

Mark was still talking and cocked his head my way.

"....and we have been tracking your trips to and from school with the kids. Watching Amy work in the garden. Nice flowers, love, garden is coming along well," he said with a grin.

"Did you want a cigarette?" He stripped the plastic off the brand Amy smoked, and opened the packet taking out the silver paper with a flourish, to release a choice of two.

I noticed Amy's hand was shaking as she reached out for the cigarette and stepped towards the balcony so she could blow smoke out of the open door. She looked out furtively, careful to keep herself hidden inside.

I felt like I was having an out of body experience. They knew everything and had been watching us for a few months, maybe since Amy arrived.

"You have two choices, Amy," Mark said. His voice was gentle. It was like he was talking about the weather, and the forecast for a light sprinkle of rain risked Amy getting her hair ruined, after all her efforts with the straightener.

"You can be charged for importing illegal substances to manufacture Class A drugs of dependence, which when proven, results in a lengthy prison sentence," Mark said.

Amy blinked at him. Her baby blue wide-eyed innocence disbelieving that this was abruptly her only lot in life.

"OR," His inflection was strong, "You testify against the suppliers AND the outlawed biker gang and we arrange witness protection for you, so you stay alive and make it to court."

Amy blanched. Her face paled.

"You don't have the evidence," she began, sounding unsure. Her addiction taunted her with illusions of invincibility. Amy thought she was in control.

To me it was obvious.

Amy's world was split in two.

Defined by a clean, white line of crack on the table.

I spoke gently to her.

"There are forks in the road, lines in the sand, times to choose. You can change everything. Be safe and protected, or be forever looking over your shoulder," I said.

Amy was silent.

I was not.

To me the choice was crystal clear.

"Amy, I don't want to see you get a bullet in your beautiful blond head, and we cannot be at risk while you play dumb," I said. It sounded harsh, but it was the truth. Every detective movie was playing in my mind. The women are always sacrificed.

"Listen to your friend, Amy, she has your best interests at heart. You can trust her completely," Mark spoke quietly.

Amy splintered in front of us.

Broken wide open, streaming the innocent tears of a scolded child.

Mark handed her a tissue and Luke rubbed her shoulder. He was also taking the opportunity to look straight down her top. He caught my eye and averted his gaze, snapping into professional cop mode.

Chapter 25

"Go home tonight, have dinner and pack your things, and we will fly with you back to the city for official processing tomorrow," Luke said.

Good cop, good cop. *Great game well played,* I thought.

I shook their hands as we left, and held Amy close, as we walked back to the car. I wondered who else might be watching us.

At home, Amy thrashed out her options.

I knew which path led to safe haven and was straight up and firm.

I also knew we were being watched. I wanted her out of the house, and for us to be completely safe in our own fresh start. We did not need any more drama this lifetime.

Amy clung to my clarity. She was drowning in lost direction, from twisted turns for all the wasted years before. She cried deep, traumatised sobs while I held her close.

"You are making the right choice, Amy, witness protection lets you live," I soothed her.

"They will kill me as soon as look at me," she moaned.

"The cops have systems in place, it is your safest option. Imagine if they charge you and then the bikers are wondering what you will say, to who and when. It puts you and your family at so much more risk. Better to disappear," I said. I had wished as much for myself many times in my life.

Amy slept in my bed that night. We tossed and turned waking early. As the children got ready for school, I called them aside.

"Amy is heading back to the city today," I said, "So, if you want to, give her a hug goodbye."

"That's good," said Rachel keen to get her mother's full attention back in focus. It occurred to me that Rachel always had more insight than I fully realised.

Dutifully, the twins held Amy in long, loving hugs before they left for school. After I dropped them off, I came back to take Amy to meet with Mark and Luke. They shook my hand. The deal was done and delivery was made.

Amy and I hugged, as the officers promised we could keep in touch.

Detective Luke took me aside and gave me a card with his number on it.

"If anything comes up, you need anything, just call," he said quietly.

I thanked him, hugged Amy for the last time and walked away.

What could come up?

Detective Brown kept in touch. He let me know how Amy was coping. She was struggling with the isolation of witness protection and was fearful being in the city again.

Before they disappeared Amy into her new life, they invited me to visit with her at a unit in the city. In her inimitable style Amy had arranged for us to have facials at the local chemist and to enjoy a Reiki session with the healer she had found close by.

During my session the Reiki healer told me that I was surrounded with love.

"You are circled by wise Aboriginal people. They are performing a sacred ceremony around your body, cleansing you with smoking eucalyptus leaves from a campfire in the bush."

I imagined the Elders around me, holding me close and wondered why they chose me.

"You will go to the desert," he said. "You have a choice to make."

I lay on the table for a long time after he finished wondering what that choice might be and who was guiding my life. I imagined the Elders with hands outstretched, curlicues of purifying smoke working magic on my life.

My life was a magical mystery tour with no miracle mirages in sight.

Chapter 26

Amy wasn't Amy anymore. She got a new name and a refurbished life when they sent her underground interstate.

Her only job was to stay alive.

Because the Detectives trusted me, I talked with Amy sometimes, always monitored.

I asked Michael to help her find a paying job beyond the staying alive gig in her new state. I trusted him to help us. We had held each other's secrets over decades and kept each other safe. He was a direct connection to the job Amy needed to get on her feet in her new life.

My children expressed their relief that she was gone. I saw them with refreshed eyes. Rachel hugged me close when I returned from dropping Amy off.

"It is all about Amy for her, Mum. You need to care for you," she said.

I hugged her tight smelling her hair and pure skin, grateful for the wise children I am blessed with.

Life returned to some semblance of normal. It was less colourful without Amy at the edges but back in balance, our tone, and our timing.

Amy left remnants in our life.

There were all the unfinished projects around the house and the matter of her silver sports car prominent in my driveway.

Her father had driven it to me, and I had taken it back to my place after they asked me to sell it. They deemed it was safer for me in my country town to shift the vehicle that linked Amy directly to her old habits. I put a sign on it and drove it to the corner where everyone selling cars in town parked. Each day I brought it back to our driveway.

Christmas loomed. Another year coming to a climax. We went back to my childhood hometown to visit with my parents. The twins were settled in the loungeroom when I walked around the block to visit my old friend Stephanie, the advertising manager from my first job as a copywriter with the paper.

We hadn't seen each other for years but she had flashed into my head, so I walked to her place after texting her on a whim.

I knocked at the door but there was no answer. Stephanie was expecting me, the lights were on inside and her car was in the driveway. I peered through the window and could see Stephanie leaning back on a weird angle on the floor.

In a flash I thought she was dead.

I focused on the scene inside. In front of her were the myriad parts of a self-assembly piece of furniture, with screws, bolts and allen keys splayed out all around her. A broadsheet of instructions was beside her.

I looked more closely. Stephanie was asleep.

Ikea DIY will do that to a person.

I knocked gently at the window and watched as she slowly roused back into consciousness.

As awareness settled Stephanie began to laugh.

Chapter 26

"Oh my God! Andrea!" she called out as she rolled up into a seated position rubbing her eyes.

We met at the front door and hugged for a long time.

"Come in!" Stephanie said. "Long time no see, want a drink?"

I followed her inside, and she made long cold glasses of fresh juice, which we took out the back into the garden, and sat under the pergola, shaded from the late afternoon sun.

"Remember that time you faxed the editor's jocks to him, after he slipped into the bed when you were asleep at my place?" she said. "Bastard! I was so scared that my husband would find his jocks on the floor and accuse me of an affair. That was hilarious! At the time it could have been deadly for me!"

We threw our heads back and laughed.

Everything is simple in hindsight. We talked about our broken marriages to the fathers of our children. We had both had twins, a boy and a girl. Synchronicities. We talked about how scared we were in our marriages, at different times, and how the resentments had grown from our husbands towards us.

Hard to understand at the time. We were both happy to be free, although also simultaneously locked in the endless custody fracas aftermath. We were sharing a parallel experience.

There were other similarities. The calling for deeper spiritual insight that was unfolding. Stephanie had been involved in transcendental meditation for years.

"I saw a healer in Adelaide," I told her. "He told me that I am going to the desert and I need to make a choice."

"Interesting," Stephanie said. "The desert, eh?"

"You know my brother's mother in law runs healing retreats near Alice Springs. She gave me a pamphlet about it. I don't think the retreat is my thing, but as it happens the flyer is on my fridge."

She returned from the kitchen with fresh drinks and the flyer, promoting a sound and colour healing retreat at Ooraminna Station in the heart of Australia.

Seven nights sleeping under the stars, immersed in the soul secrets of colour and sound and labyrinths, eating clean food, and meditating with a small group of spirit travellers like me.

What could go wrong?

I have learned on my journey to trust the signposts. There are guides and angels who support our story woven with random threads of colour. Depending on the awareness we bring to the process, it can be worth taking guidance on board to see how we grow through the lessons or insights. It is imperative to trust ourselves in the process and listen to our own wisdom.

I booked the retreat in Alice Springs and organised for my parents to care for the twins while I was away.

Amy called me before I left.

"Michael got me a job," she said. "I start Monday. Think of me in my power suit out to earn the big bucks!"

"Great, Amy," I said, and I meant it. A fresh start interstate with new challenges and people was a brilliant opportunity for her to explore. Income that didn't rely on the black market and the psychopaths that came with it. Now clean from drugs Amy was bouncing in her own energy.

Safe in her new city with a new name, a new house and far away from the bad influences of drugs, bikers, international traffickers and death visiting her doorstep.

"I'm heading to the desert on a retreat," I said. "I will be in and out of range. Take care of you there and good luck with your new job! Very excited for you." I went to say her name but didn't. Her new name still sounded unnatural coming out of my mouth.

Heading for the desert, I hit the road and expanded into the clear blue Australian sky, as I drove through the outback toward my destiny.

It was fifteen hundred kilometres and the time in the car over a couple of days settled me into myself. I arrived at the meeting place to share dinner with the people on my retreat, and the next day I left my car and joined the minibus taking us out to our campsite.

Chapter 26

Christine and Vicki who ran the retreat were amazing. The group were an eclectic range of men and women from around the world. We shared wonderful experiences including silence, toning, meditation, drumming, drawing, colour exploration, and creating and walking a labyrinth. We ate clean fresh vegetarian food. We slept in our swags on single bed frames, under the shining stars of the Milky Way, with all our belongings off the dirt and kept dry from the dewy mornings.

The week was supported by Mutitjulu Elder Bobby Randall. Bobby was a beautiful wise Aboriginal man who taught us songs, and how to track animals around our campsite. We heard the calls of dingoes in the night and in the morning, I went out in my pyjamas to find their footprints, two bigger dingoes, and a pup.

Bobby was hosting a sunset when he wondered out loud if I'd like to marry him and move in at Uluru.

I figured he was joking.

"Little brown baby," he crooned as the firelight licked our faces. The red sand caressed our feet. Every day we chose coloured aura soma bottles that were arranged on a silken stand in the shade from the sun. The bottles were all numbered and combinations related to the tree of life and the kabbalah.

I carefully walked the steps of the labyrinth which aligned with the tarot and the kabbalah.

Everything is connected.

It became crystal clear to me as I walked the labyrinth that every step I take, was my choice made from my own free will. Every move I make, every vow I take….there's a song in this!

Maureen was sixty, from Brisbane, and just a little bit crazy. We became instant soul sisters. On the final morning we woke, walked in silence to the top of the mountain and meditated as the sun rose.

Over breakfast Maureen shared her insights while looking me straight in the eye.

"I had my guides come to me during the night," she announced. "They told me that I was to cancel my flight through to Adelaide and drive with you back to South Australia." She watched me carefully and nodded solemnly.

"Oh really? Your guides told you to drive with me home?" I said, "That's cool, a girly road trip!"

"So, when we get into town later this morning, I will find a travel agent and get them to cancel my flight and I will come with you. Okay?" It was decided.

"Sure," I said.

And that was that. I trusted the process.

In Alice Springs I parked the car behind the main shopping centre, and found we were in front of a gem and crystal shop. Drawn into the place, a large clear quartz crystal caught my eye. We were buzzing after a week in the desert and the whole place started to shimmer and give us tingles.

The proprietor noticed.

"It's really heating up in here," she said, as we moved through the shop, admiring and resonating with various crystals and rocks.

Maureen looked at me over her shoulder.

"I will buy you whatever you want from here as a gift," she said, "Choose what you want, whatever draws you. It's yours."

I was standing next to the large clear quartz crystal and placed my hand gently on it again.

"I thought so," said Maureen, and indicated for me to bring it to the counter.

I checked the price.

"But it is two hundred and forty dollars!" I said.

"Perfect," said Maureen, "It is yours. For your healing room."

We made our farewells to the group and hit the road. Wide open cloudless sky, all the way from the red centre as we headed home to the beach. Wedgetail eagles circled overhead and horizons

Chapter 26

stretched forever around us. The road ribboned off into a silky mirage that looked like water in the distance. Water that never arrived.

Maureen asked me about my life and I shared my stories of love, hope, loss, and betrayal. I told her about Amy, whose sports car sat in my driveway while she made a new life with another name of her own choosing.

Maureen honed in, suddenly sharply focused and intent.

"You need to get her out of your life, Andrea," she said.

"I know, she has moved interstate under the witness protection program, and she got a job, she is off the gear now and making positive choices for her future," I explained.

"All well and good my dear, but love, light and angels won't protect you and the kids from bikers with guns and evil intentions," Maureen was strident and, on a roll, "They will fucking kill you as soon as look at you. They don't care if you are a lightworker, a mother, a good citizen or whatever. You MUST cut her out of your life. At the root. NOW!"

"Okay, I hear you. As soon as I get home the car can be transported back to her folks for them to deal with," I promised.

"Earlier is better, but as soon as we get to your home, that is the plan. Agreed?" Maureen was resolute and settled back into the seat beside me.

I looked out at the horizon of possibilities surrounding us. Clear, calm, and present.

"Agreed!" I said and turned up the music so we could sing our lungs out to the desert sky. We stopped in Coober Pedy and booked into the Underground Desert Motel.

Text messages started to come through as we got back into range.

Michael had messaged me. Amy has not been at work for days; did I have a contact number?

I took Maureen to Tom and Mary's Greek Restaurant. We were in the middle of the desert and their garlic prawns were the best the universe offered.

My phone rang. It was Amy.

"I have missed you SO MUCH," she cried, "I haven't been able to get out of bed for a week! I am SO SICK. It is like PTSD. Davey is here with me."

Davey was her latest boyfriend.

"Put Davey on the phone," I said and listened to the rustling as she handed me over.

"Davey?" I queried.

"Yes Andrea?" he responded.

"Have you given her a taste of gear?" I was straight to the point.

He hesitated.

"Don't fuck with me, mate," I said, "Have you scored drugs and given some to Amy?"

His voice had a certain whine about it.

"It was only a taste, not a big score, she was just so sick, and I thought it might help perk her up a bit, no harm done," he concluded.

"Put Amy back on the line," I commanded.

"Sure," Davey said and was gone. I could almost hear his scurry.

"Amy?" I said, "I am done. I can't do this with you anymore. I love you and respect you, but I cannot sit by while you make destructive choices with your life, choices that also put me and my family at potential risk. I will arrange to send the car back to your parents as soon as I get home, and please know that I wish you well on your journey. You have so much to offer, so much light, but the addiction dulls your flame, and it makes you and others unsafe. It is your life and your choices, and these are mine. Goodbye, Amy. I trust that you are well again soon, because you ARE strong enough to get through it."

There was silence at the other end of the phone, apart from a sharp intake of breath as she listened.

"And Amy? Fuck Davey off. He means no good and does not support your healing process. Goodbye and take good care," I finished the call.

Chapter 26

Maureen sat looking at me, eyes wide open and shining. Then she burst into her crazy laughter. Her peals of joy filled the restaurant, reverberating off the walls. Everyone looked our way with smiles on their faces.

"And THAT sister, is HOW it is DONE!" she cried.

Tears formed in my eyes.

"I love Amy and can see her promise, but I just can't put my children or myself at risk for her any longer. It is incredibly sad to see people so unaware of their own beauty and worth," I said.

Maureen watched me carefully and stood up with her arms open wide.

"I know, darling, it is hard, but people must find their own way and take responsibility for their choices. That is where their power is," she said and held me tight in heartfelt hug.

My tears fell onto her shoulder and I breathed a few times deeply in and out.

"It is safe for me to let go," I said.

"You are a very wise woman, my friend," Maureen said as she stood back, looking into my eyes as she held me by the shoulders. "It is all going to turn out alright."

That night in our underground room we slept soundly, as Mother Earth held us like babes in arms. In the morning we were on the final run home where my beautiful twins, and Mum and Dad awaited us.

On the way I received a call from Julie, our family friend.

"Hey, Andrea?" she said, "That sports car in your driveway? Of Amy's? You need to get rid of it straight away! I have this really strong feeling about it, and it is not good."

"Julie? Thank you for the confirmation, it is done as soon as I get there, I promise you, it is gone," I said.

That is how the universe works. Whispers of wisdom that we hear inside ourselves, or that others share with us, that we may choose to take on board, always trusting ourselves in the process, and operating out of deep love, and compassion for ourselves and our voice, beyond fear.

The next week I went to see my local healer. She laid me on her table in the half light and placed warm hands on my heart. She brought light energy to my chakras and soothed my being with soft words of loving wisdom.

As she worked, she told me about a beautiful red and gold dragon she saw emanating from my body.

"It is rising gently towards the heavens with a seductive sway and a beautiful smile," she said.

Fixated, she sent it to the light.

"I am watching it all the way. To make sure it had truly left its hiding place in your soul," she clapped her hands. "That's it! Gone forever."

I laid there on the table feeling calm and clear. I kept my eyes gently closed.

"It was a parasite," she explained. "The most beautiful parasite I have ever seen."

That night I called Amy's Mum. I told her about hearing from Amy's new boyfriend.

"Anna, she has left her job. She is back on the gear. Sliding down into that dark fiery abyss. You should be careful because you never know who the drugs invite in," I cautioned.

Anna listened in silence.

"Hold on" she said, there was a rustling in the background.

Suddenly Amy was on the phone. Yelling.

"How dare you question me? I am SUFFERING! STRUGGLING with post-traumatic stress. They tried to kill me with fire. It is NOT ABOUT THE DRUGS!" she screamed.

"Amy? I love you," I said, "Stay off the drugs. Get clean. Be safe. You choose. Every moment, you choose."

She hung up on me.

The next day I saw my healer at the school. We hugged.

Chapter 26

"That parasite," I said, "It was Amy, wasn't it?"

"Yes," she said.

"Why didn't you tell me?" I was puzzled.

"Because you had to work it out for yourself. Dragons breathe fire in darkness. You breathe the light of love. You are learning that you are worth loving. By you," she said.

As I walked away, I understood.

My life. My choice. My love. For me. And THEN for everyone else.

Chapter 27

In our move to the beach my spiritual exploration deepened. I explored artists and writers, modalities, and programs to support expansion of my soul.

I was introduced to a group of mature aged ladies whom I shared weekly meditation and regular Reiki healings. Our living situation with Derek had become unhealthy. He had a lot of unexpressed anger, and an expectation that as the woman I was responsible for all of the housework.

With three daughters that he saw on weekends and during holidays, plus other times as arranged with their mother, I was working full time, paying for most things, and caring for five children when they were all at the house. Derek spent his time out at his burnt-out block, rebuilding fences and planting trees.

My work took me right across the Peninsula and I discovered a special affinity for Ceduna on the Far West Coast. Ceduna has a large population of First Nations people and my work focused on opportunities for them through the development of a range of workforce development and wellbeing projects.

Chapter 27

One afternoon I visited the art and cultural centre and met with the local ladies about a mining employment preparation project we were putting together. An Elder with twinkling eyes sat next to me. She saw straight through me.

"Hey, sister," she said, "I think you need to go on a journey!"

"A journey?" I responded. "Where?"

"To here," she said, and placed her warm brown hand on my heart.

"My name is Avis," she said. "You are my sister."

Outside we sat in the shade at the front of the gallery and continued the conversation.

"There are weenas here who can take you on the journey. You will meet them," Avis said as a car arrived, and two well-dressed blonde women alighted.

Avis greeted them and turned to me.

"This sister here," she pointed at me with her gnarled forefinger, "She needs a journey with you. Tonight."

I smiled at them, incongruous in their city garb out here on the casual coast. I must have looked puzzled.

One of the women sat next to me, shook my hand, and introduced herself as Jamie.

"We are here to arrange journey work. The work of Brandon Bays. Have you heard of her?" Jamie asked.

I hadn't.

"Brandon Bays healed herself of a large tumour in six and a half weeks and has developed the Journey Method to teach and support others with their transformative healing," Jamie said. "We are here to plan a community journey workshop coming up in a few months. Avis thinks you need a journey. Did you want to come to our motel tonight and give it a go?"

That evening I collected Avis who was also going on a journey with the other woman, and we arrived early at their motel.

Parking out front, I got out my angel cards.

"Did you want to choose a card or three Avis?"

Avis smiled and I shuffled them for her. Avis chose three cards, which glowed in the ambient light.

I put on the interior light and read her the messages from the guidebook.

"Wow!" she said, "I think that is just perfect, sister! Thank you!"

Avis got ready to get out of the car and enter the motel room. Bugs flew around the light outside the door. I shuffled the cards slowly and thoroughly. Then drew three cards.

They were the exact same three that Avis had just drawn.

Avis looked at me with eyes wide.

"Our journey, sister?" she said, "It's already started!"

We laughed and I got out to hug her good luck. Simultaneously we looked at each other and winked as we each knocked on a motel room door.

Journey work is a guided and facilitated meditation and visioning process that explores earlier memories and events in our lives. As Jamie's soothing voice guided me back into my earliest memory I was back in bed, aged three with a snake coming up the leg of the bed towards me.

Dad was putting his socks on with his back to me and I was screaming for help.

He couldn't hear me.

I was terrified.

And alone.

Abandoned and ignored.

Jamie invited me to explore what that little girl needs right now.

"What tools does she need to have to resolve or heal this situation, this experience of abandonment?" Jamie's voice was calm and bright.

I held out my arms to the little girl and pulled her close. I smoothed her hair and shooed the snake away. I alerted her Dad

Chapter 27

so he could be there too, and together we held her, calming her, loving her, healing her. I gave her the tools of knowing, of calm presence, of resilience, and of seeing the lesson from a higher perspective. I saw the patterns that had pervaded my life.

When Jamie guided me out of the meditation, I was fully equipped. I felt clear and peaceful.

With gratitude I hugged her for the gift of guidance, love, and transformation.

Avis had a wonderful journey too and she talked with me about returning for the community workshop later in the month. I agreed to get a group together and come along.

Back at home I shared the experience with my meditation group and encouraged them to join me in Ceduna for the workshop. I booked accommodation which was a large house on the beach called 'Coastal Dreaming'. Their website was adorned with Aboriginal art. It was perfect.

Our eclectic, all aged group of women and some of our daughters, shared a road trip four hundred kilometres to Ceduna for the journey workshop training.

On the day of the training Rachel decided to stay back and create bracelets. Vera and her daughter stayed with her at our rented beach house.

As the workshop progressed, I was partnered with a random woman at the session so that we could practice facilitating each other's journeys. I went straight back to the dream about the approaching snake, and we did more work healing that little girl, empowering her, and holding her.

When I facilitated the process for my partner, she also shared a story about an earliest memory.

"I was travelling with my family. It was summer, and it was very hot. My mother wanted to visit a grave at the cemetery and my father parked the car in the shade. As he left to accompany Mum, he told me to stay close by the car, not to walk around, and they'd be back very soon." Her eyes were closed, and her eyelids flickered as she recalled the memory, like it was happening now.

"I got bored and restless, it was hot and sticky, and I got out of the car to look at the graves. As I wandered through the gravesites, I came across a grave with a broken headstone and a hole where the surface of the plot had caved in. As I went closer to have a look, I was just imagining the dead person drying up underground, when a large snake appeared out of the hole and slithered towards me."

Her voice was agitated as she recalled her terror.

"I ran away, stumbling and crying as I went and still the snake kept coming. Dad heard my screams and he came running from the other direction. We finally met at the car."

"I was terrified and sobbing, as I explained to Dad what had happened," she said. "He gave me a slap and yelled at me, telling me that he had told me to stay with the car, and NOW look what happened when I disobeyed him!"

"It was all my fault," she finished with a whimper.

"What does that little girl need right now?" I asked gently as the guidance prescribed. "How can we equip her with the tools and acceptance for healing that fear and rejection?"

We worked through the process and as we finished, we looked at each other with clear eyed admiration and care.

I felt amazing.

Two snakes! What are the chances?

We broke for lunch and I checked my phone. There was a message from Vera for me to call her as soon as I got the message.

I immediately dialled her number and waited until she picked up.

"How is it going?" she asked.

"Amazing," I said, "You should have come along."

"Well as it turns out I am glad I was here," she said. "Rachel was on the beach collecting shells for her collage and jewellery earlier, and as she went to come back home a large brown snake blocked her path! She was terrified. There was a man on a beach. Rachel ended up asking him for help and he accompanied her across the road to safety," Vera finished with a rush.

Chapter 27

"My God!" I said, "My journey partner and I both had sessions with a snake appearing, and Rachel has one in reality, at the same time! Is she okay? Put her on?"

Rachel came to the phone. She was breathless as she recounted her experience on the beach.

"I was so glad that man was there to help me," she said.

"I am, too, darling," I said. "I am, too."

We finished the conversation and I went to tell Avis and the other Aboriginal women in her circle about the snake on the beach.

"Wow!" said one of the ladies, "Very unusual to see a big brown snake on that beach! Never seen that before in my lifetime."

All the ladies nodded, murmuring concurrence.

Snakes and serpents are symbols for creation across the cultures of the world. It was a sign of trust, healing and support in a world where rejection and abandonment abound.

We are surrounded by magic, if we choose to notice. Most importantly, we need to be right there for ourselves, expressing acceptance and care, and be there for each other as we journey together towards healing.

Chapter 28

After we moved, Clayton sought a new court order. His application was upheld. Its terms forced me to move back to our hometown again, so that he had ease of access to Thomas. It was an outcome designed to make it easier for him but did not consider the best interests of the children and our difficult circumstances.

I hired a barrister and appealed the court order, while staying firmly in place. After an investment in many court appearances and additional fifteen thousand dollars in costs, we were successful. The access orders still stood, and I continued to pay for flights so that Thomas could share every second weekend and half of all school holidays with his father.

Early in our separation, I had seen a prominent woman on television, discussing the approach she had taken to the divorce from her husband, and subsequent access arrangements for their children.

"My children are a product of their father, and for me to undermine him, reflects directly on who they are, so whatever happens, I choose to show respect for him as the father of my children. My children are who I love more than life itself," she said. This resonated, and despite my frustration with the ongoing court conflict, I was conscious of ensuring my language and behaviour was respectful of their father. After all, they are a product of us both.

Clayton continued to make applications to the family court for changes to our arrangement as he sought full custody of Thomas. I countered his application with appeals, countless court appearances, and invested thousands in legal fees. Clayton was consistent as he showed up to make his case, dragging up sordid but by now irrelevant details we were determined to leave behind. Meanwhile his child support bill remained unpaid, and mounting.

After a few years, the court saga had gone on so long that I reached out to my former lawyer and lover Paolo. We made a time to catch up at a café while I was in the city for work.

"You are looking so well, Andrea," Paolo said as we hugged. I sat down at the table.

"It is all in perfect alignment and I deserve only good things," I found affirmations very useful to transform my experiences into valuable lessons of life where I took full responsibility for my choices and the outcomes. Positive use of language was vital.

Paolo's eyes crinkled as he laughed warmly.

"Okay," he said, "How can I help?"

I explained the family court situation. An expensive, exhaustive, and a fruitless waste of energy, particularly now that Thomas was fifteen years old and making up his own mind about his relationship with his father.

"Whose application is it?" Paolo asked, with his head tilted to his shoulder, surveying me as he considered what we once shared.

I could read his thoughts. I stuck firmly with the business.

"Whose application is it?" I repeated, confused.

I had lost track with all the to and fro, appeals, injunctions and counter applications.

"My advice is to find out forthwith," Paolo said. "It could be as simple as withdrawing your application."

"Ahhhh, brilliant, thank you, I will call my lawyer and find out," I said. "How's Ingrid?"

He smiled at me and the conversation turned to the banal. After I departed, I called my lawyer to ask whose application was currently before the courts.

She had no idea.

"I will look back through your files, and let you know," she said, "It's a very full file you know!"

"I can imagine…." we laughed with shared irony and finished the call.

A couple of hours later she phoned back, to let me know the application being heard at the next court date, was mine.

I immediately sought permission from the magistrate to link in by phone at the next hearing. At the scheduled time I was in a taxi heading into the city from the airport for work. The magistrate came on the line and informed me that the father was not in court.

"Your Honour, I understand the application we are hearing today is mine, and I would like to withdraw it," I said.

I heard murmurs in the background and papers being shuffled on her bench.

"The mother withdraws her application, and with no representation to dissent I confirm that her application is withdrawn, and the case file is closed unless any new application is filed in the future," the magistrate's voice was formal and clear. We finished the hearing within minutes. I hung up.

And that was it.

Our twelve-year saga of family court was over in an instant of ultimate clarity and letting go.

It was the last and most useful contribution of Paolo to our lives.

Thomas continued to see his father, but he was maturing quickly and his time with friends and weekend sport where he excelled, became his primary focus. He started to resist going away on weekends. Access visits faltered, became irregular, until they tapered off to nothing. The phone phobia that Clayton flailed about with, in mute avoidance of conversations fostered through regular contact meant that his relating was non-existent.

Chapter 28

Clayton faded from our lives, like the ghost who walks.

It was time to move out into our own house. Living with Derek and his children was taking its toll. His latent anger was too much for me to bear.

We needed to find somewhere to live, and fast. I was driving to Ceduna for work when I called Vera for a chat.

"Hey, we need a house. We need our own space and being in town is easier on the kids rather than having to catch the school bus to and from Derek's place. His anger management is a bit to be desired, and I think we have been through enough. He needs to sort his own shit out," I said. "Any ideas?"

"Did you know that as a state government worker you can get subsidised rent on a government house?" she replied quick as a flash.

"No! Can I?" I was amazed.

Could it be that simple?

"Sure, ring Dave at Services SA, he manages the housing and ask to be put on the list," she said.

"Awesome! All I want is a house with sea views, three bedrooms so the kids can have their own space, and close to town so they can get to and from school with ease if I am working away or whatever," I said.

"Go for it. My understanding is that they have a range of houses available. As you always tell me.... Ask for what you want!"

We laughed. Recently Vera had told me she was ready for a relationship, after many years of life as a hard-working single mother. We pondered the various ways to attract a soul mate into our lives. The spells, the intentions, the vision boards, the dreaming, the gratitude, the exercise, the internet.

I had a flash of insight.

"Let's face it sister, if the right bloke is the right bloke, he will come and knock at your door!"

We giggled and poured another wine, sitting in the newly built yurt style dwelling Vera had designed and just completed. It still had bare concrete floors, and a garden waiting to be landscaped outside.

Three weeks later Vera rang me.

"You will never guess what happened!" she exclaimed in a conspiratorial whisper. Her daughter must be around the place somewhere and the news must be juicy!

"What?!?" I asked.

"Last night there was a knock at the door, and it was the guy from up the road holding a bottle of wine. He brought it as a housewarming gift. He thought an old lady lived here!" she laughed, "We sat on the verandah and talked until three in the morning. He is recently separated with three boys and had no idea who even lived here! He just came to welcome me to the neighbourhood."

"Maybe it is one of THOSE conversations," I said. The conversation without end. Where we learn and grow, accept each other, and share adventures, with hot sex.

"Maybe it is!" she said, and we laughed.

They married, sold the yurt and built their own place to share. They developed and run three businesses together. If it is right the universe finds a way through pure love. It is always whole, complete and perfect. That's the law.

My next call was to Dave at Services SA.

"I just want a house, three to four bedrooms, with sea views!" I said, excited at the prospect.

"You don't get to choose the house, you know," he said gruffly. "You get whatever is the top of the list."

My face fell at his tone. I calmed my excitement a notch.

"Sure, we will take whatever you offer us with gratitude," I said.

I completed the emailed application and sent it back. A few days later he called.

"Come and pick up the keys to your new place, open lease," he said.

Chapter 28

"Thanks so much Dave, really appreciated," I said. We had a house!

On the way home that night I looked up the address and stopped by our new home. It was a three-bedroom house with an ATCO hut at the side, a playground in a park in front, and 180-degree sea views overlooking the bay.

We were home. We were free.

Derek grumbled as he helped us move out. He wanted it to work out, but he needed to do the work on himself, and set himself free.

Happiness is an inside job. His happiness was his own to discover. I couldn't do that for him. Not anymore.

Exactly twelve months later, after the Amy experience, it was time to buy our own place, somewhere we could call our own again. Our renovated former home in Gladstone was occupied by tenants, and their rent didn't quite cover the mortgage payments.

I looked at real estate in the paper and attended open inspections of homes on the market.

Nothing suited. They were either outside of my price range, in the wrong location, or didn't have the characteristics I wanted for us as a family.

My friend Michelle came with me, as I needed a second opinion. Someone with clear eyes, a good head and no emotional attachment to the outcome. Michelle and her husband had a few properties and she was an excellent businesswoman with real estate.

I took her to meet the agent at a house in the middle of a hill. There were views of the bay but a main road out front. The home's elevated position meant we were stuck with the small rooms in the footprint, unless I found funds for a major renovation.

It was in my price range.

The agent showed us through and then went outside to allow us time to chat.

"Small kitchen," observed Michelle, "And the bedrooms are tiny."

"Can't swing a cat," I agreed, "But it is in my price range."

Michelle nodded thoughtfully.

"Every time you back the car out down the driveway you are entering a main road, and the hill means you can't see what is coming so easily," she said.

I looked down the driveway.

She was right.

"But I can afford it on my wage," I said.

"Hmmmmm, up to you. Why don't you have another look through and I will go and chat with the agent to see what sort of interest there is in the place," she said.

When Michelle left the room, I pulled my crystal pendulum out of my pocket. At my meditation group we explored a whole range of tools and methodologies. A pendulum is one way we confirmed our own inner knowing. It tells us what we already know, even if we haven't admitted it to ourselves yet.

I calibrated and tested the pendulum, asking it a definite yes question.

Is a ball round? The pendulum swung itself clockwise. YES.

Is a ball square? The pendulum slowed to a stop and turned the other way, picking up speed and clearly turning counterclockwise. NO.

I stopped it still with my other hand.

Is this the home for us?

The pendulum began to move, slowly but surely counterclockwise. NO. I stopped the pendulum and tried it again.

A definite NO.

Frustration rose within me.

I went outside. Michelle gave me a hug and excused herself so I could talk with the agent alone. They wanted two hundred and forty-nine thousand dollars for the house.

"I'll make an offer of two hundred and twenty-two thousand dollars," I said. "Let me know what the vendors say."

Chapter 28

"Sure, it's a low offer, but at least it's an offer," he said.

That night he called me back.

"Your offer has been refused," he said, "If you'd be willing to add $15,000 dollars?"

"No," I said, "Thank you, but no."

"Fine, we will keep an eye out for you, something will come up," he finished the call.

I got angry.

What was the problem?

All we need is one house!

Why can't the house appear now that I am looking for it?

My wisdom whisper was a full shouting tantrum.

That's it! I told the universe in no uncertain terms. *I am not looking at any more real estate, or going to any more open inspections, if you want us to have a house, you show us the house!*

I went to bed and cried.

That closed the matter. I didn't cry very often.

The next day there was a wellbeing expo in town, and I went to check out the crystals.

There was a clairvoyant doing sessions and I decided to book in and give it a go.

As I sat down, I was astounded by the first words out of his mouth.

"You are looking for a house," he said, "You need something complete and easy to maintain as you travel a lot for your work. You work with Aboriginal people often and you are making a positive difference with your work. I can see the Elders around you. You are single, but there is a soulmate out there making his way towards you. It won't be easy at first, but it will all work out okay. You need to trust your voice and trust the process. It is all perfect. Just trust."

I hadn't said a word.

How the fuck could he know all that by just seeing me?

Just trust, Andrea, wisdom whispered.

That night I went out for a birthday dinner with the meditation group. One of the ladies was turning seventy-five. There were a couple of women I hadn't met before. I launched into the story of the real estate pendulum adventure from the day before.

"The pendulum said NO," I said, grumpily, "So now I have given up looking for a house and invited the universe to show me where our house is!"

They laughed at my petulance. All grandmothers, they were wise and tolerant of my impatience.

Bemused, one of the women across the table leaned in closer.

"A house? You are looking for a house you say?" she said, her raised eyebrows adorned sparkling eyes, "We are planning to sell our house and I told my husband, 'We won't need to advertise the house, the right person will come along and buy it from us privately.'"

"And here you are!"

My eyes got wide.

"Are you serious?" I asked astounded.

Janice laughed.

"I surely am!" The whole table of beautiful crones cackled with knowing laughter.

The next day I took Michelle around to Janice's home. It sat at an angle on the block, built out of deep brown brick, with a rose garden and unfenced lawn at the front.

We knocked at the door. The room we entered was exceptionally large and served as a lounge and dining room, with a fully renovated kitchen off to the side. The home had a bathroom also recently renovated and the master bedroom had a walk-in robe and ensuite. As we toured through the space Michelle leaned over to whisper.

"FEEL this house!?!" she exclaimed.

I could feel it.

Chapter 28

Calm, grounded, complete, and perfect.

There was a boomerang over the kitchen door. Janice's husband was an Aboriginal Elder.

As we got to the back door, we started to make our way outside to a beautiful undercover fernery and pergola. This space led onto another large spare room at the back like a detached granny flat.

Michelle turned to me.

"Either you buy this house, OR I will!" she said.

I asked Janice and her husband what price they were asking. It was in my range and so the deal was done. A private sale in a smooth exchange without a real estate agent or open inspection in sight.

Apparently, THAT is how the universe works. In its own perfect time and space.

We are home. Always home. We just need to trust the process, and ourselves. That we deserve all good things and can be profoundly grateful for every gift we receive, even the painful lessons we experience at the time, if we move right through, there is the promise of peace on the other side.

Chapter 29

Now I owned two houses.

Or the bank did.

One sunny Sunday afternoon I got a call from Sue my friend who still lived in Gladstone.

"Andrea? Are you sitting down?" Sue asked in an urgent tone.

What could be wrong?

"What's happened?" I asked.

"We had Tom and all the guys at our place for a barbecue and then their pagers all started going off!" Sue explained.

Many of our friends volunteered in the Country Fire Service which responded to emergencies, accidents, and incidents in the community.

"They had shared a few beers, so I drove them, and now I am standing outside your house. It is on fire!" Sue finished in a rush.

"The fire unit is on its way, and there is smoke pouring out of the hallway, but there is another accident out on the highway. Someone has been hit by a car, so the guys are stretched pretty thin right now."

Chapter 29

"Are you serious? A fire? Where are the tenants? Are they out? Is everyone okay?" My mind started to race with all the possibilities.

"I have to go! I will call you back as soon as we sort it out!" Sue finished the call.

I sat down.

Then rang my mum and dad.

Half an hour later Sue called again.

"The fire is contained and has done minimal damage. Your neighbour was out seeing off a visitor when he heard the alarm and saw smoke pouring out the front door, so he grabbed a shovel and removed most of the burning material, which turned out to be a pile of photo albums lit with accelerant in the hallway." As a clinical health professional Sue provided all the detail rapid fire.

"The TV, fridge, and other appliances have been smashed up. Your female tenant turned up and said she had left after she had an argument with her boyfriend. He has evidently smashed the place up, set it alight and then gone out to the highway. A local teacher was driving home from school. She was in the eighty zone, and he has thrown himself in front of her car. I am sorry to say that he couldn't be saved. The teacher is a mess, she tried to avoid him, by swerving this way and that, but he just kept running at her until she collided with him. She is devastated."

"Fuck." I said. What a tragedy! What a set of choices. My heart broke for her. I knew exactly what it felt like for a humdrum existence to explode into a massive shitstorm of drama in real life.

"Fuck is right. It's a big day for Tom and the crew of volunteers to have to deal with all that. Your neighbour did a good job, saving the house," Sue counted our blessings in a tragic awful situation.

"Yes, it is, please thank everyone for me. I will be in touch with my tenant to pass on my condolences and will organise an insurance claim for the house through my landlord's insurance," I said with gratitude.

"I reckon the boys will need another beer!" Sue said.

"Tell them it is on me," I said as we finished the call.

Once all the details came through, I contacted my insurer. They sent an assessor out to inspect the damage. The tenant moved to her mum's place, and I started to organise the repairs.

A letter arrived from my insurance company. It stated in the fine print of my landlord insurance policy, that the house was not covered for malicious damage.

If the house had burned down, I wasn't covered?

I rang the insurance company and they confirmed the details in the correspondence was correct.

"We are declining the claim as it is malicious damage, which is an extra for the landlord's insurance policy," the representative intoned like an automaton.

"Why have landlord's insurance unless I wanted to cover the place for damage that the tenant might inflict on the place?" I asked the rhetorical question.

"Sorry Ma'am, it's in the policy," he said.

I finished the call and cried.

I cried for my broken home.

Broken when the love of my life and father of my children left, broken by the betrayal of my second husband and turned into a crime scene, and now broken by the conflict between my tenants, their shattered relationship, ending in a man's death, and traumatising the young teacher who collided with him. Life changing every moment.

It is true that the storm is always outside. Whatever happens we can choose how we respond. Whether we are victims or victors, hurt or healed. It can take time, lifetimes, deep time, millennia, or moments. Depending on our choice.

A few weeks later I received the quotes for the fire damage. Fortunately, it was only five thousand dollars.

It could have been so much worse.

For my tenants, it WAS so much worse.

The insurance company called.

Chapter 29

"We have reconsidered your claim, and because of the quantum involved, we have decided to cover the repairs. Please proceed with your choice of repairer and we will fix up the account," he said.

"Thank you," I said, "Your consideration in the situation is much appreciated."

I hung up and cried.

The house got repaired and I put it on the market. It was time for letting go. Despite my love for that home, and the joy I got from coordinating all the renovations, I didn't even think about it anymore.

I focused on where I was right now.

Here in the moment.

Making the most of each second, with love, acceptance, hope and forgiveness in my heart.

Michael phoned me. I took the call outside the office into the sunshine. He had a cough that he hadn't been able to shake.

"They have found cancer," he said. "In my lungs. It is a secondary."

My breath caught in my throat. His whole life ahead of him. His dreams of sailing to new horizons. His children. His wife. His book.

It was not about us. We were a hazy interpretation of what could have been. A fantasy in fiction, across twenty whole years of friendship shared throughout our lives.

A few weeks later the phone rang again. It was Michael.

"I have been surfing, and there were dolphins in the waves. It was amazing. So beautiful." His voice was pensive. "I wonder when I will start to feel sick?"

Before he said goodbye, he shared the big news.

"They did more tests. They found the primary. It is in my brain."

I felt sick.

A wondrous brain. A beautiful man caught on the anchor of responsibility. Participating in a marriage of toxic interaction but committed to his vows. Until death do us part.

"I will give you a sign," he said. "I will brush past your left breast while you are sleeping, and you will know that I am gone. You will know that I have passed your way."

"I love you," I said.

"I love you, too," he said. "Always have. Always will."

We laughed. Empty but alive.

We talked again the morning he was on his way to tell his mother. He had delayed the inevitable for as long as he could. A desire to give his family time to ease the pain of his sister's passing, before the conversation no one ever wants to have with their Mum.

I was calm outside and ravaged inside. Clearly this was not about me.

We kept in touch. I sent healing energy. We talked. Soothing conversations that left nothing unsaid and everything undone.

He encouraged me.

"Write it all down," he said. "Write your book. Put your words out into the world."

I thought about how I never wanted to be in the waiting place. I could not put my life on hold in denial of my highest knowing. Michael is my teacher. I write.

Later when I called all I got was his message bank. I left messages of encouragement and friendship. I listened to his voice. I heard our eons of life connection in his tone. I know his soul.

It was Anzac Day when I woke and searched the internet, with purpose and betrayal at this life's cruel but perfect mysteries of love. I found the news of his passing just a day earlier. He had brushed my left breast in the night. Sending a whisper of wisdom through the universe to my heartbeat of knowing. Michael left this plane riding a wave of light to a new horizon. With a dolphin by his side.

Michael was perfection in the distance.

Chapter 29

When I visited the beach, I searched for dolphins surfing waves. I share the whispers of wisdom, grateful for his full acceptance of me, as I shoot my words into the stars for all to see.

For I am scared, but I am alive, and free.

Our letters are among my treasures buried deep. I hold keepsakes. I hoard the writings of people. They are our marks. Proof we existed.

Michael was my muse, my lover, confidant, and friend. I love him still. He is me.

A few weeks later, my real estate agent called.

"We have an offer on your house," he said. "Surprisingly it is from your former tenant."

My former tenant had decided that broken home was her best healing place, and she chose to purchase it for her own as a shrine to her lost love.

Life has been a lesson in learning to listen. Mostly to myself.

That small voice that says, *wear the black pants* on the evening my girlfriend later laughed as she spilled red wine my way across the table.

The whisper about the man I just met, who, so consumed with my own lack of confidence, I agreed to meet only to find his greasy hair and sweaty hands smell like loser all over again. Just like the others.

The intersections of lives with an introduction that only has meaning in retrospect, as I look at the patterns across time.

The friends that turned on me when I offended their senses, or stopped meeting their expectations, finishing chapters of relationships that moved and shifted like tides across vast expanses of sand.

I didn't need to defend myself.

I didn't need them to accept me the way I am.

My job was to accept myself.

To forgive myself.

To love myself, both my light and shadow sides.

Whole, complete, and perfect.

My job was to grow, heal and learn along the way and keep an open heart and mind.

Some of the patterns in life we can only see in retrospect. How the swirls of light and dark corners shape our existence, experienced in the lessons we learn in relationship with another.

Lessons of choice.

Of love, hope, loss, acceptance, forgiveness, and freedom.

A search for love beyond church, beyond self, beyond saving.

Where love must surely live. Even beyond death there is life in love. Love IS forever.

Forgiveness became my daily practice. Mainly of myself. It is a life passage and there was plenty to go on with.

Chapter 30

For much of my life I have been on the search for the wisdom that will guide me to the light of the truth. The epiphany. The secret. Peace, freedom, and fulfillment.

In my early days I filled my school mates up with stories of home. This was despite Dad saying that whatever happens at home is our own private business, and not to share stories.

I never understood that, as nothing really happened at home. Keeping it private never seemed important to me.

I catalogued stories of incidents and accidents, tall tales and true to regale anyone who would listen to the insights I wanted to share. I entertained, made people laugh, horrified, or justified. Sharing ideas and possibilities, dreams, and notions.

I had a lot to say in an attempt to impress the school children I shared classes with. People I assessed as so much better than me, that I needed to expose every weakness to gain their approval. I was that pain in the ass kid. Full of information that had to be collated and presented in my vain quest for acceptance.

There was no need to lie. Real life gives so many rich variances of fairy tales that play out in reality. Stories are everywhere.

At school I was never part of the crowd, and always felt on the outer. After my best friend moved towns when we were ten, I was on the constant search for her replacement, which didn't happen.

Years later, I was in the local pub for dinner and saw a guy I went to school with. He was doing some work in our vicinity and we talked about memories of mates and school days.

"I never felt like I fitted in," I confessed. "I had no friends. It was torture always on the edges of the groups that hung out at recess and lunch times at school."

"Andrea," he said. "You were so fucking bright we thought you were going to be the Prime Minister. No-one knew what to say to keep up with you."

I looked at him, eyes wide.

"Yeah? Well, that didn't help me feel like I was accepted and an okay human at the time," I said.

He shrugged.

We laughed.

I bought him his next beer.

That was a revelation.

That's the thing with humans. We get so caught up in ourselves it is a challenge to see it from any other perspective. There are SO many perspectives, and perhaps hidden in there somewhere is the truth.

I look up to my parents, who always support me whatever debacle I am delving into. They have been there to pick up the pieces, and have not intervened with any great stridency to protect me from myself. This is both a blessing and a curse, but I am glad we chose each other this lifetime around.

I am not sure parental interventions assisted me to avoid any pain, as I have always done my own thing, and we have shared a close connection and rich lessons as a result. Our family laughed a lot. It is a good survival technique.

Once my spiritual journey began to reveal itself, I was voracious in learning more. Extremely focused, I read everything I got my

Chapter 30

hands on to explore the perspectives of guides and gurus to support an expanding awareness. From my childhood of church immersion, the path became ever wider and all encompassing.

How can one brand of religion have the golden ticket to eternity?

It is too strange for that to be true.

It seems to me that belief narrows the field of what is possible because it kills off other options. The Latin origin of the word 'decide' is literally; to cut off.

On that basis, a decision or belief that something is true can limit our views, rather than expand them.

Choices must be made if we are to have any progress. I recalled the virginal adults in my youth group when I was a teenager. Waiting on a bolt of lightning from the sky to tell them what to do. Waiting for God to instruct them on their next move.

I was fourteen when I shared my perspective on a higher power guiding our lives.

"A vehicle can only be steered if it is moving," I expounded at the time.

Choices are our moves, and if we make positive choices, with good intentions, and maintain awareness and discernment, we can be guided. My life is a co-creation of choices.

To my reckoning, religion has a lot to answer for in the ways it perpetuates judgement, war, and separates rather than connects. My discovery was that love is the answer, and love IS Goddess, or God for the patriarchs in the room.

Over time, I learned to listen to myself and be attuned to signposts and guides as a part of that observance. But there have been many times I have looked outside myself for the wisdom I am seeking, a voracious learner of how to avoid mishap by taking on the lessons of others.

Chasing gurus is habit forming. The belief that someone other than me has the elusive wisdom I require. Reading took me to places beyond my imaginings and introduced ideas. Concepts slipped into place like a vital cog of recognition.

I travelled the world to learn from people and grow my understanding.

From the introduction to Doreen Virtue and Angel Therapy when my life was mired in deep crisis and trauma, where she opined that children are our teachers. The reason I had pursued motherhood despite fertility barriers and ambivalence from my husband at the time, was the love we could share and the lessons we learned as a family unit in a soul contract.

Maybe we have been together before.

My life lessons have always been about love, acceptance, forgiveness, trust, hope, and healing.

There have been opportunities to meet my guides along the way. There was the conference in Melbourne where Doreen Virtue came out, encircled with her purple Goddess robes to encourage our creative pursuits, serenaded by her most recent "Michael". Emanating pure loving kindness and imparting wisdom, that for her in more recent times, has evolved directly into Christian doctrine.

Doreen has renounced many of the perspectives of her past and has shifted from her focus on angels. Goddesses and guides are now evil deeds of the devil, and she espouses only the way of God for her future. She has encouraged her millions of followers to move track and follow Christianity. All the while encouraged on the sidelines by her rapturous husband. A Michael that replaced the previous husband also named Michael, a sign she said at the time.

It is not for me to judge. We all evolve according to our path, and all perspectives are valid and to be honoured. As long as no-one gets hurt.

Marianne Williamson's incredibly honest book *Return to Love* was life changing for me. Marianne's work with the *Course in Miracles* and the deep sharing of her journey mirrored mine.

Chapter 30

My friend Vera came over to share coffee one day and we talked about the latest book she was reading. It had just come out in bookstores.

"Amazing story," she said, "Eat Pray Love."

Eat Pray Love by Elizabeth Gilbert was lent to me. I purchased my own copy to share her memoir with others. I was with her crying on the floor as her marriage crumbled, in her backpack as she traversed the globe, searching for herself in the bottom of pasta plates in Rome, in the temples of India and in between the sheets as she fell in love in Bali. Honest, connective tissues between the hearts of mainly women across the world, that read of her discovery of love in that mystery of another.

What shone through Elizabeth's work was her primal honesty and humanity. A depiction of herself and her experiences that we all knew so well from our own lives. Our desires, dreams, and discoveries, as women excavated ourselves to reveal our light, and give space for our shadow sides as we assimilated into wholeness. It is a life work to accept and fall in love with ourselves.

I devoured that book and wished for a soul mate to save me from my broken life. I continued to make shit choices. Some for a few months and others for a few years. The men I connected with continued to teach me lessons with some well-worn themes. Things started well but over time the same scripts were staged, including rejection, abandonment, addiction, and heartbreak. A pattern.

I didn't yet understand the whispering of wisdom as my superpower. I wasn't listening deeply enough.

I continued my journey as a seeker and seer, building my strategies of self-awareness on constant lookout for guides and signposts in life. Signals that I was on the right track. I studied Theta healing, Reiki II, started yoga, and meditated, did neuro-linguistic therapy, Landmark, and hypnosis. I visited my past lives and devoured self-help and healing books. Over time I discovered I saw energy and I knew what people were thinking by the way they expressed themselves. I listened to their spirit shining through.

When I read *The Four Agreements* by Don Miguel Ruiz my heart blew wide open. He shares Toltec wisdom from the Mexican tradition. The Four Agreements are: Make no assumptions; Take nothing personally; Be impeccable with your word; and Always do your best.

Ruiz taught that everything is a construct of our perspective through our domestication, shaping our world through our choices, our yes and our no.

The opportunity came up to attend a seminar with Don Miguel Ruiz and his son to do the work of the Four Agreements. The program was being run on a cruise ship sailing from Seattle to Alaska. The twins were nineteen and still living at home. I booked in.

It was a signpost.

On the pristine high seas of the Northern hemisphere we sat in a circle at the feet of our teacher and listened to his wisdom. He talked us through his concepts. I took notes.

One of the women in the group was an experienced cruiser and travelled the world chasing gurus, spending time in their presence to expand her soul.

"You must join the spa for the trip," Kathy advised. She was from Florida and knew stuff.

"Every day you can swim and lay on the hotbeds watching the glaciers roll by outside."

Soul rejuvenation requires deep listening. I joined the spa and soaked in the pool with the myriads of mature aged cruisers travelling the world on the floating casino.

I had concerns about the conditions for the workers who served us on the ship. Mainly Filipino, Indonesian, and Balinese people who were on eight to twelve-month contracts working seven days a week, earning about $1000 USD a month. One of the men who created animal sculptures from towels on my bed each day was going to miss the birth of his first baby back in Bali.

States of total awareness can impact the fun to be found in day to day life. Against the rules which clearly stated no tipping, I tipped

Chapter 30

the staff that were sacrificing their own family time to care for us on the cruise, so those funds could be sent to their home.

Kathy could still do the splits at age seventy. She had a friend with her whose marriage had just ended and was in the seminar for some healing insights.

Each day we joined the circle. I felt ungrounded by the way the ship floated across the ocean, like I wasn't attached anywhere. I keenly observed the energy in the room and took in the lessons.

A young Spanish woman took up residence at Don Miguel's feet every session. It got weird when she laid her face in his lap, and he grabbed the back of her head, seeming to grind her into his groin as he waxed lyrical with all we needed to learn.

There was a family from the Netherlands, who had packed their woodwind instruments.

"Let's watch for the Northern Lights," I said, leading them to the top of the ship in the dark after dinner. I unleashed the daybeds where they were tethered for the night in case of rough seas. We lay under the sky while they played lutes and lyres, searching the sky for tell-tale magical flashes of greens and pinks.

There were none.

As I walked the ship between sessions, I saw Don Miguel and his son taking in the sights, as the captain on loudspeaker regaled us with unmissable moments. Don Miguel and his son never saw me once. Walking straight towards them I raised my hand to greet them. They walked past, deep in conversation, oblivious to my existence. It was like I was an invisible observer, inconsequential, not seen or heard.

I was unhinged out there at sea. Whales chased the boat, in the wash behind the restaurant. When on shore, I searched out authentic experiences. A challenge when thousands of passengers descend on tiny towns along the Inside Passage for retail ravaging.

I took a boat charter to see whales leap and otters cling together in rafts and met Teresa from Florida whose husband was fishing. Our charter boat had two 350 horsepower engines, and I was keen to see just how fast this baby rode. Hair flew from our faces and our lips peeled back from our teeth as we squealed in delight at the speed. Whales leapt from the water, breaching with joy against the snow topped mountains behind us.

Teresa and I had lunch together and she shared her battle with a rare form of cancer, for which treatment in the US was not funded.

Every day, every moment was sacred.

When I came home, I was part of crowdfunding trials and treatments with the potential to save her life. In the end they just prolonged it a few sacred years longer.

While I was there in Alaska, I wanted to see a bear.

In Juneau, I explored the walkways over the water in the old part of town where the ladies of the night used to live and service their communities with commodified loving. I happened upon a small shop with an artist demonstrating his carving craft in the corner.

We struck up a conversation as he worked. People came and went. A woman served customers while we chatted. I bought a tshirt adorned with his art.

"Did you want to join me for a coffee?" he asked.

"Sure," I said, and we made our way to the front street. As I sipped tea with honey, we shared our stories. My seminar experience sitting in the circle of the guru on the ship, and my search for bears on the shore.

"I have friends in South Australia," Douglas said.

"Cool! Six degrees of separation! The world is a small place," I said.

"I catch halibut in the summer," he said. "Did you want to see my boat?"

"Great!" I said.

It wasn't his etchings.

My newfound friend led me to the wharf area, along jetties and walkways to his big halibut boat with its cabin full of kitchen utensils, pots and pans in disarray. Ropes and pulleys scattered the deck.

Chapter 30

Douglas explained his fishing methods and deep love for the ocean, enjoyed when he wasn't creating in his studio. A shared connection with the sea. I imagined fishing in Alaska as we crammed into the cabin. The pull of halibut on the line from their habitat deep in the ocean blue.

"Time is running away, Douglas," I said. "My ship will be leaving soon."

As we walked back towards the intersection where our lives separated once more, he told me of his Inuit heritage.

"I am Native American from Alaska," he said, "Thanks for a special time today."

"Thank you!" I said and we hugged goodbye.

"I am from the bear clan," he said as we parted.

I looked deep into his big brown eyes.

"Thank YOU!" I said and hugged him again.

I had seen my bear, and shared coffee and connection.

The ship's captain blasted its airhorn a few times to warn the stragglers that departure was imminent.

I ran for the boat.

Panting up the gangway I ran into Kathy and Sally.

"What did you get up to, Andrea?" Sally asked. "You disappeared."

"I met a man from the bear clan, an artist who took me for coffee and showed me his halibut boat," I said breathless.

"Of course you did! You saw your bear!" she laughed.

We tumbled up the stairs giggling.

On the last night, another woman in the group and I chatted. She was from Boston and had known our guru teacher for years. A grief and loss counsellor, Marian was married to a heart surgeon. She invited me for Chinese dinner with her husband onshore in Victoria Canada which was our last stop.

"You guys could close the loop," I teased gently. "If they don't make it on the operating table, you can support the family through the aftermath."

We laughed.

We talked about the seminar.

"I feel invisible," I shared with them. "Like I am an observer, not a participant. I see Don and his son on the boat, and they don't acknowledge me. I have enjoyed the people in the group but feel disembodied in the group work."

"Ahhhh, we have known Don Miguel for decades. He is an old friend," She leaned over conspiratorially.

"Do you think you might be taking things personally?" she asked with a cheeky grin.

Marian's husband watched me from across the table as my eyes widened. He leaned back in his chair relaxed and smiling, his eyes crinkling at the corners with kindness.

I gasped; eyes wide as the lesson landed.

We all burst out laughing.

We cried with the hilarity of it all.

The blessed beloved humanity.

I held no judgement, just the compassion and understanding that our shared human experience delivers lessons of contrast. Chances to choose. Darkness or light, shadows or clarity, wet or dry, deep or shallow, victim or survivor. They are experiences, that as spiritual beings having a human experience we must traverse. *Why have I been such a harsh critic of myself?*

We have experienced challenges to learn and heal from. We are all perfect in our own individual and sometimes awkward ways.

It was then that my search for love outside myself took a sharp turn inward.

My search for gurus in the world was over.

I came to a stark choice, at a crossroad of broken marriages and failed love affairs.

Chapter 30

It was time to fall truly, madly and deeply in love.

With me.

I went home.

My awareness expanded through my reading and rituals, as I listened to my inner guidance with a keen and open heart. I had written gratitude lists and soul mate attributes but now I stopped looking outside myself and focused inside.

Through a life explored in the prisms of relationships with others, it was time to truly fall in love with myself. Good and proper.

I tried to marry myself on Facebook. The algorithms said no. Over some years I steadied and reflected quietly. I worked hard to support my children, to put love into the world, through my job, and into myself through my heart.

In 2009 the Federal Government advertised contracts for independent project practitioners to deliver place-based education, training and employment solutions across Australia to respond to the Global Financial Crisis.

The role was perfect, but the twins were just starting their final two years of high school, and I needed to be available for them. It wasn't a good time to be travelling so far from home.

I didn't apply.

Two years later, when the contracts were advertised again, I applied and won the role, which gifted me the opportunity to start my own business with a well-paid base contract. I worked in a great collaboration with the department representative. We hit the ground running, and got a range of projects going that supported many hundreds of people to get training and jobs.

As part of the role, we had an annual conference in Canberra, attended by the other twenty people in the same contracts across the country. I met people doing wonderful work to support people reach their innate potential. We shared ideas and friendship.

Rachel and Thomas flourished in their education and both enjoyed part time jobs during their schooling. Rachel dreamed of being a teacher, then changed course to study social work. She moved to the city for university, but after six months she returned home and studied full time externally, while holding down a full-time job in case management. Thomas won an apprenticeship as a tiler and then transferred into the carpentry trade, building a high-quality life.

It was in Canberra that I first met Jack. He made me feel safe, and was stern when one of the guys tried to take advantage, by placing unwanted kisses on my face at the dinner table, while seated with my colleagues. Jack waited until the next day, when everyone was sober again, to take him to task for his inappropriate behaviour.

We had big conversations. Jack was in a relationship when we first met, and our discussion was free ranging and honourable. We shared about our love for our children, the stories of our lives, and our dreams for the future.

The next year I didn't go to Canberra as we were launching a big project, so I didn't see the team again face to face for another two years.

During that time, my relationship with myself expanded. I had the feeling my soulmate was coming to meet me. It was true that every day it must have been closer than the day before!

It was also true that settling for someone ill-suited had not worked out so well, so I honed my patience.

I trusted myself and the process.

I swam, did yoga, and journaled. I travelled to Santa Fe and made lifelong friends, connecting deeply with Native American people who greeted me as "sister" with a hug, a random fried bread burger, or a CD of their music. I went to Hawaii and learned to hula, and met a stone whisperer who sold me a clarity crystal of clear quartz, that I wore around my neck to strengthen my voice.

At a business awards event I attended, the keynote speaker shared our table. Dale Elliott was a former pilot, who after becoming a paraplegic in a random motorbike incident, turned to comedy and business mentoring. Throughout the evening we shared a lot of stories, and much of the time we were laughing. We clicked. I hired Dale as my business mentor and travelled to visit him on

Chapter 30

Hindmarsh Island to undertake a retreat, and plan the next steps of my new beginning.

It was an incredible time. We meditated before we did the work.

We went deep, ever deeper.

Dale asked me who I was being, and my question for life.

Who do I choose to be? Who shows up? What am I thinking with, my head or my heart?

I considered whether I filtered through compassion.

Do I walk in their shoes as I walk in mine? Or do I arrive in judgement already decided on a position?

A stance based on some assumption or historical experience that overtakes the present moment, and projects my past into my future.

We talked about wonder.

"What about fearlessness, beyond death? Not after, but now," Dale mused.

"I feel beyond death already and am open to a new adventure. Not to deny the fantastic journey of unfolding into presence as life is. And perhaps it is pure ego to think that we have got this. This knowing of a bigger expanse of wonderment beyond this being," I said.

"Really all we have is a series of nows. Manifesting in pure presence. Here now," Dale said.

He was right. Eckhart Tolle is right too. Incredible teachings and so much power in being present.

Deep breathing helps. If I focused on my breath, I couldn't think about anything else, which brought me immediately into presence.

"Writing is presence," I said. "It is witness to being. A mark of evidence that consciousness exists here. It frees me from me. Because as I write, as anyone can write, I express the Onesoul that I am, that we are. The facet of being in this presence that mirrors all others' potential for being."

"Who are you being now?" Dale asked.

I pondered. The loving mother. I am her. The struggling single mum. I am her. The shoplifter. I am her. The grieving wife when the marriage crashes but he doesn't have the good manners to die. I am her. The listening friend, soft shoulder to lean on in times of trouble. I am her. The daughter navigating life with thought for her parents and their loving investment. I am her. The teasing sister. I am her. The aunt interested and with an opinion of care to share. I am her. The team member who shows up in uniform to play every game. I am her. The lover, the chef, the cleaner, the weaver of life. I am her.

These were some of the myriad of reference points for who I am being here now. In this life.

"I am me. Having a human experience. Spirit witnessing the amazing manifestation of itself as consciousness. Pure awareness of being," I mused.

One thing I knew for sure. I needed more than four hours of sleep a night to be healthy in that process with Dale, excavating my soul, exploring my reason for being, guided by my mentor.

The deep questions Dale posed.

"What is the message? Where is the magic?" he asked.

"Being the presence of pure love. Clear light," I responded.

We discussed our observation of the currency of gossip. The times when some script which judges another person's circumstance is running rampant, unchecked, and nasty. Exposing that lack of acceptance for self, through the judgement for the other. So, it goes on. We mirror each other. Judgement invites judgement.

"It is so easy to step in," I said. "Who do I want to be? Pure creative presence. An expressive me. With love. Breathing from my heart centre and working here now. Trusting that this moment is the perfect time. For it is here now."

I looked at Dale sitting beside me in his wheelchair.

Then I had a revelation.

Chapter 30

"Trust is a space. Where nothing happens. And anything CAN happen. So here I am. In the space of trust," I exhaled, feeling clear. I detached, released, and expanded simultaneously.

Dale smiled at me.

"Are you able to be free in your daily expression of yourself?" he asked.

"I am," I replied. "I am enough. Love in action, in motion and in stillness. A simple expression of wonder, of receiving and giving, of finding, discovering, and experiencing. Honouring self to transform the experience of me in the world. Gentle, open, free. To be me." I felt lighter.

"Andrea, when people read your book, how do you want them to feel?" Dale asked.

I pondered and looked out the window at the sun setting on the water, pure golden pink.

"I want them to feel forgiven," I said.

Dale smiled.

"You know that's what they say about the Bible?" he said.

We looked at each other and laughed out loud for a long time. Safe in a space of trust, where nothing happens, and anything can happen.

On June 30, 2013 I sat in the dark alone. I created an altar, lit a candle, and shuffled affirmation cards. Reflecting on the ten years since that dark night of my broken soul and the incredible healing and transformation since, I expressed deep gratitude to the universe, the Goddess, the Mother that holds us to her breast. Broken by circumstance and healed by intention, my children and I survived. We have expanded our hearts, shared our dreams, and have thrived to support others to heal and grow.

I felt self-contained and complete. Proud of Rachel and Thomas and their incredible achievements, but mostly of the compassionate, wise human beings they are, and the ways they have healed themselves and contributed to the healing of others.

I decided to buy a bigger boat. As fishing has been the lifeblood of our family adventures it was time for this woman to have her own vessel. After my penchant for white goods got me into the second marriage mess, I was determined to be independent and buy my own boats. Putting it out there for man with suitable boat was way too risky in my experience.

Sadly, my friend Kate's beloved husband had recently died, and she offered me first option on his boat. When I checked it out, I discovered it was aluminium and slightly too small to get to the Sir Joseph Banks Group of islands. Our annual holiday destination for family fishing expeditions since I was five years old, The Group has gifted us many incredible moments of connection with family, friends, Mother Nature, and her fruits of the sea.

I called my brother Sean for advice.

"Andrea, get yourself a boat big enough to get to the Group. It needs to be fibreglass, so you are safer in the water. Do it once and invest properly, and you will have the boat for life," he said.

I drove four hundred and sixty kilometres towards home after meetings. On the way I called my girlfriend Nerissa to tell her how Kate's late husband's boat wasn't going to suit my needs.

Nerissa and I had become close after we met at work when I transferred to the coast. She was my fishing and foodie buddy. We had shared lots of adventures in the little tinny gifted me by a friend. The tinny I lay under in the sunlight, to patch the pinholes and prevent her taking in water, and we shared time in the ski fish combination boat I bought next from a beautiful old farmer, both not big enough to get us to the Group safely.

"I saw a boat here in Tumby Bay for sale. It was poking out of the shed around the corner, I will see if I can locate the owner and get back to you," Nerissa said. I continued to drive in the golden light.

Half an hour later she called back.

"A local guy named Sammy owns the boat, and he lives close to the boat ramp. Why don't you stop in on your way home and check it out?" she said.

Chapter 30

It was sunset when I arrived in Tumby Bay, and started knocking on doors near the boat ramp, to find the guy with the boat for sale. After meeting his neighbour, I was guided to knock on the correct door and met Sammy. He looked surprised to see a woman in business attire at dinnertime, enquiring about his boat.

"I have had it up for sale on the internet, and haven't had any interest, so I am trading it in for a caravan. We drive to the city tomorrow to make the trade," Sammy explained as he led me to his shed.

Inside was a five and a half metre fibreglass Caribbean Concorde, in pristine condition, glowing white with deep blue trim.

"I bought it brand new, and have rainwater rinsed it after every trip, before I park it in the shed," Sammy said, as I hoisted my skirt, clambered up onto the trailer, and climbed in.

She was beautiful. Sparkling white, low hours and with all the extras a fisherwoman could want.

"How much?" I asked. She was a gorgeous boat, worth upwards of forty thousand dollars.

Sammy watched me carefully, and his head tilted to the side as he started doing sums in his head. It took a little while before he spoke.

"I have been offered a deal on it as a trade in for a caravan, if you pay me what I have been offered, it saves me towing it, and if you can pay cash, I'll take twenty five thousand dollars," Sammy said.

"That sounds perfect," I said. I had just that much cash in the bank. "It's my birthday next week, and this can be my birthday present to myself."

I figured I deserved it.

I scaled down from the boat and shook Sammy's hand. We had a deal.

I stood back to admire my soon to be new boat. I took some photos to show Dad and Sean. Her name was on the side.

About Time.

As I drove home in the darkening sky, I called Dad who immediately offered to visit when I collected the boat, so we could try it out together, with a plan to head straight to the Group on her first expedition, with me as captain.

We launched her at the Tumby Bay boat ramp and drove across the open ocean to the sanctuary of the Sir Joseph Banks Group of Islands. It was when we had cast our lines into the deep emerald sea that I looked closely at the backs of the seats. Embossed in the clean white seats were eagles. About Time had eagles as her totem too.

It was mid-2014 and we were called to Canberra for the final conference of our contracts. Conservative Tony Abbott had been elected Prime Minister and planned to cut the program we ran, despite its significant success with job outcomes for highly disadvantaged communities and jobseekers, and its relatively small budget.

Jack was at the conference, too. He is a very well-considered and highly regarded professional. I speak before I think most times.

I swear with irreverence as my middle name. When the department counselled us on appropriate social media protocols at the conference, I raised my hand to ask a question.

"Does that mean I am not allowed to build an Abbott proof fence on my Facebook?" I asked innocently, having posted a meme on the subject the week before.

The presenter was stunned into silence, while my colleagues laughed at the delicious naughtiness of me saying out loud what many were also thinking.

As the conference concluded, I shared how fortunate I felt to have already won some other consultancy work. My mind was made up.

"I am going to hang loose and not try to find a job," I announced to my colleagues. "I will stay self-employed and see what comes my way."

I loved the freedom of it, and the ways the universe provided me with opportunities to use my skills to make a difference, working

Chapter 30

on a range of different projects across Australia. We scattered to the far corners of Australia to plot our respective next moves.

Somehow, I ended up on Jack's call list. He phoned randomly for a chat to see how I was going.

His long-term relationship with the mother of his children had concluded through mutual agreement after a long period of unhappiness. He had a list of people he called, including his mother, adult children, and a few friends.

Once it was announced our contracts were officially ending, my phone rang. It was Jack.

"A small group of us are going to get together in the Tweed and look at planning consultancy opportunities. Would you like to join us?" he asked.

We had all connected strongly through time spent together and respected each other's work ethic and style. Starting a national consultancy that combined our skills was a brilliant opportunity for us all beyond our current contracts.

"Sure," I said, thinking that while I was there, I could catch up with Penny in Queensland.

I hung up to make a call to her, but it turned out that Penny was planning to be away on holidays.

I called Jack back to discuss my options.

"It's a long way to come for a weekend," I said, "I was thinking of making a holiday out of it."

"Why don't you divert through Sydney on the way back, and I can show you around the regions I serve in New South Wales?" Jack asked.

I still didn't see Jack as a prospect. He is a warm, intelligent, kind man. Older than me by ten years, and somewhat formal in style. I had been doing the work. Falling in love with me. Not focused on the love of relationship that had distracted me in the past. I was thinking from my heart space. Breathing and grateful to just be me.

The work to be complete in myself, outside of any reference point in relationship, was significant.

There have been years of singledom, celibacy, healing rituals, and quiet reflection. Dark days and long nights where I processed the experiences offered, berated myself, succumbed to a brief time of self-flagellation then let go through forgiveness. To be present as pure love. An adventure in being I treasured.

I had long ceased viewing my success as an individual through the prism of relationship with some significant other, and anyway, that approach had not served me well up to now. Single and celibate suited me just fine.

When I arrived in the Tweed at Terry and Jen's place, I was led upstairs via their massive wine cellar straight into a four-course gourmet meal overlooking the water outside.

Renee, her partner, and children were there. Jack sat at the other end of the table, sipping wine, and sparkling with wit that crinkled his eyes with shared laughter.

As the weekend progressed, I realised I could feel Jack standing next to me. There was an electricity between us, and discussions about how we activate and embody compassion for people and the planet. He glowed.

On the second morning before breakfast I confronted him on the balcony where he was seated with a coffee, taking in the view.

"I think we need a chaperone!" I said.

We laughed.

He said nothing.

Throughout the weekend we all walked each morning. Our track took us along the water to the oyster farm and back. We jumped over puddles on the way.

Terry had formerly worked in tourism in the region and the itinerary included lunch at the art gallery and the restaurant at Mount Warning, a sacred Aboriginal place. We were transported by limousine to share a long table dinner at the beach, where we enjoyed a Shakespeare play at interval.

It was there after dinner at the beach that Jack asked me to dance. It was a Michael Jackson number. Jack can DANCE! He is an in-

Chapter 30

credible dancer. He only knocked over the chocolate fondue fountain once.

On the way home in the car Jack held my hand. Then as I went to bed, he pulled me aside for a kiss.

That night I knew my whole world had changed.

I couldn't sleep as I processed what was happening.

I had navigated myself to know exactly who I am and where I was, and here he was on the horizon rising up to meet me. I had a deep knowing that the soulmate I had yearned for was here with me now.

His name was Jack.

Jack shared that after his relationship had ended, he needed a new place to live. He put a call out into the universe.

Please show me a house to live in and a partner to share my life with.

Later that day the neighbours across the road dropped in to announce they were taking a sabbatical for twelve months to Europe and needed someone to housesit. Eyes wide, Jack offered, and they helped him move his things into his new home straight across the street.

Now here we were, just months later together, in a blossoming relationship that instantly felt forever.

Chapter 31

Scintillating conversation began that took us places beyond the horizons. Jack was an adventurer, always posing options of new places to go, or experiences to share. He was thoughtful, kind, wise, compassionate, and loving. As our relationship unfolded, we shared our deepest desires, fears, and foibles. Hearts opening wide we stepped into a balanced interaction.

There are continual small sticking points and challenges, differences, and discussions which we talk through to the end of time. Jack doesn't let me get away with anything, and I return the favour. There were no shadows here.

As we lived in different states of Australia, two thousand kilometres apart, we began to commute to see each other. We talked every single day, often for hours.

When I visited Jack, we walked his dog around the lake near his home. We collected shells on the shore and watched the yachts on their moorings, shifting as the wind flowed around them. The water of the lake was like glass, mirroring the sky, then in the afternoons, the breeze whipped up the surface into a series of small waves that chopped against the vessels in the bay.

When Jack visited my home and we walked our dog down to the beach, we climbed over ancient rock formations with seams

Chapter 31

of black lava solidified in place, gleaming feldspar, sparkling from within their form.

Nights were sleepless and full of conversations and when we were together, lovemaking. That sacred time of getting to know each other in the dark. Soft whispers and gentle touching. Giggles and sighs. Sharing secrets of dreams and the regrets of deep shame. Nothing was off limits.

Jack is a lucid dreamer who travels in his sleep to far flung places of magic and mystery. Vivid recollections that include characters and costumes took our explorations into deep time and space.

Within a few months it was clear this was a forever thing.

It was later in 2014 when a friend approached me and suggested we stand as candidates for the local government council elections.

"We should run together, get in there and shake things up," he said.

"Sounds like fun!" I said with a vague idea about the process and how to go about it.

Four years earlier for the previous election, a friend I worked with had shared his intention to run for Mayor. I was extremely excited about the prospect of a change because of the infamy of the longstanding Mayor at the time. My friend asked me to be part of his campaign team, which I did, and after implementing a range of shared ideas, he was duly elected.

This result finished the controversial and polarising career of the man who had made international headlines when he stated in the media that children of mixed marriages were mongrels.

My Mum was visiting Cambodia to see the child they supported through World Vision when that news broke. It got our city international attention for all the wrong reasons.

Four years later the local media got wind of my intention to stand for election, and asked if they could do a piece highlighting the need for more women in decision making roles in local government, to balance the predominant male elected member body to date.

Subsequently a front-page story ran in the local paper, with me and my friend in the photograph, announcing our intention to run as candidates for the upcoming Council election.

When it came to the deadline for nominations, my friend had other priorities and didn't fill in the form. There I was, my intentions exposed in the media and abandoned by my friend.

I decided to complete the nomination process, and for my campaign I created a Facebook page, which I shared through my local social media channels.

That was it.

My relationship with Jack continued to flourish. We started working together as consultants, combining our skills and love for solutions with care for our community, and enjoyed the freedom of working for ourselves doing good work with good people.

It was October, and my daughter Rachel and her boyfriend Lee had booked a trip to Bali.

There was an unexpected knock at the door one afternoon. It was Lee. I put the kettle on, and we sat at the kitchen table. I could feel an air of seriousness around him.

"I have a question to ask you, Andrea," he began. "As the mother of your beautiful daughter."

Whooaahhh, I thought. *This IS serious.*

"I am seeking your permission to ask Rachel to marry me," Lee said.

He looked deeply into my eyes, searching my face to ascertain my immediate response.

I was deadpan.

My mind turned to the promise and potential of fresh love, coupled with the joy and happiness it brings. From my vantage point, I knew that promise could tarnish with time and lack of attention to everyday choices that keep a healthy relationship alive.

I understood my own part in those choices and had done much healing reflective work to accept responsibility for myself in the breakdown of my relationships. The resentments I had displayed,

Chapter 31

the unexpressed anger and disappointment that had tainted my interactions in my first marriage to the father of my children.

Forgiving myself was a daily practice. For all manner of transgressions.

"Will you treat her with respect, love, and compassion?" I asked. "Will you grow together as equals, and ensure her space to be herself? Will you be faithful and honest? Even if it means being vulnerable yourself?"

Lee was earnest.

"I will," he said.

"And you are committed? There is no other person who might distract you from love and a long-term commitment with Rachel?" I asked.

"There is no-one else. I love Rachel with all my heart and soul and will care for her with everything I am," he said.

His eyes had started to fill with tears. His love was written all over his heart.

"Lee, you both have my heartfelt blessing. Thank you for coming to speak with me about your love for Rachel and I wish for you both the best that life can offer you," I said.

We hugged and cried.

We never got to drink that cup of tea.

Lee planned to surprise Rachel with a proposal on their way to holiday in Bali. He had booked the artist whose original song had accompanied their first dance. The musician would secretly fly over on the same plane to serenade Rachel as she entered the arrivals hall and Lee got down on one knee to pop the question. Flowers would be placed on the carousel by baggage handlers behind the scenes.

Lee was a true romantic.

Lee took me to see the ring he had selected at the jewellers.

A beautiful solitaire diamond on an elegant white gold band.

Their trip to Bali was imminent.

After a big day fishing in my boat, I cleaned up and got straight into bed without any dinner.

I had missed a call from Rachel during the day and as I settled back onto the pillow, the phone lit up with Rachel's name.

I answered the phone.

"Mum?" she said quickly. "We are on speaker, Lee's here, and we have something to tell you."

"Yes?" I said. "Sorry I missed your call today, I was fishing."

"That's okay. Mum? We are pregnant. We are expecting a baby," Rachel finished with a rush.

I sat bolt upright in bed.

"Wow! Really? Congratulations! How exciting! I am so happy for you both," I said.

"I have been feeling REALLY SICK," said Rachel.

"That happened for me too, but it passes. What amazing news! I am SO EXCITED for you!" I said. "It is the most amazing, challenging, and inspirational thing we can do in this life. We learn SO MUCH!"

Rachel sounded tired.

"Thanks, Mum, it's good that you are happy about it," Rachel said.

"Have a good rest darling and if there is anything you need, let me know," I said. "I love you both very much."

"Thanks, Andrea," said Lee and we finished the call.

I couldn't sleep. The thought was clear.

I can feel a girl coming for Rachel and Lee.

Eventually as I drifted into sleep, I dreamt of a pink vintage car I was getting detailed. I visited a family friend and her husband told her that her mother had died. The grief was overwhelming. Then my friend brought her father to me. I held him tenderly and he shone with the understanding of love forever.

In my dream I said, *"At this moment your mother is being born."*

Chapter 31

In the morning I woke and wrote it all down in my journal.

"I feel a girl for Rachel and Lee. A gift of life and love, healing, and perfection," I wrote.

My phone lit up. Rachel had sent me a message.

"This is perfect as it is."

And so it was.

The local government election happened. There were ten spots and in the first preference votes I was running a dismal fourteenth. My colleague who had run for Mayor for the second time was elected in a landslide.

Invited to celebrate on election day, I dropped in after softball. When I entered the house, our re-elected Mayor was wearing a fur cape and a mock crown, placed on his head by his friends.

He removed the cape and draped it around my shoulders with a flourish.

"You next," he said. "I anoint you as my successor."

We laughed at the incongruity of it all.

I went home to shower and then returned to the celebrations at the Mayor's home. He was jubilant to be elected for his second term. Later the count had progressed, and other elected members dropped in. I was out of the running. Coming fourteenth with only ten spots, there was no possible way I could be elected now.

"Where was your campaign?" the Mayor asked. "I thought you'd poll really well."

Now that we were here, I was disappointed.

"I made a Facebook page," I countered.

"It's a pity because I was looking forward to working with you," he said. A sentiment echoed by the other successful candidates, who gathered on his deck overlooking our beautiful city, nestled on the sea, twinkling with light.

The Mayor took me into his study and prodded his computer into life. Printing out the preference report, he showed me how it worked.

"There is no way you can win from here," he said. "I am sorry to say."

He patted my shoulder.

I was forlorn as I went home. I thought of all I could have done to increase my vote.

Now that I had missed out, I realised I wanted it.

Really wanted it.

I called Jack for our usual late-night chat. Jack was convinced I'd be elected. I thought he was deluded.

The counting moved to preferences, and by Wednesday I still hadn't heard anything. I wrote in my journal.

"I am letting this go now. Trusting is the new black. The universe continues to protect and guide me in its wise plan for the investment of my energy. That I might be that wise. That I might be so clear about what I choose to create. What I choose to invest of me. What I choose to step up for. That I might consider the choices I make. That I might free myself to write, to travel, to be with Jack, manifest, heal myself, change the world. And so it is."

As I took our dog for a walk on the beach, I considered the choices I make without consciously choosing. I thought about how I invest my energy.

I talked myself out of the equation.

I thought about how the universe moved each person's pen stroke on a voting slip through their choice, that designed my present and planned my future.

How it is all perfect. Whatever the outcome.

How not winning can still be a win.

I convinced myself there on the beach with the dog that I didn't want it anyway.

I let myself off the hook.

I let go and fell into trust.

When I got back to the house, I put the kettle on.

The phone rang.

Chapter 31

It was the deputy CEO of the Council.

"Andrea?" she queried.

"Yes," I said.

"Congratulations. I am ringing to let you know that you have been elected in the tenth spot for the next term of Council. You came in very strongly on preferences," she said.

I sat down with a bump.

"Thanks so much," I said.

I think, I thought.

I might have exclaimed "FUCK!" before I had fully finished the phone call.

The Mayor rang.

"Wow! You came in from the clouds! Never seen that before in my life! On those numbers I was sure you were totally out of contention," he laughed.

"Thanks. I look forward to working with you," I said.

"Likewise!" he said as we finished the call.

I rang Jack with the news.

"I got elected, tenth spot, after it looked like I was out of the running," I said.

"I told you it was so," he said calmly. "I could see it."

And so it was.

Jack and I had been considering where we might settle to be together full time, as the commute interstate was expensive, and time apart interminable. Life is short and we both had big plans about how we wanted to contribute to a healthy happy world, together.

"Looks like I am staying in South Australia," I announced. With the announcement of my daughter's pregnancy and the strokes of those voter's pens, my imminent future had been decided.

Jack helped me shop to buy an outfit for my first Council meeting.

A classy black and white number. Not a shade of grey in sight.

Like my life seems sometimes.

When I listen to what wisdom whispers.

And watch long held dreams slowly moving into view, to come true.

"I will move to be with you," Jack said.

Six months later he did.

Rachel gave birth to our first grandchild in June of 2015. The beautiful baby girl I felt coming through the universe to meet us. Rachel and Lee had a second daughter in 2018. We share sacred time as a family, caring for ourselves and each other as part of our village. The people who have been there for us, across deep time, like my parents and brothers, for decades like my children and many friends, and for sacred moments of shared humanity with people that we resonate with, as we reflect each other along the way. Some who still walk beside me, and some that have moved on with the flow.

Thomas moved out aged twenty-six, a qualified carpenter and tiler with his own business, five years shy of the promised aged of thirty-one. He confided that he had waited to make sure I was properly looked after.

I wondered if he was waiting for me to expand enough to adequately care for myself. My relationship with Jack continues to evolve, and I figure my children approve. In the end that doesn't matter, it is what I think and feel that counts for my life.

What wisdom whispers is my truth. I listen with an open heart.

My higher self has wisdom to share. As I attune, I finally understand I am worth it.

What you see here in me, is you.

Epilogue

Mother Earth April 2020

The whole planet has shifted into a slowdown, lock down, physically distanced, home isolation in the face of a global pandemic that kills many each day around the world. *What Wisdom Whispers* was poised to be launched at the SALT Festival, an annual ten-day celebration of art, innovation, culture, and creativity we were part of birthing almost half a decade ago. Four weeks from opening we cancelled, as the restrictions of the global pandemic and Australia's response became clearer daily in a dynamic environment.

Life as we know is changed forever.

Life as we know it changes every moment. Every time we make a choice, we listen deeply, we honour the community over an individual, and with every step and breath we take.

Change is the constant we can rely on.

I found a goal card I completed at a motivational session some years ago. By April in 2020 my goal stated "I am happy and grateful that......my book is published and resonating with people to support their healing. I am travelling the world to share stories and healing."

It is April 2020 and *What Wisdom Whispers* has sat resting in my laptop for over six weeks. No one is travelling anywhere at all. Borders are closed, and the most fortunate of us have sheltered in our cocoons.

I feel lethargic, like I am moving in honey. Everything is not important or urgent right now. A beautiful friend who I approached to assist with the book cover design has been sending me updates, and our ideas and vision become clearer with each version Claire creates. I have Zoom connections with Bella-Marie in Montana US. Bella is the artist I met on Facebook when she posted the painting of Sacred She, who graces the cover. She has no name, but I know She needs a capital letter to herald Her, any time She is mentioned.

It was before my fiftieth birthday in December last year, that I saw Her image. I knew I had to have Her in my life. Bella was getting set for an exhibition and had posted some images online. I reached out to enquire, and while ferrying paintings to the venue Bella kept leaving Her home. By mistake. Bella messaged me to say that the painting didn't seem to want to be shown as part of the collection.

Maybe She was meant for a different journey? Maybe She was meant to travel to Australia? Maybe She was meant to travel the universe? Maybe She would help change the world?

Bella explained that She had been channelled after a sound healing retreat in Chimayo New Mexico, and that she comes with sacred dirt from the place.

"She is Forgiveness," Bella wrote. I couldn't tear my eyes away. I made a financial exchange, and Bella shipped Her to arrive before my birthday. She hangs on the wall in my studio. Heart and womb connected with knowing trust. She trusts Herself. She forgives Herself. She graces the cover of this book with Her presence.

Forgiveness. My life work. To forgive myself. To forgive him, and her, and him, and me again. It is a daily practice, moment by moment, of awareness, insight, patience, understanding and hope. Trust is a space where nothing happens, and anything CAN happen.

Epilogue

I tidy up loose ends.

I forgive my girlfriend with whom I shared a bonded friendship. A healer with presence and potential. Perhaps frightened of herself and her infinite power, she abandons the friend of the moment, or the mission or the decade, after taking what she thinks she needs.

An affronted aftermath of unfinished business, imagined slights, a miscommunication not able to be discussed, never to speak again. She retreats, hopefully to learn the lesson of acceptance that only she can give herself, because deep acceptance of self will break the pattern, which sees her rejection of those who love her.

Rejection that manifests because she thinks that is what she deserves. She creates the abandonment to prove she is unworthy and blames separation on the imagined transgression of another. It prevents having to look or listen too closely, to grow into the next steps of the full forgiveness of self, when blinded by the illusion it is always someone else's fault. It is a pattern. I see it in myself.

I wrote a letter. Honest and frank, exploring what had gone wrong. I got a typed note back. "Our friendship is strong no longer," she wrote. I recognised the intricate textures of convoluted story constructed to prove one is right, which automatically makes some other wrong. There is a whole world of hurt manifested around us, based on being right, and making others wrong. Wars are made of these misconceptions.

These stories keep us safe, but they are illusions.

I see clearly. For she is me. I forgive me. I forgive her. It is all just a story we made up to learn a lesson.

Always of love and forgiveness.

I forgive myself for the confrontations of sadness and confusion that unexplained endings in relationship present. I forgive myself the time invested to twist conclusions around in my heart and mind in fruitless attempts to make sense of what has occurred. I forgive myself my sadness. I look for my blind spots from alternative angles. I want to understand and take responsibility for my actions, inaction, lack of sensitivity, my brash voice that might inadvertently hurt and not bely the compassion I feel at heart.

I forgive the man who was a close confidante, whose family, career and dreams I supported only to be rejected with distance and unexplained disgust. We were so close once. Before Jack entered my life. This friend read a piece of my writing I shared with him way back when. He called me and told me to stop driving my car immediately as he had something important to say. I pulled up on the side of the highway to listen.

"You have got it going on, you must heed the call to write and put it out into the world," he said then.

But now he doesn't speak to me anymore. I made a meeting a few years ago to talk through what had happened. I wanted to discover what I had done wrong. How had I offended him so surely? To ask why his family look the other way when they see me.

"What stories have you told them?" I asked, "All I have done over time is to support you all and I cannot understand this anger. Please explain where it springs from?"

"I can say whatever I like to my family," he said. "That is my business." He looked at me with a mixture of disdain, unveiled derision, and a spark of insight.

"You are a force of nature, Andrea," he said. And that was that.

I forgive me. I forgive them. Their story isn't mine.

I move on.

In our home we have a wall hanging.

It says:

"In the end what matters most is: How well did you live? How well did you love? How well did you learn to let go?"

I let go. I release into the space of trust.

Letting go gives some illusion that there was some control to start with. The greatest gift of my life this time around is the stark lesson is that all is out of control. I have choices. Action I make, responses to circumstance I create, and outside any influence by me, the surprise twists and turns life offers every moment.

Epilogue

Because shit happens.

Like global pandemics that shut down continents, countries, and economies. We respond with community, connection, clarity, and patience. It is simple really. Stay home and wash our hands.

And save lives.

Like marrying a man who chose family violence, and the man who perpetrated against my children.

I take responsibility for not loving myself enough. As a result, I made poor relationship choices. A lack of self-worth so dark I put my own children at risk. A pattern of rejection repeated until I learned the lesson, and life school's curriculum moved onto new studies of love, hope, patience, trust, grace, and forgiveness. Ever deepening in a growing awareness of everything and nothing at all.

Mum always says we get to choose how we respond. I am fortunate to have a wise, kind, funny, compassionate mother and father. Blessed indeed. I am ever grateful for the friends and family who accept me just how I am. Who love me enough to give frank and fearless feedback and forgive me when I miss the mark. When I open my mouth in a moment silence was golden. When I write it down and tone is taken some other way than intended. When I take it personally, and forget whatever you say, says more about you than me, every time.

I am learning to listen more deeply. Mostly to myself. To the kind wise voice and the gut feelings where my soul resides.

I feel deep gratitude for the gifts life gives me. Whatever is in my bank account I appreciate the reserves of abundance overflowing in my life. I notice and give thanks for the warm shower, our clean water, a healthy home that I share with my life partner Jack, who is mostly all grown up. It is refreshing to share life with an adult who is also aware, and always kind at his core. Thoughtful and curious about the world, a lucid dreamer who travels the astral planes, and returns each morning to discuss with me his adventures of the night.

I love. I hope. I forgive. I trust. Sometimes I forget. Then I remind myself again. And start over. Patience is that other virtue I am learning.

The words wisdom whispers are a guide to our healing. They have been to mine. Whether it is the wisdom of the shared soul, or an individual effort, it can be hard to discern, but I prefer to think of it as collective energy. Grace and love dressed as hopeful protection if only we are aware enough to tune into the messages we are gifted, follow the guidance, and trust we are cared for in the process. That it is bigger than us, and our life thread makes the quilt complete.

What wisdom whispers is worth listening to. Wisdom whispers its sweet challenges of life. If we only linger long enough to listen.

To trust ourselves and our voice.

To love ourselves, accepting our failures as lessons, forgive ourselves and others, so we may let go and move on. There are always challenges in this human experience. May we grow and expand to learn fuller expressions of love.

When we listen to what wisdom whispers, we are set free.

Free to be me. Free to be you.

For you are me, and what I see in you is me. The great mirror ball on the dance floor of life.

What grates, what grows, and what delivers insights and joy.

It is everything I am. Everything we are.

We are one. One soul having the range of human experiences in the illusion that we are separate.

ONESOUL.

It is when we come together with common purpose, compassion, and care, that we can heal ourselves and each other, and our Mother Earth that holds us. We come home.

What wisdom whispers is a reminder of who I am and all I can be. Just like you.

It is safe to be.

Epilogue

Love.

That is what wisdom whispers to me.

www.ingramcontent.com/pod-product-compliance
Lightning Source LLC
Chambersburg PA
CBHW020314010526
44107CB00054B/1837